KT-413-005

Flaubert and
an English Governess

FLAUBERT AND AN ENGLISH GOVERNESS

The Quest for Juliet Herbert

HERMIA OLIVER

CLARENDON PRESS · OXFORD
1980

Oxford University Press, Walton Street, Oxford OX2 6DP
OXFORD LONDON GLASGOW
NEW YORK TORONTO MELBOURNE WELLINGTON
KUALA LUMPUR SINGAPORE JAKARTA HONG KONG TOKYO
DELHI BOMBAY CALCUTTA MADRAS KARACHI
NAIROBI DAR ES SALAAM CAPE TOWN

Published in the United States
by Oxford University Press
New York

British Library Cataloguing in Publication Data

Oliver, Hermia
Flaubert and an English governess.
1. Flaubert, Gustave – Relationships with women – Juliet Herbert
2. Herbert, Juliet
I. Title
843′.8 PQ2247 79–41142

ISBN 0-19-815764-9

Text set in 11/12 pt VIP Garamond, printed and bound in Great Britain at The Pitman Press, Bath

TO KATHARINE DUFF

Incomparable friend and co-researcher

Foreword

Although the trend in literary criticism nowadays leads away from the 'biographical fallacy', many scholars and critics – not to mention the general public – keep searching for the '*secret du génie*' not only in the text itself, but also in the life of its creator, in the circumstances of its genesis, publication, and reception. No surprise therefore, if along with many formalistic studies of the Flaubertian text, quite a number of works should appear which concern themselves with the novelist's biography, correspondence, and papers.

Most of the 'secrets' of Flaubert's life have been discovered and studied, in a more or less satisfactory way: we still don't know what really happened between Élisa Schlésinger and Flaubert in the 1840s; nor do we completely understand the reason for his break-up with Louise Colet in 1854–5. But one feminine presence in his life could hitherto be only the subject of wild guesses: Juliet Herbert, who lived at Croisset from 1855 to 1857 as governess to Flaubert's niece Caroline. *Flaubert and an English Governess* fills this gap brilliantly. Through a painstaking and thorough search in London archives, Miss Oliver has uncovered all the basic facts concerning Juliet and her family; through an equally meticulous search through Flaubert's papers, she has been able to reconstruct in great detail Juliet's relations with the Flauberts up to the novelist's death in 1880. The figure of Juliet Herbert looms high in Flaubert's later years, much higher than was thought. That he was her lover is very likely; in any case, her 'gracieuse' person, to use Louis Bouilhet's term, was very dear to Flaubert for many years, as they played Hero and Leander across the Channel. Unfortunately, Miss Oliver's exhaustive research did not yield the greatest prize: Flaubert's letters to Juliet and Juliet's letters to Flaubert. Are they lost for ever?

Good research brings what I would like to call its bonuses, and *Flaubert and an English Governess* does not throw light only on its two main characters. While reading Flaubert's letters and notebooks, Miss Oliver rectifies many faulty readings, and corrects many erroneous datings. While focusing her research on Juliet Herbert, she also deals with other English acquaintances of the Flaubert family: 'Miss Jane', who was governess to Flaubert's sister Caroline in the 1840s, is *proved* to be the same person as Mrs Farmer, often mentioned in later letters; new information is brought about the Collier family; not to mention original discussions of such enigmas in Flaubert studies as Miss Braddon's novel *Charlotte's Inheritance*, the Calves' Head Club, or Émile Bergerat's *Le Chèque.* Miss Oliver also devotes a chapter to the study of Flaubert's character, which shows a very keen and very wise understanding of the novelist's personality: no easy task!

Miss Oliver's quest was very successful indeed for Juliet Herbert, and also for Gustave Flaubert.

Jean Bruneau

Acknowledgements

This book owes so much to three people in particular that no expression of gratitude could be adequate. Before the book was written, Professor Jean Bruneau gave encouragement, made invaluable suggestions, and generously contributed information without which it would have been impossible to discover two posts held by Juliet Herbert and her sister Marianne. Despite his own heavy commitments, he also read the first draft of the manuscript, which thus benefited from some crucially important interpretations and criticism. My indebtedness to Dr A. W. Raitt, of Magdalen College, Oxford, who had been equally generous in passing on information, is limitless. He has uncomplainingly read all the drafts, redrafts, and redrafts of redrafts with minute attention and I have benefited from his knowledge, constructive suggestions, and keenly critical mind, and not least from his kindness in sparing me time to discuss the book and in correcting my often defective translations. This book has additionally benefited more than most from skilled editing that has exposed obscure passages, excrescences, insufficiently scholarly statements or expressions that have fallen short of the *mot juste*. For all these reasons I am deeply indebted to the editors of Oxford University Press. My co-researcher, Katharine Duff, has not only been responsible for many fruitful suggestions but has also, in countless unselfish ways, made it possible for me to write this book. Needless to say, I am myself responsible for any errors.

I owe a particular debt of gratitude to Monsieur Francis Ambrière, who courteously took so much trouble to reply to a letter from an unknown stranger, thereby enabling me to clear up one of the innumerable *petits mystères* surrounding Juliet Herbert, and my co-researcher and I both want to thank Monsieur Jacques Suffel, Conservateur-adjoint of the Bibliothèque Spoelberch de Lovenjoul in Chantilly, for the friendly welcome and practical help he gave us. We gratefully acknowledge the kindness of Monsieur Lucien Andrieu, the distinguished secretary of Les Amis de Flaubert and curator of Flaubert's library at the Canteleu-Croisset Mairie, who showed us a book containing an inscription by Juliet Herbert. We also want to thank Sir John and Lady Conant, of Lyndon Hall, Rutland, for positively welcoming us to rummage through their attics and for passing on an enquiry to the Leicestershire Museums, Art Galleries and Records Service.

We jointly extend thanks to the following institutions and firms: the Bibliothèque historique de la ville de Paris (and to Mlle Verlet in particular), the Bibliothèque nationale, the British Library, Chelsea Library, Messrs Christies, the Guildhall Library, the Greater London Council Historical Library and Record Office, the Institut français du Royaume Uni, the London Weather Centre, the Musée Carnavalet, the Public Record Office, the Royal Institute of British Architects' library, Somerset House, Messrs Sotheby, the Taylorian Institution, Oxford, the University of London Library.

We owe a special debt to the biographical, literary, and genealogical collections in the London Library and to its open-access system which made it possible to search for an unindexed item in the *Mercure de France*.

East Molesey,
May 1979

Contents

List of Illustrations

(between pages 146 and 147)

Introduction

The Quest for Juliet Herbert

Juliet Herbert was an Englishwoman who went to Croisset, the Flauberts' home in Normandy, as one of the governesses of Flaubert's niece, Caroline Hamard. The little girl's mother (Flaubert's sister) had died soon after she was born and her father, Émile Hamard, showed signs of mental derangement after his wife's death. This is why the child was brought up by her grandmother, Mme Flaubert, and her uncle Gustave. But while it has been known for a long time that Juliet remained on terms of friendship with the Flaubert family after Caroline's marriage to Ernest Commanville in 1864, that Gustave went to London several times to visit her, and that she paid several visits to Paris to meet him, until quite recently only those who could study Flaubert's autograph letters and one of his notebooks could learn even so much as the duration of her relationship with Flaubert, for two important reasons. The first is that although the relationship did in fact persist until the year of Flaubert's death, 1880, no single letter they wrote to each other has as yet been found. The second reason is not only extraordinary but is also one that cannot fail to arouse suspicion of a relationship which Caroline Commanville wished to hush up: it is the systematic suppression of even the most trivial references to Juliet in the published texts of Gustave's letters which appeared during Caroline's lifetime (she died in 1931). Until her death, she exerted a tight control over all the unpublished Flaubert manuscripts, which she had inherited.

Caroline's own favourite niece, Mme Lucie Chevalley-Sabatier, who in 1970 published a book on *Flaubert et sa nièce Caroline*, believed that the reason why Caroline did this was because, when she was sorting his letters after Flaubert's death, she felt resentment at discovering that the ties between her uncle and her governess were closer than she had believed.[1] Professor Benjamin F. Bart, whose biography of Flaubert was published in 1967, believed that the reason for the suppressions may possibly have been that Juliet or close members of her family were still alive.[2] (The first four-volume edition of Flaubert's correspondence, which did not contain the letters to his niece, appeared in 1887–93; a fifth volume, *Lettres à sa nièce Caroline*, was published in 1906.) The question of the suppressions and of the disappearance of the large number of letters Flaubert and Juliet must have written to each other is discussed in Chapter X, but it is notable that no direct mentions of Juliet in Gustave's letters hint at any relationship beyond one of friendship, with the possible exception of one phrase in a letter of 1872 (see p. 117). The interpretation of the relationship as one that a Victorian might wish to hush up depends on passages in letters that Caroline never saw and which never mentioned Juliet by name, although those which do mention her often show that she was in Paris at much the same time as these passages were written.

The first published edition of Flaubert's letters which did include references to Juliet (there are very few of them) was the four-volume *Supplément* to the Conard edition of the *Correspondance*, which appeared in 1954, but as a matter of policy this supplement excluded the letters previously published in the Conard edition. Consequently to date the only edition to include all the letters and to restore the suppressed passages is the regrettably expensive and hence not generally available *Œuvres complètes* published by the Club de l'Honnête Homme in Paris in 1971–5, which is not always reliable in its dating of the letters. This edition includes also the notebooks (although with many serious misreadings), and in one of these a skeleton diary of a visit to London is reproduced, which is an indispensable source for Flaubert's relations with Juliet. Mme Chevalley-Sabatier's book, based largely on Caroline Commanville's unpublished memoirs, *Heures d'autrefois*, contains a brief but valuable description of the Herbert household in 1870, when Caroline spent some time in England, but it does not give the Herberts' address. Several of the unpublished letters written to Flaubert by his close friend Louis Bouilhet, which are preserved in the Fonds Franklin-Grout in the Bibliothèque Spoelberch de Lovenjoul at Chantilly, include mentions of Juliet, and these too are an essential source.

Yet the sum total of the knowledge that can be derived from these published and unpublished sources remains slight. We still know nothing more of Juliet than the fact that she was a governess whom both Bouilhet and Flaubert found attractive. We do not know exactly when she went to Croisset, how old she was then, when she left the service of the Flaubert family, or how long she lived. The scrappy evidence in the letters and the skeleton diary does no more than hint at a relationship which may have gone beyond friendship, and from the passages in the letters which do not mention Juliet, it is only possible to deduce that they may refer to her. Hence interpretations of the nature of the relationship between Gustave and Juliet differ widely. Professor Bart, who has so far given the fullest treatment to the relationship (based on Flaubert's and Bouilhet's autograph letters and the skeleton diary), believed that this was 'surely the most tender and the longest and deepest' of Flaubert's many relationships with women.[3] This is a surprising statement. By far the longest of his relationships with any woman was that with Élisa Schlésinger. He met and fell in love with her in 1836, and in 1872 he was still addressing her as 'ma toujours aimée',[4] while the earliest possible date when he can so much as have set eyes on Juliet was 1854 or 1855 (see p. 62), and Professor Bart believed that it was not until 1857. There is, too, much on record to demonstrate that Gustave loved Mme Schlésinger, his first love, more deeply and tenderly than any other woman. He himself twice used the metaphor of a buried Roman road in his heart to describe the persistence of his feelings for her.[5] On the other hand, there exists so little evidence of the true nature of his relations with Juliet that on that basis alone it is scarcely possible to assert that it was a love affair. The conclusion so far reached by that most impeccable scholar Professor Jean Bruneau goes no further than to describe Juliet as Flaubert's 'grande amie',[6] and the late Dr Enid Starkie maintained that although many critics had assumed that Juliet became his mistress, they 'are able to bring no evidence whatsoever to support this theory'[7] (an astonishing statement from one who studied the autographs). Without adducing evidence, the CHH edition of the *Œuvres complètes* states categorically that Flaubert became Juliet's lover.[8]

It was precisely the absence of any factual knowledge about Juliet and the conflicting interpretations of her relationship with Flaubert that suggested that the time had come to try to do two things: first, to try to discover at least the identity of the Herbert family and, if possible, some concrete information about Juliet, and second, to review such evidence as exists in the light of what is known about

Flaubert's character and his relations with other women who were important to him. For in examining such fragmentary evidence, one is in the position of the archaeologist who is patiently attempting to reconstruct the whole design of a mosaic when most of the tesserae have disappeared. It is then only on the basis of a knowledge of the totality of the designs used in mosaics of the period that it is possible to indicate the outline of the vanished pieces. In this instance, the only part of the design that is to some extent known is the kind of man Flaubert was and the importance in his life of friendships and also of his relations, other than casual ones, with women. Yet it is rash indeed to attempt to delineate such a complex character as his; moreover, the remarkable quality of the scholarship that Flaubert's writing has attracted makes it presumptuous for anyone who has not had a long apprenticeship in Flaubert studies to enter this field. But, in the absence of all the letters they wrote to each other, the indications of Juliet's character remain so slight that it is mainly only through a knowledge of the kind of man, and writer, Flaubert was that it is possible to make any reasoned deductions of the role she played in his life. This book tries to present the available evidence objectively, to make it possible to conclude whether or not she was his mistress and whether, if she was, she meant more to him than the many other women with whom he had more or less casual affairs. Was Juliet someone to whom he could have written, as he did to another woman he loved: 'Do you not feel that between us there is an attachment superior to that of the flesh and even independent of the fondness of love?'[9]

When it occurred to me that it might be possible to trace the Herbert family history by means of census returns and parish registers, provided that it might be possible to discover where they lived, I was fortunate enough to find that an old friend, Katharine Duff, was as enthusiastic as I was myself to make this attempt, and since she rather more than fully shared in the research we embarked on, from now on when I write 'we', it is to indicate my co-researcher, who also took an equal share of the work we did in Paris and Chantilly in the spring of 1978; for it soon became apparent that it would be necessary to make a thorough examination of the notebook (preserved in the Bibliothèque historique de la Ville de Paris) in which Flaubert's skeleton diary appears, and also of Bouilhet's unpublished letters.

The only datum we could find when we embarked on the quest

for Juliet Herbert was the sole private London address which appears in Flaubert's correspondence; 311 King's Road, Chelsea, which headed two letters written in 1866, and which the editors of the *Supplément* thought was doubtless her address – rightly so in the opinion of the CHH editors.[10] We therefore began by searching the 1861 and 1871 census returns for the King's Road. When that search proved negative for no. 311, we searched elsewhere in the King's Road in case the figures might have been misread or misprinted, but we found no Herbert family in that road in either of these two censuses. Of course it was possible that the Herberts might have moved, for population mobility is one of the hazards encountered in using census data, but we thought it worth while to try to discover if there existed any other clue in the published letters and notebooks, and so we went carefully through the CHH edition. In volume 8, which includes some of the notebooks (known as *carnets de voyage* and *carnets de lecture*), this edition reproduces (on p. 313) a loose leaf torn out of another notebook (a 'feuillet arraché sans pagination') which Flaubert had inserted in *Carnet* 7. (*Carnet* 7, described as 'Notes de l'année 1860', contains notes for the Carthaginian novel *Salammbô*.) On this loose leaf Flaubert had written down two or three addresses, without names attached to them, and some bus numbers. (It had vanished from the MS *carnet* by the time we examined this in Paris in May 1978.) The address which riveted our attention read '13 Millmain Row, Chelsea, Londres'. We concluded that 'Millmain Row' meant Milman's Row (now called Millman [*sic*] Street), a short street leading from the King's Road to the Thames. It was not until many months later that we found 'Milman Row 13, Chelsea, S.W.' on the verso of a folio of an unpublished letter in the Lovenjoul library (which has been dated July 1860) by Flaubert's friend, the more accurate Louis Bouilhet.[11]

The 1851 census for Milman's Row[12] revealed that 'Caroline Herbert, Head', school mistress, aged 48, and her daughter Adelaide, 'daily governess', aged 20, were living at no. 13, while the 1841 return showed that no one of the name of Herbert appeared at that address then. We were able to discover from London directories that a Mrs Caroline Herbert kept a 'ladies' school' at 13 Milman's Row from 1848. We had one piece of great good fortune in this research: at the time of the 1861 census,[13] Caroline Herbert's sister, Emma Harris, happened to be staying with her; as she had no occupation, she apparently had independent means. We now knew

Caroline Herbert's maiden name. Our excitement in finding in the same return Juliet, then aged 31, described as unmarried and a governess, may well be imagined. Adelaide too was still present.

The last census return we were able to consult (since the 1881 returns will not be available until 1981) was that for 1871,[14] when not only Adelaide and Juliet but also Marianne (aged 45, unmarried) and Augusta (aged 44, unmarried), both Caroline's daughters and also governesses, were in residence. Until we read this census roll, the name of the fourth daughter was unknown, since in 1870 when Caroline came to London during the Franco-Prussian war (see Chapter VIII) and later described the Herbert household, only two of Mrs Herbert's daughters were living with her, Marianne (spelled 'Mary-Anne' by Mme Chevalley-Sabatier) and Adelaide, who was not named but was described.[15]

Since all three census returns revealed that Mrs Herbert and her daughters had come to Chelsea from Marylebone, it was now possible to consult the Marylebone parish registers, which are kept in the Greater London Council Records Office. The registers of St. Marylebone Parish Church baptisms reveal that Caroline Harris, daughter of Joseph and Mary Harris (unforgettable biblical names) was born on 16 October 1802,[16] and according to the marriage registers of that church, she married Richard Herbert on her birthday, 16 October 1824.[17] At this date no further particulars (of occupation or address) are given, but the register of All Souls Church, Langham Place, baptisms for 1829 yielded the information that Juliet, daughter of Caroline and Richard Herbert, builder, was born on 27 April 1829 and was baptized on 21 May that year.[18] This time an address was given: 16½ Old Cavendish Street.[19]

We admit to an initial reaction of some incredulity that Juliet Herbert, as the daughter of a builder, came from the artisan rather than the professional classes. It seemed far more probable that the father of a woman who held Flaubert's interest for so long a period would have been more highly educated, like Mr Brontë. Even though the age of Caroline Herbert tallied with the ages given in the census returns, to ensure that there could be no possibility of error, we searched the All Souls Langham Place baptism register again. We found the birth of Adelaide Wilhelmina on 15 July 1831 to Richard and Caroline Herbert (same address and occupation).[20]

It was this that prompted us to search for information on the building industry in the early nineteenth century, and in particular to consult Hermione Hobhouse's masterly life of Thomas Cubitt. It is important to state at the outset that the small master builder of that period bears little resemblance to the contemporary jobbing builder. He was usually the designer of the buildings he put up and was responsible for contracting for the services of the various tradesmen, so that he needed capital. (This was sometimes arranged by subcontracting.) But he was not necessarily an educated man. As a contemporary lampoon (quoted by Mrs Hobhouse) put it, he might only have 'served his apprenticeship to old Plumbline, in Brick-lane; got up the Carpenter's *Vade Mecum* by heart; had a little smattering of drawing from Daub the painter, and then set up in business for himself.'[21] Mrs Hobhouse's book also led us to suspect that there might be some relationship between Richard Herbert and William Herbert, the large builder who lived in Farm Street, Berkeley Square, in the 1830s and had sawmills at Grosvenor Basin, Pimlico. We then began to search the Middlesex Deeds Registers, which indicated that there was a relationship between them. As is described in Chapter IV, the land deeds not only established the fact that Caroline Harris was the daughter of a poulterer but also revealed that Richard Herbert was bankrupt in 1832. (Who could better sympathize with Gustave after the Commanville financial disaster than the daughter of a bankrupt?) To try to discover what happened as a result, we searched the Public Record Office bankruptcy proceedings and found a very dusty file for Richard Herbert.

We also searched the national death registers, which are particularly refractory research material. They do not begin until 1837, so that it is impossible to trace the death of anyone before that date without knowing the parish in which that person died. (Nor are all parish registers in the custody of the GLC.) Moreover, it is not until a comparatively recent date that the registers give any information at all beyond the name, date, and place of death. To find out any further particulars, even the age of the person whose death is registered, it is necessary to purchase certificates – we fruitlessly purchased three certificates in the hope that they might prove to be those of Juliet's father, mother, and aunt (Caroline Herbert's sister). These difficulties arose because the name of Harris is exceedingly common and the name of Herbert common enough. Fortunately the combination of Juliet and Herbert proved to be almost unique, and we succeeded in acquiring a copy of her death certificate.

Our final quest was for wills, and these proved very rewarding. After ascertaining the date of William Herbert's death from his obituary in the *Builder*, we were able to find his will in Somerset House, and this not only confirmed the supposition of the relationship between William and Richard but showed that they were brothers. Since we had also learned from Mrs Hobhouse's life of Cubitt that William's daughter Elizabeth had married Cubitt's lawyer, James Hopgood, we were able to find a copy of her will as well, and those of Caroline Herbert and all her daughters.

We believed that it was relevant to this study to discuss the English governesses employed by the Flaubert family before Juliet Herbert went to Croisset, and we suspected that there was a connection between the 'Miss Jane' (as she was called) who was the governess of Gustave's sister (also called Caroline) and the Mrs Farmer, described in various editions of the correspondence and in biographies as a friend of Mme Flaubert's, whom Gustave and his mother visited in London in 1851 and who also recurs quite frequently in the Flaubert family history. Thanks to discovering an address for Mrs Farmer in 1851, we were again able to make use of the census returns, and succeeded in proving that Miss Jane and Mrs Farmer were one and the same person, for Miss Jane married a Richard Farmer. And since, when Caroline was in London in 1870, she wrote one letter that has been published, we were able to find that she lodged for some of the time with the family of an Italian sculptor.

In this book it has often been necessary not only to trace the family histories of some of the minor characters who played, or sometimes might have played, some part in Flaubert's life during the period with which this study is concerned, but it has often been crucially important – and still more difficult – to discover their whereabouts at a particular date. One example is Herbert Collier, Gertrude and Harriet's younger brother, whom Flaubert met at Trouville in 1842 (see pp. 33–6), for it was necessary to ascertain whether it was Herbert who in 1868 sent Flaubert some material he used when he was writing *L'Éducation sentimentale*. Herbert proved particularly elusive. He was absent from the 1851 census return (when the Colliers were back in England) and is not listed in any of the London directories or in Burke's *Landed Gentry*. Fortunately he is listed as a colonel in Burke's lesser-known *Family Records* (1897), but he seems to disappear from the *Army Lists* after 1863. It needed further research to discover that from November of that year he transferred to the Indian Army and was in India when this material was sent to Flaubert. The research we undertook on the Collier family also to answer the question why Gustave made no attempt to get in touch with Gertrude during his visits to London in 1865, 1866, and 1871, happily enabled us to discover fresh information about this family and Gertrude's husband Charles Tennant, which supplements Philip Spencer's article 'New Light on Flaubert's Youth', published in 1954, and also Professor Bruneau's publication of Gertrude's unforgettable letter on *Madame Bovary*.[22]

The question remained, who *did* send Flaubert the information he wanted? As will be seen (pp. 97–101), this was a French translation of an article in a popular reference work, written by hand and obviously sent with a covering letter. Many years ago René Dumesnil had access to the manuscript and the letter, and reproduced a photograph of the MS in a pictorial anthology entitled *Flaubert et L'Éducation sentimentale*, published in 1943, while in the text of his edition of the novel he quoted one phrase only of the accompanying letter, but he did not indicate the provenance of these documents. Hence all there is to go on is the handwriting and one vitally important clue in the brief phrase quoted from the letter: the writer addressed Gustave as 'tu' (see p. 98). The person who sent this matter was therefore very intimate with Gustave, and that at once ruled out Gertrude or Harriet Collier, then respectively Mrs Charles Tennant and Lady Campbell of Barcaldine (who in any case can be eliminated on other grounds). The Colliers' cousin, Hamilton Aïdé (who was with them at Trouville in 1842), the Victorian dilettante *par excellence*, writer of verse and novels, painter in water-colours (who even exhibited travel sketches), and composer of settings from his own verses, did not address Gustave as 'tu' in a letter that has survived, but even so, it seemed necessary to make quite sure that it was not he who got up this information (and for once addressed Gustave so familiarly). There seemed only one way to do this – to discover a sample of Aïdé's handwriting and compare it with the MS reproduced by Dumesnil. That we succeeded in doing (see pp. 98–9), and can confidently state that the notes sent to Flaubert were not in his hand.

Another family important in this study is the Conant family of Lyndon Hall, Rutland. It is not difficult to trace their history, but there was a problem in discovering where they were in 1871, for this was unknown either to Sir John Conant, whose helpfulness we gratefully acknowledge, or to the Leicester Archives, which hold the earlier family records. This time we relied on the deduction that with so many daughters of or approaching marriageable age, the family was likely to have come to London. As will be seen (chapter VII), this proved to be the case, but the information was not easy to find since they are not listed in any of the ordinary London directories. It was also material to find out where Turgenev was in the summer of 1865 (for letters of his in the earlier part of that year seemed to indicate that he was in Russia) and again, where he was in 1871 (because of a statement implying that he was in Paris – see p. 114). Indeed, it is not too much to say that our research was often made more difficult by the plethora of what may be termed false clues – from the King's Road address onward, not least a note by the late É. Gérard-Gailly stating that Caroline's governess made out a 'cheque' in Gustave's favour in which she pledged to pay 'her person' (see Appendix II). Gustave himself unwittingly left one major false clue when he wrote the wrong year at the head of the skeleton diary of a visit to London. Since this remains the most crucial evidence so far found for his relations with Juliet, and since the wrong year is repeated in the only published version of this diary (in the CHH *Œuvres complètes*), it was necessary to devote a good deal of time to dating it correctly, after a careful examination of the manuscript in Paris, when too, on the basis of local knowledge and research on the Farmer family, we were enabled to correct some serious misreadings.

Flaubert's correspondence is indispensable for those studying his life, character, aims, methods, and step-by-step progress on the novels and tales. The letters are also superb in their spontaneity, and their broad spectrum makes them a valuable source for students of nineteenth-century France. But until Professor Bruneau's definitive Pléiade edition of the correspondence is complete – at the time of writing, only the first volume, ending in May 1951, had appeared – there are problems for those who try to use the letters to piece together Flaubert's life. The nine-volume Conard edition, published in 1926–33, not only lacks a very large number of the letters (including all those which were suppressed by Caroline) but the texts were bowdlerized, and in both it and the *Supplément* numerous letters have been misdated. This arose because (as Professor Bruneau explains in the Pléiade edition), with certain exceptions, Flaubert wrote the day of the week and the time of writing at the head of the letters but not the month or the year, so that dates had to be assigned on the basis of other information (and for this reason appear in parentheses). Two authorities have done careful work on redating – É. Gérard-Gailly in two series of articles, and A. F. Jacobs in three series (see bibliography). The CHH edition claims to have made use of both series to redate letters it publishes,[23] but research done for this book has revealed that this is not always the case. For example, it perpetuates such major errors as an 1869 visit to London by Flaubert (no. 1732) and a visit by the Farmer family to Croisset in the same year (no. 3688), when in both cases the right year (as Gérard-Gailly noted) is 1867. Since it has been necessary to use the CHH texts for all letters later in date than June 1851, in known cases of discrepancy between dates we have added the phrase 'redated by Gérard-Gailly' to indicate the letters listed in his series of articles (published in the *Bulletin des Amis de Flaubert* in 1965, 1966, and 1967), for it is these letters that are drawn on in this study. But since the CHH edition sometimes offers no explanation of why it has occasionally opted for a date which differs by one day from the Conard date, and since in one instance of a letter Flaubert had himself dated the CHH reading proved to be wrong when it was checked with the autograph, it is necessary to state that until the Pléiade edition is complete, strict accuracy does not seem attainable. Flaubert's friend Louis Bouilhet likewise did not date his letters precisely and his letters have been dated, often very tentatively, by the Lovenjoul library. We have sometimes indicated that redating is necessary.

For Flaubert's letters, serious students must use the Pléiade edition for the following reasons (to list only the principal ones). (1) This edition gives the exact provenance of each letter; (2) no one can do without Professor Bruneau's superbly well informed notes; (3) this edition contains, as well as Gustave's letters, autograph letters or, when these do not exist, the copies made by Mme Chevalley-Sabatier of letters of Flaubert's family; (4) it contains also extracts from Maxime Du Camp's letters to Flaubert and to Louise Colet as well as her 'memoranda', together with extracts from letters written by Alfred Le Poittevin to Flaubert; (5) the preface includes a history of the publication of Flaubert's correspondence (which also deals with Caroline Commanville-Franklin-Grout's legacies of the documents she inherited and the discovery of Louise Colet's

'Memoranda'); (6) the preface likewise contains essential information on Flaubert's accentuation, punctuation, and dating; (7) there is a valuable chronology (although at the time it was compiled, an earlier error in dating caused the omission of Flaubert's 1865 visit to London). It will, however, be many years before this edition can be completed, and in the meanwhile there seems to be a crying need for a calendar of the letters, if only because the failure of the CHH edition to be consistent in redating means that all dates it gives should ideally be verified by reference to the two series of articles on redating. Since the articles list the letters by their Conard numbers, a careful researcher needs to be able to consult simultaneously the CHH edition, the Conard edition and its supplement, and the relevant numbers of two periodicals – an extraordinarily difficult and time-consuming task.

If the limitations of the nature of the evidence we have been able to disinter about Juliet and the Herbert family beg some of the major questions concerning her character and education, even so, it is striking that one scrap of paper, the loose leaf inserted in *Carnet* 7, can reveal so much, and we believe that in fact her family circumstances do at least indicate that she is likely to have been as unspoilt as Flaubert's mistress the beautiful Louise Révoil, who became Louise Colet, was spoilt from her earliest childhood. We think too that the story of Juliet Herbert, the governess who became a cherished friend of a very distinguished writer, and who remained his friend after he had become a celebrity who was also taken up by royalty, is the more remarkable when one knows her parentage, and the fact that her mother and all three of her sisters were likewise compelled to become governesses. Flaubert's devotion over more than two decades to a woman of such a humble family, during which he could count among his friends the most notable authors and many other distinguished men and beautiful women of his generation, is a tribute to both of them and reveals, we believe, another facet of his many-sided character.

What we hope above all is that this book may succeed in eliciting some further knowledge of Juliet, perhaps some family letters or photographs or even oral tradition. It may be too much to hope for another discovery such as the quite recent one of the papers of Louise Colet which Professor Bruneau relates,[24] but there must still remain the hope that in some attic or bank a box containing Flaubert's letters to her and the inscribed copies of the books he and Bouilhet gave her may still come to light.

I Croisset at Mid-century

On 26 June 1851, when Flaubert had only just returned from a journey with the traveller and writer Maxime Du Camp to the Near East, Greece, and Italy – a journey which lasted nearly two years and which made Flaubert 'one of the most widely travelled writers of his century'[1] – his mistress Louise Colet boldly visited Croisset uninvited. Though she claimed to have previously met Mme Flaubert, Gustave's mother, on a street corner in Paris, she had certainly not been introduced to her. In her record of this visit, Louise described the 'charming English-style two-storeyed house in the middle of a green lawn', with only an iron gate and the road between it and the Seine. This 'white and smiling house' with its Swiss-style farm backed on the hill slopes which were crowned by 'the celebrated château of Canteleu'. When she went through an outer gate, left ajar, she was struck by an air of peace, well-being, and opulence. Beyond another iron gate she saw the lawn and its flowers, and, through open windows, several people dining. She believed she even saw Flaubert.[2] Although she did not gain admittance to the house, as will be related (p. 44), Flaubert met her in Rouen later that evening.

Gustave's father, the renowned Dr Achille-Cléophas Flaubert, master and chief surgeon of the Hôtel-Dieu, the municipal hospital of Rouen, had bought this house, downstream from Déville in the canton of Canteleu, in 1844, when the country property he owned at Déville was to be developed for the railway.[3] Croisset, a few miles from Rouen, was the first village – a mere cluster of houses – on the banks of the Seine between Rouen and Le Havre, and the house was situated on a great bend of the river, with wooded islands strung out in the channel. It stood almost at the water's edge, on a hillside which rose to the wooded slopes of Canteleu, with its church and Louis XIV château, its terraces and gardens laid out by Le Nôtre but modernized before the 1850s. The Flauberts' house was long, low, and white, mainly eighteenth-century, but enlarged and modernized in the early nineteenth century, and parts of it were much older – the seventeenth-century pointed roofs and gothic windows could be seen from its courtyard.[4] It had several acres of land, with its own small farm on the left of the house and on the right a narrow part of the garden with a terrace walk which went up the hill, planted with magnificent limes. Flaubert claimed that Pascal had once visited the house and walked and meditated under these trees.[5] Extending, behind the house were lawns and flower-beds and the rose hedge from which Flaubert had cut flowers to send to Louise in the first phase of their love-affair. Higher up the slope were the vegetable garden and an orchard which George Sand called 'mon cher verger' and advised Flaubert (fruitlessly) to visit every day for exercise.[6]

At the water's edge was the little Louis XV-style summer-house, with windows looking on the river, which has alone escaped destruction and is now a small museum. Here very often, Flaubert's niece recorded, she, Mme Flaubert, and Gustave sat on the balcony: 'night came, little by little; the last passers-by had disappeared; on the towing path opposite the silhouette of a horse, drawing a boat which moved soundlessly, could scarcely be seen'; in the river mist two or three eel-fishers' boats left the shore.[7] On that farther shore were fields where cows grazed, and a wooded hill. Du Camp described it as one of the most beautiful landscapes to be seen in Normandy.[8]

Although some of Gustave's friends alluded to Croisset as if it belonged to him, in fact it belonged to his mother who, when she died, left it not to him but to her grandaughter, his niece, with the proviso that Gustave was to continue to keep his study and bedroom during his lifetime. Mme Flaubert had indeed made over the finest room in the house for his study. It was a splendid corner room on the first floor, with five windows. Three faced the long part of the garden, with its lawns, flowers, trees, and the terrace walk, and the other two faced the river, in summer framed in the leaves of a great tulip tree.[9] From these windows he could see, so close that it looked as if their yards were going to touch the walls, the great ships sailing up to Rouen or returning down to the sea. Flaubert 'loved looking at the silent movement of the ships gliding on the great river and leaving for all the countries one dreams of'.[10] From that window too he could see on the left the myriad Rouen steeples and on the right the hundreds of factory chimneys of Saint-Sever, which 'vomited their festoons of smoke into the sky'.[11] He could hear the river and the clanking chains of the steam tugs or the sailors singing as they weighed anchor to sail with the tide.[12] Flaubert's letters return again and again to the murmur of the Seine, the wind soughing or roaring, rain pattering on the leaves of the tulip tree, moonlight whitening the water while the islands were black – those islands Emma Bovary saw from Bois-Guillaume as great motionless black fish.[13] Or the letters depict the garden at all seasons and Flaubert's special love of the spring violets and primroses. No wonder that when he was on the Nile in February 1850, he missed a less ancient river, the lime-tree terrace where he walked in a white dressing-gown in summer, his little primroses and the great wall carpeted with roses.[14] 'Your house, your garden, your citadel are a dream,' George Sand wrote.[15]

Flaubert's study so precisely reflected his character that it is fortunate indeed that it was described by such admirable observers as the diarists Edmond and Jules de Goncourt, Zola, and Maupassant. Since Flaubert had no time for ornaments or, so Zola says, for pictures (he nevertheless made minute descriptions of pictures in the numerous galleries he visited), his study was bare except for his books, housed in oak book-cases with twisted columns, which occupied the whole end of the room, an immense divan covered with cushions, the splendid white bearskin turning yellow (so often mentioned in the letters), a gilded Buddha dominating the great circular writing table covered with green baize, and some chairs. Flaubert wrote in a Louis XIII-style armchair upholstered in green morocco leather. On the table was an inkwell in the shape of a toad and a large copper platter with Arabic inscriptions on the rim, on which he used to throw his hundreds of goose-quill pens and used papers.[16] A bust of his sister Caroline by the fashionable sculptor James Pradier stood on a pedestal between two of the windows. On the mantelpiece was a yellow marble clock crowned by a bust of Hippocrates, and beside it portraits of old friends. There was a copy of Callar's etching of Bruegel's painting of the Temptation of St Antony. He had seen this painting in Genoa in 1845 during the family wedding journey after his sister's marriage, and it was the initial inspiration of his own *Tentation de Saint Antoine*. On the bookshelves or fixed to brackets on the walls were some souvenirs of his travels – Egyptian amulets, primitive arrows and musical instruments, bead necklaces, a small African headrest, two mummy feet black-polished by a naïve servant, strange paper-weights. The mountains of notes were kept in cardboard boxes. As Edmond de

Goncourt said, this interior was 'the man, his tastes, his talent . . . one thinks of a barbaric core in the artist',[17] and as Zola said: 'For us, all Flaubert was there.'[18]

The books, at the time of his death totalling some 700 volumes, were, of course, all-important. Writing from Constantinople in December 1850, Flaubert told his mother (who had asked when he thought of marrying) that he was resigned to living as he had done, alone, 'with his crowd of great men who took the place of a circle', and with his bearskin, 'being a bear myself'.[19] Among these 'great men' were, of course, the Greek, Latin and French classics, Shakespeare (two French translations but an English copy too), Byron and Scott, at least some Balzac, *Don Quixote*, works by French historians, and more exotic books such as G. Pautier's *Livres sacrés de l'Orient* (1840), F. Creuzer's *Religions de l'Antiquité* (1850–1), Chardin's *Voyages . . . en Perse et autres lieux de l'Orient* (1811), and Volney's *Voyage en Égypte et en Syrie* (1825).[20] Besides the Bible, then or later the library included the works of the marquis de Sade, and over the years was to become considerably augmented by the books written by his friends, among them the Goncourt brothers and George Sand (whose gift of her seventy-two volumes must have taxed the capacity of those oak bookcases), Zola, and several younger writers. Already in the 1850s there would have been a copy of Bouilhet's long poem *Melænis* (first published in the *Revue de Paris* in 1851 and as a volume in 1857), and this Flaubert would certainly have proudly shown to Juliet Herbert who, as will be seen, was admired by its author.

Flaubert's study adjoined his bedroom and was connected with the other rooms on this floor by a long corridor. There were few rooms, as we know because he sometimes warned friends, if they were accompanied by maids, that he had no room to put them up, even after his niece's marriage. The great dining room, in full view of the Seine, was in the middle of the ground floor, opening on the garden by french windows flanked by two other windows. It was here that Louise Colet had seen the dinner party on Flaubert's return from his travels. Other than the heavy provincial family furniture, the only concessions to décor were reproductions of 'antique' (no doubt Greek) bas-reliefs hung on the walls of the staircase.[21]

It was at Croisset on his return from his travels that Flaubert was to spend his whole life until in 1856 he acquired an apartment in Paris where he spent the winter. For five years he saw almost no one except his mother, his niece, her governess, one or two close friends, and for the two remaining years of his life his uncle Parain.

Mme Flaubert, the most important person in Gustave's life, has sometimes been prejudged by the much-quoted description of her by Gertrude Collier, based on their meeting in Trouville in 1842. But Gertrude was writing forty years later, at the request of Flaubert's niece, and her memoirs could hardly have excluded hindsight. She portrayed Mme Flaubert as 'grand and solemn' and looking as if she never smiled: 'she seemed to have had some great sorrow in her past and to be expecting some great sorrow to overtake her in the future'.[22] Now that Professor Bruneau has included some of Dr and Mme Flaubert's letters in the first volume of the Pléiade edition of Flaubert's letters, it is at least possible to point to the evidence of Mme Flaubert's letter to Gustave in August 1840 saying that no one missed more than she did '*le gros diseur de bêtises*',[23] which hardly consorts with Gertrude's unsmiling portrait; nor does our knowledge that both parents allowed the children and their friends to enact blood-and-thunder dramas on the billiard table seem to go with a grand and solemn manner.

What Mme Flaubert seems to have shared with her husband was his rationalism because, herself the daughter of a physician, brought up (because she was an orphan) by her godfather, the then master of the Hôtel-Dieu, she is believed to have been a free-thinking deist.[24] Hence she too may have contributed positively to Gustave's Voltairian rationalist upbringing – it was she who taught her own children to read and write. Flaubert's niece Caroline (who first married Ernest Commanville and later married Dr Franklin Grout) says that she transmitted to him his impressionable nature and almost feminine sensitiveness 'which so often overflowed in his great heart and sometimes brought tears to his eyes at the sight of a child'.[25] This therefore describes Mme Flaubert's nature too. In 1863 the Goncourt brothers described her vitality and also, beneath her wrinkled features, 'the dignity of what was once great beauty',[26] and George Sand found her charming when she visited Croisset in 1866.[27]

But Mme Flaubert had indeed suffered greatly. She had lost two children before Gustave's birth (one only six months before), and another after he was born. The health of two of her three remaining children, Gustave and his gifted and beautiful younger sister Caroline, gave her much cause for anxiety. Then, in 1844, Gustave had so serious an illness that his parents first feared that he might not survive, and ever afterwards Mme Flaubert lived in dread of further attacks. After his return from his travels Gustave dared not ring his bell for fear of hearing her run panting upstairs in apprehension.[28] Only two years after the terrible attack of 1844, and within two months of each other, her husband and Caroline died, the latter of puerperal fever within a few weeks of the birth of her baby girl. Flaubert told Edmond de Goncourt that this unimaginable double blow turned his mother into an atheist overnight.[29]

Since the Flauberts' eldest son Achille had already married and after his father's death was surgeon-in-chief (but not master) of the Hôtel-Dieu, in her grief and desolation Mme Flaubert had no one but Gustave to turn to, as he fully realized: 'My mother has no one but me, only me, and it would be cruelty to leave her', he wrote in July 1847.[30] They had between them to bring up the baby (another Caroline), since her father, Émile Hamard, showed signs of mental instability immediately after his wife's death. Unable to do without Gustave when he and Du Camp set off on a walking tour of Brittany in 1847, Mme Flaubert arranged to travel by coach with the baby and meet them in the chief towns. When, in October 1849, Gustave did leave her for the long journey to the Near East (again with Du Camp), he described the day of departure as 'an atrocious day', the worst in his life. He wept all the way to Paris in the train and all but turned tail, visualizing his mother in tears, with the corners of her mouth turned down.[31] But of course it was a heart-rending parting for her, and of course he realized it. She can hardly not have wondered if she would ever see him again alive, and she would, he knew, often be at Croisset 'all alone in this great house and in this great garden looking at the little girl running about breathless on the lawn'.[32] The incomparable letters he wrote to her while on his travels indicate not only his belief in her devotion to him but the reality of her educated interest in all he was describing. That she evidently, later, read his books attentively we know from his report in December 1852 that she had found a scene in *Madame Bovary* that was identical with one in Balzac's *Médecin de campagne*, which Flaubert had not read: 'the same details, same effects, same intention, so that you would think that I had copied it if, without boasting, my page were not infinitely better written'.[33]

The stigma attached to Flaubert by Du Camp, Louise Colet, and some biographers of being too much tied to his mother's apron strings does not take sufficient account of the sympathy for his utterly bereft mother on the part of a man who certainly was unusally responsive to all misfortune. That he had also something of what is these days described as a mother-fixation (though in a far less acute form than Ruskin or Proust) seems undeniably true. Like Balzac, whose Mme de Berny was almost twice his age, Flaubert preferred maternal women.

First, on holiday in Trouville in 1836, he fell in love deeply, romantically, and initially platonically with Mme Schlésinger (then, unknown to him, living with the music publisher Maurice Schlésinger, whom she later married) when he was fourteen and a half and she was twenty-six; and then, in 1846, passionately but less romantically with Louise Colet, ten years older than he was. And writing to a friend from Naples in 1851, he explicitly said that he had been offered young girls but that he was interested in 'mature women, large women' and was frequenting an establishment where '*maternal* pleasures' were provided.[34] But there is no evidence that it was because of his mother that Flaubert never married; it seems that she even encouraged him to marry. He refused because he believed that marriage was an inevitably 'bourgeois' step (part of a career, having property and children) and, above all, that it would upset the hard-won equilibrium he needed as a writer – the artist had to be 'a monstrosity – something unnatural'.[35] Moreover 'the idea of giving birth to someone fills me with *horror* . . . I would rather perish than transmit the ennui and ignominies of existence to anyone.'[36]

Mme Flaubert clearly did not have the temperament to help her overcome the death of her husband and daughter. 'My mother is still inconsolable,' Gustave wrote in June 1846, and the same year he told Louise Colet that she did not know what it was to carry the burden of such despair alone.[37] Next year he wrote, 'If you knew . . . what my life is like! When I come down in the evening after an eight-hour working day, my head full of what I have been reading or writing, preoccupied and often on edge, I sit down to dine opposite my mother who is sighing over the empty places while the child starts shouting or crying.'[38] She was also a worrier, who when she had nothing to worry about invented anxieties.[39] She was delicate and suffered much from the migraines which seemed to run in the family, but at least sometimes her illnesses mysteriously disappeared when the doctor came.[40]

Professor Bart maintains that Mme Flaubert ruled her son

'through a total dependence on him and through the unremitting threat of the pain it would cause her were he ever to make her less than the centre of his life',[41] but a careful examination of the evidence does not seem to bear this out. At the time of her life when she needed him most, she did not stand in the way of the eastern journey once persuaded that it would benefit his health, nor (as Professor Bruneau has shown) was it she alone who was responsible (as Du Camp alleged) for the abandonment of the original project of extending this journey to Persia.[42] It was Gustave himself who gave her the choice of seeing him again in September 1850 instead of February or March 1851, and Mme Flaubert advised against the visit to Persia not only because she wanted to see him sooner but also because there were disturbances in that country and on grounds of cost. She certainly made no attempt to stand in the way of his later visits to England and Tunisia. What seems to lend colour to Professor Bart's view is Flaubert's description of his mother's expression when he found her waiting for him on the station platform after he had spent a night out (with his mistress) without announcing that he would not be returning. 'She made no reproach but her expression was the greatest reproach one could make.'[43] From the daily arrival of letters at Croisset, she is bound to have known what he was up to, but she was not straitlaced; as Gustave told Louise, once in Le Havre when his father wished to revisit a former mistress of his, Mme Flaubert and her three children waited for him in the street for an hour, but without any trace of jealousy or resentment.[44] It is far more likely not that she was shocked by his morals but that when Gustave did not come home she feared another attack, for this was September 1846, a mere two years after the first critical attack of a recurrent illness (see p. 32).

What she did for him, with incomparable devotion, was not to interfere with his working habits. As his niece's description of life at Croisset tells us, "the habits of the house were subordinated to my uncle's tastes, grandmamma having, so to speak, no personal life.' No sound must be made until 10 a.m. Only after Gustave had looked at his post did he knock on the wall to summon his mother, who at once ran to sit by his bed until he got up.[45] What could not have been foreseen was that as his mother aged and became very deaf and increasingly fragile, she would prove a burden to him, and especially after his niece's marriage, he did resent the more tyrannical habits she developed in her old age. When he went to

Paris, for instance, she was in the habit of insisting that he should fix the date of his return in advance, and as late as 1871 she was nagging him to come back, provoking him into saying 'it seems to me that *at my age* I have the perfect right to do what I want once a year'.[46]

The element in their relationship which Flaubert came to resent deeply was caused by the temperamental difference between his extravagant nature and her financial prudence. Mme Flaubert seems to have rubbed in the fact that she paid the then enormous sum of nearly 28,000 francs for the eastern journey.[47] But Gustave evidently spent a good deal himself on the frills, for when he wrote to his close friend the poet and dramatist Louis Bouilhet in December 1850, he told him 'entre nous' that this journey had severely cut into his slender capital,[48] and he had earlier told Bouilhet that he and Du Camp could not afford to get to Persia, but 'entre nous, remarque-le *entre nous*'.[49] As Professor Bruneau explains, Flaubert never spoke of his financial problems to his mother.[50] Although Dr Flaubert had left the family well-off, Gustave believed that if he had invested the capital differently, they would have been better-off.[51] After his father's death, it was Mme Flaubert who carefully invested Gustave's portion of the inheritance, and he had enough to live on without earning anything at all while he was living at Croisset. Gustave himself had no financial acumen whatsoever. Since he was unknown when he sold the rights of *Madame Bovary* to the publisher Michel Lévy for five years for 800 francs plus a premium of 500 francs, which Lévy spontaneously offered him in August 1857[52] (a fair price for a first work), he did not reap the windfall profits which resulted from its becoming a *succès de scandale* after his acquittal following a trial for immorality and blasphemy. As he had to pay the costs, he maintained that he was actually out of pocket on the deal. It was not until 1862, when he succeeded in selling *Salammbô* for 10,000 francs, that Flaubert might have been able to live on his income. But from the time he set up in Paris, first (in 1856) at 42 boulevard du Temple, and became a social celebrity, his expenses and his extravagance soon far outstripped his income.

In 1865 he had to confess the extent of his indebtedness to his mother, who was compelled to sell a farm to bail him out, and she would certainly have preached a sermon about this. We know from her letter of 10 February 1865 to her lawyer Frédéric Fovard that Mme Flaubert was seriously worried, not only about how to clear his present debts but about the future, for 'if he has not been able to live on 7,000 francs this year, after spending a large part of it with me, where he pays nothing, how will he manage later?' And on 2 March that year she told Fovard that she could not spare the 5,000 or 6,000 francs he needed without serious embarassment.[53] That she must have told Gustave as much in no uncertain terms (the parallel with Baudelaire and his mother is close) we know from his own letter to Fovard, in which he said 'nothing is more painful for me than constantly to have to ask my mother for money',[54] and in 1866 he asked his friend Jules Duplan (head of a commercial firm in Paris) to try to raise a large loan for him, explaining that he was anxious that his family, particularly his mother, should not know about this.[55] There were ample causes for friction over what in 1847 Flaubert had termed this 'hippogriff' money.[56]

Mme Flaubert does seem to have had a cold manner, and her niece said she was a little alienated by this and by the fact that she was not given to caresses. When little Caroline was scolded, it was to her uncle she ran, into those great arms opened to hug her.[57]

By the 1850s the Flaubert family circle consisted of the Achille Flauberts and, at first, Flaubert's uncle François Parain, a widower who was a goldsmith and jeweller of Nogent-sur-Seine and who regularly visited Croisset after the death of his brother-in-law, Gustave's father. Parain seems to have shared something of the salt in Gustave's own nature. Writing to him from Rhodes in October 1850 Gustave said: 'It seems to me that young Bouilhet is indulging a little in immorality in my absence. You are seeing him too often. It is you who are demoralizing this young man.'[58] Gustave was very fond of 'l'oncle Parain' and sincerely mourned him when he died in 1853.

Parain's daughter Olympe had married Louis-Théodore Bonenfant, an advocate at Nogent, in 1830, and the Flaubert and Bonenfant families spent almost every summer at Nogent or the Bonenfants joined the Flauberts at Trouville. There were two Bonenfant little girls – yet another Caroline (*b*. 1831) and Émilie-Apolline (*b*. 1833), who had died in 1841. Achille had married Julie Lormier in 1839 and they had a daughter called Juliette, born in 1849, who was to marry Adolphe Rocquigny. It is not surprising that Gustave did not hit it off with Achille. There was nearly nine years between them, so that Achille had already gone to Paris to study medicine when Gustave was old enough to go to school, and after being separated during the whole of their childhood, they did not know each other at all intimately. Clearly there were temperamental differences too; Gustave termed his brother 'bourgeois' and even described him and his wife as behaving almost 'as indelicately as possible' when they were at Croisset in August 1847.[59] Unlike Gustave, Achille was anti-clerical – Caroline described his sardonic laugh at the arrival of her Friday eggs.[60] But Achille rallied to Gustave's side during the *Madame Bovary* trial.

When Gustave returned from his eastern travels in 1851, his little niece was five years old. As will be related in the following chapter, he and Mme Flaubert had already decided to combine a visit to the Great Exhibition in London with finding an English governess for her, but this governess was only to teach English and music. Mme Flaubert had already taught the little girl to read and write and Gustave, with a gusto charmingly described by Caroline in her *Souvenirs*, began teaching her history and geography. He taught her history in his study, she sometimes on the bearskin and he relaxed in his armchair, smoking a pipe and polishing his nails. We do not know her age when he would begin by asking her what she remembered from yesterday's lesson and she was able to reply that she knew the history of the Theban generals Pelopidas and Epaminondas, but of course when he asked her to recite their histories she made mistakes, and there followed his own thrilling account, which he succeeded in making amusing as well. In this way he taught her all ancient history, never in a talking-down-to-the-children style, and the geography lessons were equally fascinating, islands, bays, gulfs, and promontories being modelled in the garden. But Flaubert instilled discipline too. From the age of 10 Caroline had to take notes and was never allowed to drop a book half-way through; he trained her to follow through an idea as well. Since she was his pupil, he did not want her to have the unsystematic mentality, the lack of will to follow up, which was 'the attribute of persons of her sex'.[61] He characteristically wanted her to have the qualities of 'un honnête homme'.

The old servant Mademoiselle Julie, who had come to the Flauberts when Gustave was four and remained with them (in fact she outlived him) must be counted as part of the family circle. Julie was a born raconteur of stories and folklore of the region on the eastern borders of Normandy where she grew up. She was also unusually well read because a bad knee had kept her in bed for a year, and she delighted Gustave when, five years before his own death, in an 'exquisite' conversation he had with her, she was able to discuss Marmontel and *La Nouvelle Héloïse* with him – as many women, and even many men, would not have been able to.[62] She played some part in the most sympathetic character Flaubert depicted, the devoted Félicité in *Un cœur simple*, the tale he originally wrote for George Sand, but it was of the essence of Flaubert's method to study real people and documentation not to reproduce them but to use them as a springboard 'to rise higher', as he told Léon Hennique in February 1880.[63] It is for his mastery in transforming real-life personages or actual events while at the same time conveying verisimilitude that Flaubert is so much admired.

II Gustave Flaubert 'Nel Mezzo del Cammin'

J'aime à la fois le luxe, la profusion, la simplicité, les femmes et le vin, la solitude et le monde, la retraite et les voyages, l'hiver et l'été, la neige et les roses, le calme et la tempête; j'aime à aimer, j'aime à haïr. J'ai en moi toutes les contradictions, toutes les absurdités, toutes les sottises.[1]

Flaubert wrote this discerning summary of the contradictions in his character when he was 18 or 19. The contradictions are revealed also by a glance at one of his manuscript pages, because the commonly held view of Flaubert is that he was a pessimist, but graphologists maintain that lines written by pessimists slope downwards. Not so Flaubert's. Again, it is commonly believed that he was a misanthropist, but Maupassant ('mon élève'), who knew him intimately, said truly that his misanthropy was not innate.[2] Indeed, Flaubert's devoted friendships ('I never permit anyone to say anything more evil about my friends that I would say to their face'),[3] those 'great paternal arms'[4] which welcomed the friends who gathered for the Sunday afternoons at the Paris apartments he rented from 1856, are at the opposite pole from the character of the true, soured misanthropist. Unlike misanthropists too Flaubert was endlessly interested in and curious about people. Maupassant recorded that he took the liveliest interest in the people who passed Croisset on the boat and observed them through opera glasses.[5] Everywhere he went, on boats or on trains, Flaubert's sharp eyes were noting people: 'a young svelte creature wearing an Italian straw hat and a long green veil'[6] or that woman celebrated for making such a deep impression on him in front of St Paul-outside-the-walls in Rome, because she resembled Mme Schlésinger.[7]

In fact the view of Flaubert as a pessimist and misanthropist springs from his novels since, with few exceptions, the characters in them seem either what is usually termed lacking in moral fibre or, at worst, capable of petty meannesses, monumental stupidity, even barbaric cruelty. Flaubert's superb letters seem to reveal a quite different and infinitely more attractive personality; although of course they too do not fail to chastise *bêtise* and often lament the detestable features of contemporary French society, they are the letters of a man devoted to his friends and his niece, ever sympathetic to those in trouble, ready to expend hours at a time to try to comfort a middle-aged spinster who suffered from religious doubt or to criticize, in great detail, unsolicited manuscripts sent to him, a man bubbling over with infectious enthusiasms, with all the spontaneity and engaging inconsequential humanity – evinced in his urgent need to eat venison pie and drink dry white wine after examining sixteenth-century stained glass windows[8] – of the author he found most delectable, Montaigne. It was part of his so contradictory nature that he combined a sombre view of life with the exhilaration shown time and again in the letters. As his niece perceived, he had a mercurial temperament, at times expansive, at other times seemingly enveloped in the vague melancholy of the Nordic peoples.[9]

And he was a pessimist and misanthropist in respect of the age he lived in. Born in 1821, under the restored Bourbon monarchy which was overthrown by the revolution of 1830 – a revolution Flaubert always remembered – he was in Paris and actually witnessed the 1848 revolution which overthrew the July Monarchy of Louis-Philippe. Hence most of his adult life coincided with the July Monarchy and the Second Empire under Louis-Napoleon (who assumed the title of Emperor in December 1852). Then, following the disastrous Franco-Prussian war of 1870, the Third Republic was to outlive Flaubert. The July Monarchy and the Second Empire were pre-eminently periods of industrialization (especially in Normandy), of financial speculation, and of the identification of the government with the richer classes (the 1834 uprising by the Lyon silk weavers was crushed by royal troops). The seamier side of life in France in the nineteenth century was richly documented in Balzac's novels, and although Balzac died in 1850, many of the characters he portrayed in his 'comédie humaine' continued to flourish throughout Flaubert's lifetime.

What Flaubert disliked most was not only the industrialism which 'has developed ugliness in gigantic proportions'[10] but the triumph of materialism, the success of *arrivistes*, the 'constant proof of mediocrity, of banality, of stupidity'.[11] It was this that he designated by the elastic term 'bourgeois' and ceaselessly inveighed against, although, as Jacques Suffel has pointed out, in this he was a bourgeois despising bourgeois,[12] as were the *fin-de-siècle* English writers and artists. It was this 'bourgeois' victory Flaubert portrayed in the pharmacist Homais in *Madame Bovary*, and it was the received ideas of the bourgeoisie that he lampooned in *Bouvard et Pécuchet*. He was not 'anti-establishment', although one of many novels he had planned to write, *Monsieur le Préfet*, was inspired by his hatred of authority and officiousness.[13] But Flaubert had no illusions about any particular class having a monopoly of *bêtise*. 'La Démocrasserie', as he termed it in a letter to Taine of November 1866,[14] would probably be worse. It was precisely this outlook that enabled him to write an account of the 1848 revolution in *L'Éducation sentimentale* which is admired as a valuable historical document as well as a great work of imagination.

Flaubert was not alone in his revulsion from French politics:

> The intelligent man must view a nation as an immense majority of imbeciles. . . . Nothing more than that, neither progress nor principles, but phrases, words, humbug – that is what, little by little, we discern in this present age which, one day, will be history . . . . Revolutions, the merest house-moving. The corruptions, passions, ambitions, and baseness of a nation and a century are a mere removal from one flat to another, with breakages and expense. Political morality, none whatever; success is the only morality. . . . People take risks . . . for the sake of a job. . . . This, in the end, leads to an immense disillusionment, a weariness with all belief, a tolerance of any regime.[15]

So wrote his friends Edmond and Jules de Goncourt in 1863, and this was precisely echoed by Flaubert when he said on 14 March 1868 'one feels that a change of regime would bring nothing new'.[16]

If Flaubert was not what is nowadays called left wing, his 'very warm heart'[17] made him sympathize with the oppressed and with the sufferings of others, as is testified in his letters and at many points in his novels – for example in the dispassionate account of the reasons why Rosanette (in *L'Éducation*) became a prostitute, and in Frédéric Moreau's defence of the Arabs in an outburst in the house of the banker Dambreuse (for we know enough of Flaubert to feel that here he was in sympathy with his character) – and this at precisely the time when France was 'pacifying' Algeria.[18] This warm heart, this feeling of being 'brother in God with all that lives, with the giraffe and the crocodile as [much as] with man',[19] show how different the real Flaubert was from the caricature of the dissector of Emma Bovary.[20] Flaubert could and did use a scalpel, especially to uncover layers of hypocrisy and vanity, but it must be a cold-hearted reader who is unable to sympathize with Emma and Charles.

Flaubert also deplored the contemporary progressist view of a civilization he termed as a 'lying and hypocritical vampire',[21] infecting the face of the globe. 'Woe on this aridity of civilization which desiccates and withers everything which springs up to the sun of poetry and of the heart.'[22] 'In your immense pride, you have wished to subdue nature,' Satan says in *Smarh*, which he wrote in 1839.[23] Though he was too much of a Voltairean rationalist to be a believer, no one was more conscious of the void left by the collapse of Christian belief: 'We have tried everything and we repudiate everything' but 'an immense anxiety gnaws us' and 'we feel around us a sepulchral chill'.[24] He devoted many years of his life to his researches for and to writing and twice rewriting his *Tentation de saint Antoine* which, set in the third-century Alexandrian world, the age of the heresies, was in part an exploration of religious faith manifested in world religions, including Buddhism, viewed in his own age of scientific positivism and scepticism. This was his favourite work,[25] but he liked to repeat, with Montaigne, that one must 'sleep on the pillow of doubt'.[26]

'It is true that I am not easy to know', Flaubert told Louise Colet in October 1846,[27] but at least those of his friends who knew him best are reliable witnesses of the salient facets of his complex character. To set against the pessimism and misanthropy is Maupassant's record of his gaiety:

> He liked pranks, jokes which were carried on for years. He often laughed, with a happy, frank, deep laughter, and this laughter seemed more natural and normal in him than his exasperation with human nature. . . . He enjoyed living, and he lived fully and sincerely.[28]

The Goncourt brothers endorsed this and immortalized Flaubert's portrayal of 'the drawing-room idiot' in their journal, describing how he transformed himself into 'a formidable caricature of imbecility', and in 1861 Edmond wrote wishing that Flaubert could send 'the childlike ring of your merriment' by post.[29] This was the side of Flaubert that had delighted his family during his boyhood and which they greatly missed when he was not with them. 'How I wish you were here', Caroline Flaubert wrote in May 1839; 'how many opportunities you would have to make me laugh with your jokes.'[30]

His friends recorded too the hot temper which could explode, but again as Zola put it, 'his great angers subsided like milky soup' when it comes off the boil.[31] What struck them all was 'a goodness which is put to the proof at every instant' – unless one had written an incorrect, slovenly, or ambiguous phrase, for he was 'cruelly on the look-out for ridicule'.[32] He was totally without jealousy (even of other lovers of his mistress) or bitterness. In February 1862 he discussed with the Goncourts the virulent personal attack on him published by his former mistress. They noted his absence of bitterness or resentment.[33] And he gave the impression of being transparently honest. Du Camp – not always an unprejudiced witness – said 'he never lied' and in fact was easily duped because he could not imagine anyone practising deception.[34] Yet if it is true that he never lied, he was not above practising deception – for which he had a native talent – to conceal his own most private affairs, and it was he who devised a stratagem for enabling Hugo's correspondence to bypass the censors when Hugo was a political exile. He likewise took the precaution of having the letters of his mistress Louise Colet sent to Du Camp and redirected in another envelope. (Did he think of some similar ruse to avoid comment on the number of letters from France which Juliet must have received?) As will also be seen, the impression he gave of being wholly uncalculating was likewise not in all respects true.

For Flaubert, unlike Turgenev, the physical side of love was important. Although he was no Don Juanesque seducer of young or virtuous women (and the attraction between him and Juliet, then aged 30, must have been mutual), he was a sensualist who, as a young man, had been inveterate in the pursuit of sexual adventures – in the brothels of Paris and the Middle East and Italy, with actresses, with at one period of his life two concurrent mistresses. But he seemed not bent solely on physical gratification, as is witnessed by his much-quoted phrase 'woman is the arch to the infinite'. And he retained an affection for some of the women with whom he had casual affairs; for instance, he recommended the actress Béatrix Person for a part in a play and tried to help her when, later, a young man wished to marry her, against parental opposition. But Flaubert was also, as Enid Starkie perceived when she quoted passages suppressed in the published letters, at times taking steps 'to prove my virility'.[35] That he was capable of uniting love and passion with physical desire we know from his relations with Louise Colet (see p. 42), even though by the time he met her his passion to write in his particular way took first place. The austerities of his monkish life at Croisset while he was studying and writing no doubt intensified carnal desire, and whenever he was in Paris he seemed to compensate for the months of abstention. However, the taste for sexual adventures was shared by many of his contemporaries; again as Jacques Suffel has said, Flaubert's friends, Alfred Le Poittevin, Du Camp, and Bouilhet, all shared 'une morale assez libertaire', in part a legacy of the eighteenth-century literature on which they were reared.[36] Compare James Boswell. And Turgenev's formidable mother took it for granted that he would catch what she called 'man's illness'.[37] Like Gautier, whom he much admired, Flaubert loved also bawdy stories, and his letters abound in scatological expressions. When he was writing them, after strictly disciplining his prose during an eight-hour working day, he felt, as Dumesnil put it, like a boy out of school.[38] For this Rabelaisian side was so rigorously excluded from the novels that the seductions of Emma Bovary have to be inferred, since they are not even described.

What might be considered a darker strand in his nature was his cult of the works of the marquis de Sade – in the often-quoted phrase by the Goncourts, he had a mind haunted by Sade.[39] This is undeniable, but in that close-knit literary clique in Paris, where no secret did not become common property (and was duly noted in the *Journal des Goncourt*), no hint of any sadism in Flaubert's life, as opposed to his writings, has been reported – in contrast to Proust, who vented his sadistic feelings on rats.[40] The strain in Flaubert which drew him to Sade found expression above all in *Salammbô*, but far from repelling the public of the 1860s, the novel was all the rage; this streak in Flaubert's nature clearly did not shock French society of the time or seem a horrifying perversion. It is salutary to remember too that this many-sided man charmed his friends by the childish and innocent side of his character,[41] and who was more understanding of children than the man who could write of his niece's doll: 'Mme Phipharô, who will obstinately stay under the trees, has caught a slight cold from one of the yellow leaves falling on her head; she is coughing a little and I fear for her chest.'[42]

Another important side of Flaubert's character, deriving both from the fact that his generation were the heirs of romanticism and from his – related – dislike of contemporary France was a lifelong taste for the exotic, above all for 'distant travels in the countries of the South'.[43] 'Will I ever', he had asked when he was 21, 'set foot on the sands of Syria, when the horizon is a dazzling red, when the earth rises up in scorching spirals and eagles soar in a burning sky?'[44] Nothing could have seemed more unlikely when, in 1844, Flaubert was literally struck down by what has been diagnosed as epilepsy (despite the absence of some of its most characteristic manifestations such as convulsions and biting the tongue).[45] This illness was decisive in putting an end to the law studies his father had prescribed and the career Flaubert had envisaged as 'a deputy public prosecutor in a small provincial town'.[46] Thanks, however, to his friendship with Du Camp, and to Du Camp's readiness to take the not inconsiderable risk of travelling with Flaubert, in 1849–51 they together visited Egypt, Palestine, Syria, Lebanon, Asia Minor, Greece, and Italy. Contrary to what has sometimes been said, this tremendous journey by no means cured Flaubert of his *Wanderlust.* In 1859 he was 'troubled by the idea of a journey to China'; it would have been easy to go with the French expedition if he had not a mother who was beginning to grow old. Travel was still 'the best thing in life'.[47] Because of his mother, and also because he lacked sufficient money, except for a brief visit to Algeria and Tunisia in 1858, he never again went farther from France than Belgium, Germany, Switzerland, and England. But his great journey with Du Camp had made him sufficiently 'Arabophil' to declare, on returning to Alexandria from Cairo in July 1850, 'Alexandrie m'emmerde' – because it was full of Europeans.[48] Bedouin life, as he saw it, appealed to him as the embodiment of all that was the very antithesis of an age mirrored in Ingres's portrait of Mme Moitessier, in her sumptuous gown, wearing the heavy jewelry then in vogue, 'not the prisoner of her over-heated, over-upholstered Second Empire environment but its personification'.[49]

Like the Elizabethan gallants who returned from the Grand Tour full of affectations, Flaubert after his eastern journey took to wearing *chez lui* vast red-and-white striped breeks and in summer a long Nubian cotton shirt which, with a tarbush or light silk skullcap, gave him something of the air of 'a Turk *en négligé*'.[50] No wonder that the Rouennais who went to La Bouille for Sunday lunch returned disappointed if they had not been able to see, from the bridge of the steamer, 'cet original de M. Flaubert' standing in his tall window.[51]

His appearance was remarkable enough without such fancy-dress (which in fact he wore to be comfortable when writing). To his great sorrow he had lost the hair on the top of his head during that eastern journey and had begun to put on weight while sailing down the Nile ('I am getting fat in an ignoble way', he had told his mother in February 1850).[52] But Flaubert was still a very striking figure. Like his friend Turgenev, he was a giant, and he carried his height proudly. He had the broad shoulders of a powerful swimmer, and his remaining, very fine hair fell in curls on his shoulders. His large sea-green eyes with their long lashes and rather puffy eyelids were his most prominent feature. He had full cheeks, a ruddy complexion, and rough drooping moustaches, 'à la Vercingétorix'.[53] He had a stentorian voice and was given to sweeping gestures which at times made him seem to fly from one to another of his guests as he crossed his Paris apartment in a single stride, his long gown floating behind him.[54] Yet one can still discern in Nadar's photograph something of the diffidence of his brother's boyhood portrait of him at the age of 12.[55]

Flaubert valued friendship above all, but by the time he had returned from his travels with Du Camp, one of his closest friends, Alfred Le Poittevin, had died (in 1848), and another (a school friend), Ernest Chevalier, had – to paraphrase Millamant in *The Way of the World* – from Flaubert's point of view 'dwindled into a husband'. And the friendship between him and Maxime Du Camp, once so close that they exchanged rings in token of 'some kind of intellectual betrothal',[56] was distinctly cooler since on their return the ambitious Maxime, who had become a joint editor of the *Revue de Paris*, was vigorously pursuing success through journalism and courting the right people, while Flaubert was interested only in writing in such a way as to satisfy his own exacting criteria. This demanded such rigorous concentration that he was unable to leave Croisset until he had completed his first published book, *Madame Bovary*. At this period in his life his closest friend came to be Louis Bouilhet, a former medical student of Dr Flaubert's, who had thrown up his medical studies to write, supporting himself by taking pupils. A brilliant classicist who had been his contemporary at the Collège de Rouen (although they did not become friends), Bouilhet's classical background made him an ideal critic, on whom Flaubert came to depend absolutely.

An early friendship which was to play some part in Flaubert's later life was that with some members of the Collier family he had first met at Trouville in 1842.[57] The family of Captain (later

Admiral) Henry Collier had come to live in France in 1823, after serious financial losses. When Flaubert met them, the youngest son, Herbert, and four daughters were at Trouville, both the elder sons being in England. With the Colliers was Captain Collier's sister Georgina, widow of George Aïdá,[58] and her only surviving son, Charles Hamilton (always known as Hamilton Aïdé). Gustave and his sister Caroline became close friends of two of the Collier sisters and Herbert, later to become a colonel in the Hussars, used to call him 'papa'.[59] When he was a law student in Paris in 1842–3, Gustave was a frequent visitor to the Colliers' house at the Champs-Élysées Rond-Point, where he used to read aloud to Harriet, who had a back ailment and was a patient of Dr Flaubert, but (according to him) he resisted her mother's attempt to ensnare him.[60] As Gertrude's later memoirs show,[61] she and Harriet were both enamoured of the handsome young Gustave and were rivals for his affections, and Harriet gave him her portrait which he hung in a place of honour on his chimney-piece at Croisset, but it was Gertrude to whom he wrote warmly when she told him in November 1846 that they were returning to England ('You are mingled with so many things in my intimate life').[62]

On leaving France, the Colliers first went to the Isle of Wight where, at Ryde, in 1847 Gertrude (then aged 27) married Charles Tennant, an attorney and solicitor who was a writer on political economy and was twenty-four years her senior.[63] In 1832, on the death of his elder brother, he had inherited Cadoxton Hall, Neath, Glamorgan, a property which had been purchased by his father, who had also purchased Rhydding estate and started the formation of an inland navigation system known as the Tennant Canal. He was very briefly (and not, as has been stated, for many years) MP for St Albans – from October 1830 till June 1831, but he was not re-elected to the Reform Parliament.[64] They lived at 62 Russell Square, which had been Charles Tennant's London home since at least 1841. Captain Collier (whose wife died in October 1850),[65] Harriet (aged 27), and Clementina (aged 24) were living at 25 Upper Grosvenor Street from 1850 if not earlier,[66] but Herbert, who does not appear in the 1851 census return, was probably away at school. As will be seen, in 1851 Gustave visited Upper Grosvenor Street when he and his mother came to England and had a sentimental reunion with Harriet; he was thus chagrined to learn of her marriage to Sir Alexander Campbell of Barcaldine in August

1855 ('the angels of my youth are turning into housewives').[67] He did not see Gertrude then, but this may not be because there was an estrangement (caused by the sisters' rivalry for his affections) but because Gertrude already had a two-year-old daughter called Alice and a nine-month-old baby called Beatrice.[68]

Gertrude and her husband continued to live in Russell Square until the end of the 1860s (they had four children by 1861, when Charles described himself as land-owner and mine owner).[69] It would thus have been very easy for Gustave to have called on her when he visited London in 1865 and 1866 (see Chapters V and VI), but he made no attempt to do so. A possible explanation of why he did not is that she had alienated him by her opinion of *Madame Bovary*. The inscription in a copy he sent her (after asking Hamilton Aïdé for her address in June 1857)[70] included his 'hommages d'une inaltér. affection' but, as Professor Bruneau says, the letter she wrote on 23 June 1857 'defies comment': the Victorian Englishwoman echoed the French prosecutor.[71] It was not for nothing that Gertrude was to be the only person in the world her son-in-law H. M. Stanley had ever felt afraid of,[72] and Gustave's affection must indeed have been unalterable to survive such strictures as 'I cannot understand how you have been able to write all that' in which 'there is nothing *beautiful* or good!' and 'I find . . . the *talent* you have put into this book doubly *detestable*'.[73] (The address on this letter is given as 62 Rupert Street, but this must be a misreading of 62 Russell Square, arising from the older form of the letter s and the abbreviation 'Sq.', for 62 Rupert Street was the address of the John O'Groats Hotel and Tavern in Soho – emphatically not somewhere Gertrude would be found.) In 1860 Gertrude sent Gustave a copy of *Adam Bede* (no doubt for his edification). It is then astonishing to find that two years later he sent her – of all books! – an inscribed copy of *Salammbô* (on which her comments are unimaginable). Thus her letter of 1857 had not caused a break in their relations. No letter of hers on *Salammbô* has been recorded, so that it is possible that she then wrote in such terms that he felt no desire to see her when he was in London, but it is equally possible that when, in 1865, he was visiting the British Museum (literally a stone's throw away), he was, as so often, concealing his own private affairs.

The Tennants moved to Richmond Terrace, S.W.1, at the end of the 1860s, where Gertrude eventually became a notable social hostess and her daughter Dolly's wedding to H. M. Stanley (whom she married on condition that he did not part her from her mother) was on a scale surpassed only by royal weddings.[74] Gustave could, again, easily have called on her when he was in London in 1871 (see Chapter VII), but he neither called on her nor on her father, then Admiral Collier, who at 79 had set up with a second wife, aged 25, and was living with her and their four-year-old daughter at 25 Ryder Street, St James's.[75]

Another youthful relationship with a woman which continued to play some part at various periods with which this book is concerned is that with Mme Schlésinger, believed by Gérard-Gailly and some other authorities of an earlier generation to have been Flaubert's sole love, but – as Professor Bruneau first pointed out – the evidence of Flaubert's letters to Louise Colet, of what he reported to the Goncourts, and of a letter Du Camp wrote to him seem to show that this *grande passion* ended in 1843–4.[76] It has already been mentioned that when the young Gustave first met and fell romantically in love with Mme Schlésinger she had not yet married the music publisher Maurice Schlésinger, and she could not do so until after the death of her first husband in 1839. While Flaubert was a law student in Paris during 1842–4, he spent a good deal of his time with the Schlésingers. Professor Bruneau has suggested that at this period his love for Mme Schlésinger underwent a great change, Gustave then perceiving that his passion was cooling while she was the more attracted by the personality of her young lover.[77] Jacques Suffel believes that in 1848 there are indications that the love affair no longer remained platonic,[78] yet it is notable that in all the letters Gustave later wrote to her he always addressed her as 'vous', whereas Louise was 'tu' (unless they had had a serious quarrel). Whatever did happen between them in 1842–4, Gustave continued to cherish the unforgettable impression of this passionate love (as will be seen, it was otherwise with Louise Colet), and – most important – this relationship with Mme Schlésinger was the 'springboard' for Frédéric Moreau's love of Mme Arnoux in *L'Éducation sentimentale*.

In 1852 the Schlésingers moved from Paris to Baden, but family troubles caused Mme Schlésinger's mental derangement. She was first interned in a mental hospital in March 1862, then from August 1863 lived with her family once more, but was finally interned again in July 1875; her daughter's resentment at finding that she had been illegitimate certainly played a part in this derangement.[79]

Flaubert, with his masterly powers of expression and as a student of character, excelled in flattering some of his women correspondents so subtly that it has occasionally been believed that he was in love with them, not excluding Princess Mathilde – a woman who, as the Goncourts well knew, expected gallantries from her men friends. When, however, one finds that Flaubert was capable of writing virtually the same letter to several of his women friends on the same day, and when – as will be seen – it becomes apparent that in the interests of gathering data he was capable of less subtle flattery, it seems necessary to exercise a degree of scepticism in respect of some superlative expressions of emotion aroused by beautiful women among his acquaintance, such as Jeanne de Tourbey, the mistress of Prince Napoleon ('Plon-Plon'). Yet this is emphatically not to say that he was not also profoundly emotional and responsive to feminine beauty, which is precisely why it is sometimes difficult to know when the emotion expressed is altogether genuine or not.

Any woman who was to have, and was to continue to have, a closer relationship with Flaubert than one of friendship, and a deeper relationship than one primarily on a sensual level, would have to understand and believe in Flaubert the writer. Unless, like Mme Flaubert, she could realize that for him what he called 'art' took first place, the relationship must inevitably founder. As he told one woman who failed to understand this, 'You regard this subject as something secondary, something amusing between politics and the news? I certainly don't'.[80] It is therefore of some importance to indicate the kind of writer Flaubert was and why the way he wrote demanded, at least at times, the life of an anchorite.

When Flaubert had returned from his travels with Du Camp, he faced a crisis as a writer, and since he was first and foremost a writer, this (and not his illness) was the major crisis of his whole life. This great turning-point had occurred before he and Du Camp set off, for it was then that Flaubert had read the first version of the *Tentation de saint Antoine* to Bouilhet and Du Camp. He had particularly learned to trust Bouilhet's judgement, so that the shock to him when Bouilhet told him he had better burn the manuscript and never speak of it again may be imagined. They also told Flaubert (according to the sole record of this occasion, made by Du Camp, but not at the time) that he should renounce subjects of this kind, which lent themselves to 'phrases, grandiose images, and metaphors', and adopt a down-to-earth subject like Balzac's *La*

Cousine Bette or *Le Cousin Pons* and a natural style, without digressions. It is not true (as Du Camp related) that they suggested that he should write the story of the Rouen health official whose wife poisoned herself (the immediate source of *Madame Bovary*) since this incident had not yet occurred. Du Camp's account of Flaubert declaiming 'I will call her Emma Bovary' at the Second Cataract was either inspired journalism or it applied not to the celebrated Emma but to the heroine of another tale Flaubert was meditating.[81]

Such was the result of three years of study and writing. Poor Flaubert even wondered (at an early stage of the eastern journey) whether he would write at all when he got back;[82] this 'terrible blow' had made him excessively timid,[83] but a little later he told his mother that something new was germinating in him, 'perhaps a second manner?'.[84] The 'second manner' was to emerge, slowly and painfully, in the writing of *Madame Bovary*, which he began (but no more than a synopsis) on 19 September 1851, shortly before his visit to England with Mme Flaubert already mentioned. The real-life incident was suggested to him by Bouilhet after Flaubert's return to Croisset from the eastern journey.[85]

The main reason for the slowness was because the petty provincial subject-matter was not just against the grain – for Flaubert loved subjects which gave scope for exaltation and lyricism – but one which disgusted him. 'This book is killing me. . . . No one will ever get me to write about bourgeois things again.'[86] But also this was the first of Flaubert's books which forced him to make plans and scenarios, both overall and partial ones, i.e. to work at the structure of the book – he had himself recognized that the structure of the first *L'Éducation* left much to be desired.[87] Then there was the stage of writing drafts (1,800 pages of these drafts are preserved in the Rouen municipal library), followed by more careful writing (which in some cases meant starting again a dozen times), that in turn followed by revision, which often started at the end and returned step by step to the beginning. What Flaubert was doing was not only to blaze a new trail in imaginative literature – because *Madame Bovary* was, as Baudelaire perceived, far removed from the commonly held view of realism as 'a minute description of accessories' instead of a new creative method[88] – he was also forging a new technique and, finally, a new style. He had to find a totally new way of writing, one which meant continual discarding, curbing his natural tendency to exuberance (the description of Rouen seen by

Emma from Bois-Guillaume was condensed from a whole page to fifteen lines after six successive redrafts and corrections),[89] and remorselessly excluding all comment or explanation by the author. At the same time – even more difficult – he had to avoid flat writing. It was also, in his view, of the utmost importance that his prose, while remaining 'très prose', should have the rhythm of poetry. (Hence everything he wrote was declaimed aloud.) He believed that it was very original to try to write about everyday life as if it were history or epic; this was perhaps 'a great attempt'.[90] Still more difficult, this new style had to be exactly right, not just to satisfy its author's exacting standards but to be precisely in character. One example is revealing. He discarded the image of a handful of broken sea-shells to describe Emma's comparison of her earlier dreams with reality because Emma had never been to the seaside.[91] This illustrates too what he was later to describe as the necessity to transport oneself into one's characters and not to attract them to oneself.[92] And, finally, there were scenes which required detailed technical knowledge Flaubert knew he was far from possessing. Hence his care to consult his brother and a publication on the pathology of club-feet, to consult the family solicitor (and, as will be seen, to draw on Mme Pradier's memoirs) for the financial transactions, and so on. Professor Gothot-Mersch rightly says, 'one can see in this rigorous preparation evidence of the conscientiousness with which Flaubert surrounded his work and his readers.'[93] This reflected also his essential modesty. As he told Louise Colet in October 1846, since he was no Shakespeare or Byron who could 'reproduce the universe', and was not so eccentric as to fill a book with himself alone,[94] it was essential to be scrupulously correct in all the detail in his books. Hence, later, the fifty-three works he consulted between March and May 1857 for *Salammbô*[95] (and this was only the beginning), the whole library of writings by socialists, quantities of newspaper files, visits to a porcelain factory and treatises on pottery etc., when he was preparing to write the final version of *L'Éducation*. Though he told George Sand that he regarded 'technical detail, local information, the exact historical side of things as very secondary',[96] he took infinite pains over it. No wonder that as early as 1853 he was to exclaim 'But life is so short.'[97]

Thus the popular view of Flaubert the writer toiling for weeks over a single sentence is no more than a half-truth, and Du Camp's later allegation that his brain had been impaired by the illness of 1844 is a slander devoid of foundation – as Du Camp well knew, Flaubert had written the 541 pages of the first *Tentation* (*after* this illness) very quickly (between 24 May 1848 and 12 September 1849) and, as he also knew, Flaubert was pouring out hundreds of letters, many several pages long, with the utmost fluency during their travels. (His first letter from Egypt, eight well-filled pages long, was written in less than two hours.)[98] What Flaubert had become, since the rejection of the first *Tentation*, was – in the words of Maître Sénard, who defended him at the trial – a man who 'devoted his life to study, to letters'.[99] As he himself had put it in 1846: 'Note that one manages to create beautiful things by dint of patience and long energy' and 'for me, love is not the first thing in life but the second'.[100]

Flaubert maintained that he wrote for himself alone ('I have no need to be sustained by the idea of any recompense'),[101] and in respect of his own advancement he seemed to be the reverse of calculating – in 1852 he scorned Du Camp's advice to him to move to Paris in order to become known: 'Success seems to me to be a result and not the aim'.[102] Yet the Goncourt brothers, who had heard (with 'tout Paris') of Flaubert's attempt to drive an impossibly hard bargain with Lévy for *Salammbô* – he tried to extract 20,000–30,000 francs from Lévy and was only slowly induced to agree to 10,000 francs – noted that 'there is something Norman, thoroughly cunning . . . I begin to think, at the core of this fellow, so open in appearance . . . turning up his nose at success with so much show'. They observed too that Flaubert was 'surreptitiously' working for his own success better than anyone and launching *Salammbô* 'with a modest demeanour' at exactly the same time as Hugo's *Les Misérables*,[103] yet it was Flaubert who had said that the true man of letters should devote his life to writing books for which he should not even seek publicity.[104] As was so often the case, Flaubert's complex character embraced the twin poles of total disinterest and of a calculating shrewdness which enabled him also to advise Louis Bouilhet exactly how to set about courting the right people to get a play of his staged in Paris. Having written a book (and sorely needing money) he did do his best to obtain the maximum financial reward and to work for its success, but what is infinitely more important is the truth of his statement that he wrote for himself. To perceive how totally uninfluenced by any thought of popular success he was when he was planning and writing, it is sufficient to recall that it was his unflattering portrait of the 'men of my generation' in *L'Éducation sentimentale* that was an important reason for its unhappy reception.

Flaubert could be far more calculating not for his advancement but in the service of his ruling passion, literature. Here there was one notorious case of 'Je prends mon bien où je le trouve'. One of his childhood friends, possibly related to him,[105] Louise Darcet (nicknamed Ludovica), had married the sculptor James Pradier, who in 1845 was compelled to obtain a legal separation from her because of her flamboyant adulteries and financial entanglements. On 8 December 1842 Flaubert's friend Le Poittevin had advised him to seek her out ('She can give you some useful hints . . .'),[106] and Gustave did so when he was visiting Paris before the family journey to Italy for his sister's honeymoon, shortly after the Pradier separation. He told Le Poittevin on 2 April what a beautiful study he was making of this 'femme perdue', whom he flattered by declaring that he was 'the champion of adultery', adding a celebrated phrase: 'All this demands to be written, enumerated, painted, engraved.'[107] Ludovica had certainly become his mistress by August 1847,[108] despite his liaison with Louise Colet, which dated from July 1846. It is not known how he came into the possession of a manuscript of unknown authorship entitled the *Mémoires de Madame Ludovica* which relates, ungrammatically and almost illiterately yet not without talent, Ludovica's life when she was married to Pradier. As Douglas Siler shows, the MS must date from the end of 1846 or later.[109] It was originally discovered in 1947 by Gabrielle Leleu (the librarian of the Rouen library) among the *Madame Bovary* dossiers, and Flaubert had marked passages which he was to use in this novel. It has been supposed that it is not impossible that Ludovica herself provided this very important document to her lover,[110] a suggestion which seems to receive strong support from an autograph letter which was sold at the Hôtel Drouot sale on 18 and 19 November 1931. In this letter (item 193) to Gustave, Ludovica refers to the information she sent him on the procedure of bailiffs in the matter of distraining the goods of a 'cocotte'; the letter ends affectionately 'Je te saute au col, à toi'.[111] Indeed, her generosity to her lovers is reported in the *Mémoires*, but if she did give this manuscript to Flaubert, he must at least have asked her for it. It may well be one thing to exploit one's mistress as a model – Alexandre Dumas *fils*, also Ludovica's lover, did this in his *L'Affaire Clemenceau* – but another to acquire and draw on a highly intimate account of her private life. Yet the way Flaubert transformed this tale of a fashionable Parisienne into that of a provincial girl so educated that she was unable to love her dull, country doctor husband beautifully demonstrates the distance between any model and every character he created, and if his use of Ludovica's memoirs may seem a little cold-blooded, it after all recalls Montaigne's 'les abeilles pillotent deçà delà les fleurs; mais elles font aprez le miel, qui est tout leur; ce n'est plus thym, ny marjolaine; ainsi les pieces empruntees d'aultruy, il les transformera et confondra pour en faire un ouvrage tout sien.'[112]

There was one other person who was extremely important to Flaubert from 1846 until the early 1850s – Louise Colet.

Nicknamed 'the Muse', Louise was a southerner from Aix-en-Provence who had married an unsuccessful musician in order to come to Paris. She was herself a poet and writer of plays and novels and, in the words of Jean Bruneau, she began the most brilliant of literary careers in Paris under the ægis of the distinguished philosopher Victor Cousin, whose mistress she became and who believed that he was the father of her daughter Henriette.[113] Flaubert met her in James Pradier's studio – it was entirely in character that she called Pradier Phidias and Pradier, not noted for respecting women, called her Sappho – when he went to Paris in the late summer of 1846 to commission Pradier to make a bust of his sister Caroline. Louise had (not without influence) won two Academy awards for her poems, in 1839 and 1843, and was in receipt of a government pension. Also through Cousin, in 1842 she was received by the ageing Mme Récamier and had set up a salon on the Récamier model – in 1849 she installed herself in the same street as the famous Abbaye-aux-Bois. Described as ravishingly beautiful, Louise was at the height of her fame when Flaubert was unknown and all too recently oppressed by the death of his father and sister and by his long, debilitating illness. It is not difficult to imagine her impact on him. Hence he was to tell her that after his *grande passion* for Mme Schlésinger, he had put on one side his soul, which was reserved for 'Art', and on the other his body – but 'then you came and upset all that'.[114]

From her point of view she did not upset it nearly enough, not only because of Flaubert's mother (though she did constitute a real obstacle) but because she had the misfortune to fall in love with Gustave when he had already decided, as he told Le Poittevin on 19 June 1845, that a normal liaison would take him too much out of himself and make him re-enter active life, which had been harmful to him every time he had wanted to try it.[115] As Bruneau and Ducourneau put it, after the great crisis of 1843–5, Flaubert renounced living to depict life.[116] (During the first phase of their relationship he was doing intensive reading for the first *Tentation*.) It is, however, legitimate to doubt if the eventual outcome would have been different if Flaubert had behaved more like a normal lover, for it is plausible to see in their relationship something of

> Two strangers from opposing poles
> Meet in the torrid zone of love.[117]

Not only was Louise tempestuous; she was also possessive and jealous, even of the friends of Gustave's youth – the 'fantômes de Trouville', as she derisively termed them. And Flaubert was certainly to become increasingly aware that they had radically different views of 'art'. It was evidently sharply disillusioning when it was 'Sappho' who declared, when they were together at Mantes, that she would not give her present happiness for the glory of Corneille,[118] and on a later occasion, in a poem she had written for him, preferred some *tableaux vivants* she had recently seen to the paintings by Rubens, Titian, and Raphael which they were imitating.[119] However, the first break in their relations did not occur until, in March 1848, Louise announced the news to Gustave that she had taken a lover and was pregnant.[120]

Next year she learned only from a newspaper that Flaubert was leaving for the Near East, and of his return only from a compatriot then in Paris. By that time her circumstances were totally different. On the death of her husband Hippolyte on 21 April 1851 she lost his salary (through Cousin, he had been employed at the Conservatoire), her government pension had been reduced, and in 1849 she had lost and had to pay the costs of an unsavoury lawsuit because, it was alleged, she had induced the blind Mme Récamier to give her the letters of Benjamin Constant, which she began to publish on 11 May that year, immediately after Mme Récamier's death.[121] She was in financial difficulties, and it is hard to believe that she was entirely disinterested when, as described above, she descended on Croisset uninvited but was refused admittance because 'Monsieur

Flaubert' was at table with strangers.[122] She was told, however, that if she would inform the maid of her address in Rouen, 'Monsieur' would go to see her there.

Until the comparatively recent discovery of the 'lost suitcase' of Colet papers recorded by Professor Bruneau,[123] the only version of this visit was one given by Louise herself when, in 1856, she published her transparent fictional attack on Flaubert, *Une histoire de soldat*, incidentally claiming that she had entered the Flauberts' house and remained there for two hours, only to be thrown out by Gustave. Instead he met her in Rouen, as he had said he would, but now it was a very different Gustave from the young man she first met in Pradier's studio: his travels had made him far more self-confident and independent. He advised her to marry Cousin. Louise noticed his self-possession – when, sobbing, she said 'Perhaps we will never see each other again', 'Why not?' he coolly replied.[124]

Their relationship was in fact renewed – but on his, mainly literary terms, and with diminishing warmth and increasing acrimony – until 1854. The world owes Louise an immense debt of gratitude for this renewal in their relations, for she was the recipient of and she preserved many hundreds of letters, even when they were very wounding to her. Those he wrote between 1851 and 1854, in which he explained his work on *Madame Bovary* step by step, are of inestimable value for all students of Flaubert's work, and one must regret (with Professor Bruneau) that he apparently did not have such an intelligent and devoted mistress when he wrote the later novels.[125] But, as will be seen, he did have, in Juliet Herbert, another woman with whom he kept in touch for over twenty years, who was almost certainly his mistress, and whose intelligence impressed not only Flaubert but also, in Du Camp's words, that 'impeccable critic' Bouilhet. It cannot be doubted that he and Juliet must have written numerous letters to each other, and Gustave may have described at least some of his literary aims and methods to her, but unfortunately these letters do not appear to have survived. (The question of their likely destruction is discussed in Chapter IX.) It is true that after the publication of *Madame Bovary* Flaubert was no longer 'the hermit of Croisset', reaching out (like Thomas Jefferson at Monticello) for human contacts, for the publication of this novel brought him many friends. But he was a man who needed women confidantes. As the existing correspondence shows, at this later period there were other such confidantes (especially George Sand, Mme Roger des Genettes, who frequented 'the Muse's' salon, Amélie Bosquet, herself a writer, and Mlle Leroyer de Chantepie, his correspondent who suffered religious doubt), but among letters he wrote to Juliet Herbert, seemingly there were ones of cardinal importance which, if they could be found, would undoubtedly constitute 'the most important contribution that could be made to the published correspondence'.[126]

It would not be difficult to write a treatise on the features in Louise's and Gustave's characters which, despite genuine passion and despite her intelligence, made this relationship one which more often exasperated Flaubert than it was life-enhancing. Here a very brief résumé must suffice, so as to indicate the pitfalls any other mistress needed to avoid. Du Camp, often an intermediary between them, was right when he advised Louise to accept Gustave as he was because her efforts to try to change him would be fruitless, since 'work was his whole existence', and he would never consent to be interrupted 'even for an hour'.[127] If she wanted him to visit her, she should not reproach him or weep: 'in this respect he is like all men; he does not like recriminations and he detests tears'.[128] But Louise (as we know from Flaubert's letters) was incapable of taking this advice. And Flaubert was, as he told her, 'tired of *grandes passions*', which did not consort with 'this long patience demanded by the craft'.[129] Could she not enjoy the pleasure of their being together and of writing from time to time, of seeing each other with beaming faces and open hearts?[130] Above all, for him love had no right to be in the front rank of life; it should remain in the background: 'there are other things in one's soul which are . . . nearer the light, closer to the sun.'[131]

III English Governesses at Croisset

English Governesses in Fact and Fiction

'Sixteen years had Miss Taylor been in Mr Woodhouse's family, less as a governess than a friend,' Jane Austen wrote in *Emma*, first published in 1816. Even so, Emma Woodhouse pitied Jane Fairfax, who was to have become a governess, when she 'considered what all this elegance was destined to, what she was going to sink from'.

Miss Taylor was fortunate because she was employed by a family looked up to as 'first in consequence' in the nearest village; Mr Woodhouse belonged to the landed gentry or English county families. Governesses employed by such families or by the aristocracy were as a rule far better treated than those, a little later in the century, employed by members of the Victorian middle class – the class concerned with maintaining its social distance from its employees – or by manufacturers, farmers, and tradespeople (as in George Eliot's *Middlemarch*). It is true that in a large and wealthy titled family, governesses and children were usually segregated from the parents, whose social life dictated this segregation, but, for example, the head governess of the family of Viscount Belgrave (eldest son of the first Marquess of Westminster) accompanied the family on their tours of Germany and Italy in 1835–6.[1] She was paid £70 a year (compared with the £50 a year earned by the coachman and cook-housekeeper). The second governess was certainly paid less, and there were frequent changes, possibly because the head governess was difficult.[2] The lot of a governess in a middle-class family tended to be unenviable. In her *Memoirs and Essays* published in 1846, Anna Brownell Jameson noted that the occupation of a governess was 'the only means by which a woman not born in the servile class can earn the means of subsistence',[3] and in George Eliot's *Scenes of Clerical Life* (1858), friends of Janet Dempster excused her marriage to a drunken scoundrel as she had nothing to look to but being a governess. According to tradition, the governess was supposed to be a 'lady', preferably the daughter of a family whose fortunes had been ruined or of a clerical family, as in Anne

Brontë's *Agnes Grey*, for 'the daughters of clergymen grew up with the fate of a governess before them from their infant days'.[4] As a writer in the *Quarterly Review* put it,

> The real definition of a governess, in the English sense, is a being who is our equal in birth, manners, and education, but our inferior in worldly wealth. . . . There is no other class which so cruelly requires its members to be, in birth, mind, and manners, above their station in order to fit them for their station.[5]

At a time when women were indeed debarred from all other 'non-servile' employment, the consequence was what might be called a bear market – an over-supply of governesses, which reduced their already meagre salaries, out of which they often had to support other members of their families. The 1851 census recorded (for the year 1850) 24,770 'ladies' registered as governesses.[6] The situation resulting from too many poorly educated young women hiring themselves out as governesses inevitably depressed their wages and resulted in their being treated with contempt. In mid-Victorian England at least the lot of the governess was often pitiable. Her duties were undefined and indefinitely extensible, to include also needlework, etc. No wonder Charlotte Brontë referred to 'governess drudgery'.[7] And the governess was often relegated to a remote attic room, eating meals in the schoolroom either alone or with the children, an isolation increased by the unwillingness of many employers to allow her visitors and by her equivocal social position, for she was beneath her employers but above their domestic servants who, well knowing the attitude of the employers, were often insolent. Again the *Quarterly Review* neatly pinpointed this situation: 'She is a bore to almost any gentleman, as a tabooed woman to whom he is interdicted from granting the usual privileges of her sex'; she was a bore and reproach to most ladies, since 'her dull, fagging, bread and water life' put their pampered idleness to shame; the servants invariably detested her; her pupils might love her 'but they cannot be friends'.[8] Charlotte Brontë reported that when one child in her charge said he loved her, the mother exclaimed in her presence 'Love the *governess*, my dear!'[9] Or, as in *Agnes Grey*, some children behaved appallingly, but the attitude of the parents denied the governess any authority. The governess also lived in constant fear of dismissal, and if she could not get another post, and in her old age, she usually faced destitution. When, as a first step to reform, the Governess's Benevolent Institution opened an asylum for aged workers in 1847, there were 90 candidates for four annuities of £15.

It is however notable that the governess abroad not only escaped the often intolerable English hierarchical social system but, as Nabokov's memoirs relate,[10] was usually treated as a family friend. The *Quarterly Review* noted (in 1849) that foreign life was 'far more favourable to a governess's happiness' since 'in its less stringent domestic habits, the company of a *teacher* . . . is no interruption – often an acquisition.' And since there was no 'untitled aristocracy' abroad, foreigners did not feel it necessary to maintain 'that distance which the reserve of English manners and the decorum of English feelings exact'.[11]

As for the training of governesses, sometimes they had none, but by 1850 innumerable little private schools for girls were in existence because if unmarried women became governesses, married women and widows opened such little schools. They needed little capital; all that had to be found was house rent, a few cheap tables and chairs, a blackboard, one or more hack pianos, and a supply of cheap textbooks, often rented out to pupils.[12] The entire equipment could be purchased for a song from one of the all too many failed schoolmistresses, for there was a very high turnover: even Christina Rossetti and her mother were unable to make a success of running a school, first in London and then in Frome in 1851–3.[13] The education provided was usually of an abysmally low standard – the Victorian attitude to women was epitomized by Mrs Anna Sewell in her *Principles of Education*, when she argued that girls were 'to dwell in quiet homes, amongst a few friends; to exercise a noiseless influence; to be submissive and retiring'.[14] In all but exceptional schools they had to learn by rote what James Bryce called 'the noxious breed of catechisms'.[15] These included Lindley Murray for grammar, the *Child's Guide to Knowledge*, and above all Miss Richmal Mangnall's *Historical and Miscellaneous Questions for the Use of Young People* (1800) and its companion volumes on French and German history (which netted their author £150,000). Sums were worked out of a book with no explanations; half a column of spelling was learnt daily from another book; needlework, plain and fancy, was taught, and French and piano lessons were given, probably by visiting masters, since parents insisted on piano and 'accomplishments'. (It will be recalled that Charles Bovary wanted his daughter to have parts, to learn the piano.)[16] As Miss Pinkerton, in *Vanity Fair*, informed Amelia Sedley's parents: 'In music, in dancing, in orthography, in every variety of embroidery and needlework, she will be found to have realised her friends' *fondest wishes*.' (Dancing was no doubt an 'extra' at Miss Pinkerton's Academy.)

Girls in the lower middle classes usually went to school when they were nearly 10 years old and had learnt little at home except how to read and how to hold a needle. After two or three years of the syllabus described above (and it was much the same for all social classes), the course was extended to include chronology, geology, and mythology, with other branches of general information which the pupil learnt by memorizing the answers in *Mangnall's Questions* or some similar 'catechism'. Attendance was frequently interrupted by being required to mind the baby or even by wet weather; it continued until the girl was 14 or 15. Everything except music, and in rare cases French, was taught by the same mistress, though she was sometimes helped by a younger sister or by a governess. Classes consisted of four or five children standing round the mistress to repeat their lesson, while the rest of the school (seldom exceeding 20–25 pupils) sat here and there sewing, doing sums, or learning the 'catechisms'.[17] Although by the 1850s higher educational institutions were being developed for boys, girls were still relegated to such small private 'academies'. As will be discussed later, some were of course better than others, especially after the start of the reform movement and the opening of Queen's College in 1857 and Bedford College in 1848, which initiated a consciousness of the importance of intellectual training for women, even though at the time these two colleges were only secondary schools, with a cumbersome, ineffectual lecture system. However, evening classes were sensibly started for governesses working during the day, and girls could choose from an extraordinarily wide range of subjects, including modern languages, mechanics, geography, and geology.

The Flauberts' English Governesses

Dr and Mme Flaubert took the education of their children very seriously. As has been mentioned, Mme Flaubert herself taught them until it was time for them to go to school. Gustave went as a boarder to the Collège de Rouen in 1831, when he was nine, and his sister Caroline was at a pension at much the same age, as we know from a letter Gustave wrote to her in July 1845 (when he was 24) recalling their childhood and incidentally asking if she remembered the time when he went to fetch her at her pension, when she was wearing her little green velvet hat.[18] At that pension she made friends with an English girl, Caroline Anne Heuland,[19] who with her younger sister was described by Gustave in his *Mémoires d'un fou.* (This meeting seems to have disposed him to like, in English girls, 'a natural carelessness and freedom from all our proprieties', which might be taken for coquetry but which he found as attractive as ceaselessly receding will-o-the-wisps.)[20]

Caroline must have learnt English at this pension for although the first mention of her having an English governess does not occur in the correspondence until April 1841, in 1842, when she was 17, she spoke perfect English.[21] (She was in fact very well educated; she was taught music by Orlowski, a friend of Chopin, and she had an Italian master.)[22] Possibly this English 'governess' was more of a companion, to brush up her English, than a governess proper – what today would be called an *au pair* girl. She was called 'Miss' or 'Mlle' Jane, or occasionally 'mimiss' by Caroline. Except on one occasion, Gustave always referred to her respectfully as Miss or Mlle Jane; on that single occasion he seems to have referred to her disrespectfully as 'la jeune Fargues',[23] and this may have been her surname. (If it was, she seems likely to have been of Huguenot descent, since there were families of that name settled in London at the time.)[24] She evidently gave satisfaction until December 1843, when there was a sudden, inexplicable change in her behaviour. Caroline complained of her total indifference, of the fact that she never changed her dress and one could see her camisole through the holes in her sleeves – in front of visitors, at that. She had also taken to spending all day in her room, practically never coming down except for meals.[25] It is not surprising that she left, sobbing, in January 1844, fetched, it seems, by a cousin.[26]

Yet although Miss Jane was apparently dismissed, she was still treated as a family friend. The Flauberts manifestly totally lacked the humiliating social discrimination inflicted by most English employers of governesses. In March 1845, after Caroline Flaubert's marriage to Émile Hamard, Mme Flaubert sent her 'Mlle' Jane's address.[27] Writing to his mother from Cairo on 4 December 1849, three years after Caroline's death, Gustave advised Mme Flaubert to go to England next spring; it was understood that she would visit

Miss Jane, to whom he sent 'mille compliments', asking his mother to tell her that he often thought of her.[28] When, after dining with the consul in Jerusalem in August 1850, a Beethoven sonata was played, it brought back a vivid memory of 'my poor sister' and the little drawing-room, 'where I see miss Jane bringing in a glass of sugared water'. It filled him with sadness and pleasure.[29]

Miss Jane was indeed still to play quite an important role in the lives of Mme Flaubert, Gustave, and his niece, Caroline Hamard. It has been mentioned (p. 8) that she married a Richard Farmer, and it was she who was the Mrs Farmer whom Gustave and his mother and little Caroline visited in 1851 when they came to London. It would not have been possible to have made this discovery had not Louise Colet been in touch with Victor Hugo.

Louise had originally written to Hugo to thank him for defending a poem of hers submitted to the Academy. She met him when she visited England in 1851 (just before the Flauberts' visit) and they wrote to each other from that time. In order to bypass the censors (for Hugo was living in exile in Jersey after the 1851 *coup d'état*), she suggested in 1852 that he should address his letters to Jules Simon, then in Essex Street, London, who would forward them to Flaubert.[30] (Simon, one of the 'men of 1848', later a minister, was president of the Conseil d'État in 1876.) But Flaubert realized that if they were discovered, it would have serious consequences for his brother as a government official, especially since the letters often arrived in torn envelopes revealing Hugo's handwriting.[31] Since also Simon left London, Flaubert evolved a strategy whereby Hugo's letters should be posted to Mrs Farmer in London, who would then forward them to him. Writing to Hugo on 2 June 1853 he said: 'I know a family of good merchants in London to whom you could, from Jersey, address your letters. They would open the first envelope . . . and then put the letter in a second one – which would thus bear their English handwriting and the London stamp.' Mme Colet's letters would go the same way, through him.[32] A little later he wrote to tell 'the Muse' that all the precautions had been taken: 'My mother has written the address herself'.[33] In his letter to Hugo, beneath Flaubert's signature appears 'Mrs Farmer, Upper Holloway, Manor road no. 5, London'. (Hugo, who believed that Gustave Flaubert was a *nom de plume* for Louise Colet, wrote suitably affectionate replies; he had lost the Farmer address by October 1853.)[34]

The Upper Holloway address enabled us to search census returns and directories for the Farmer family. Unfortunately the 1851 census does not seem to cover 5 Manor Road, but a Richard Farmer appears at that address in the 1857 and 1858 London and suburban directories. By the time of the 1861 census,[35] when the family had increased, he had moved to Tottenham Lane, Hornsey, also in North London. He was then aged 34, and described as an iron and tin merchant, born in Clerkenwell. Not only was his wife's name Jane, then aged 36 (and so about 18 at the time when Miss Jane went to the Flauberts), but of their three children the youngest, then aged six, was called Caroline – surely to commemorate the visit of little Caroline Hamard in 1851, which will shortly be described? This evidence likewise fits the description of Mrs Farmer as 'my mother's former governess' by Flaubert's niece in her unpublished memoirs, *Heures d'autrefois*.[36] The Clerkenwell origin precisely corresponds with the family of Charles Farmer, also an iron and tin merchant, who later had as well a general tool and metal warehouse at 92 and 93 St John's Street, Clerkenwell. (He can be traced in the London directories from 1819.) Richard's wife Jane was born in Lambeth, according to the census return. No family could better match the 'good merchants' of Gustave's letter to Hugo. And if any further evidence is required to support the hypothesis of the move from Upper Holloway to Hornsey, that too we have been successful in tracing, because local knowledge enabled us to decipher a word described as 'illisible' in the only published version of Flaubert's skeleton diary of a later visit to England.[37] This diary specifically mentions a visit to 'Mrs Farmer' at 'hornesey' (see p. 150).

The Farmers remained friends of the Flauberts. In May 1861 Gustave sent 'Jane' a photograph of Caroline;[38] in 1867 the Farmers visited Croisset, Gustave remarking to Caroline after they left that he was not sorry to get back to work again.[39] In 1870, as will be described in Chapter VII, Caroline stayed with them when she came to England during the Franco-Prussian war.

Gustave was naturally deeply concerned about the education of the only child of his much loved sister. Although she was only four in 1850, Caroline Hamard already had a governess then, after whom Gustave inquired when he wrote to his mother from Beni Suef on 14 February that year.[40] According to Professor Bruneau, she was undoubtedly an Englishwoman, who only remained at Croisset until

October 1851,[41] but it seems more likely that she may have left when Mme Flaubert joined Gustave in Rome in April 1851, leaving Caroline with the Bonenfants (contrary to Gustave's wishes). Mme Chevalley-Sabatier describes how impossible she became after the unaccustomed company of other children, and Gustave told Uncle Parain in January 1852 that all the time they were in Paris (after their return from Italy) 'Lilinne' behaved diabolically.[42] On their return to Croisset the decision was taken to go to England to seek one of those governesses 'firmly trained for their role, indispensable for the education of young persons of good family'.[43] Already on 24 November 1850, writing from Constantinople, Gustave had advised his mother to find such a governess, but herself to take a hand to the fullest extent possible and to supervise character and common sense in the widest sense of the term. Since first impressions never fade – 'we carry our past within us for life' – he feared above all a 'moral corset' for the child.[44]

In going to London, he and Mme Flaubert were also able to take advantage of the opportunity of seeing the Great Exhibition, which had just opened when they arrived there at the end of September. As Caroline Commanville Franklin-Grout related in her *Heures d'autrefois*, they descended on the Farmers (then, as we know, still living in Upper Holloway), and since the little girl was frightened by the street noises, she was usually left at the house. 'I did not enjoy myself at all in the English "home" of Mrs Farmer, confined to the nursery with very small "babies", not even being allowed to pick a flower in the garden – I who had been absolute mistress of those at Croisset.'[45] In the nursery (as the census revealed) there were then two Farmer babies, the eldest a little boy of about one and a half. Highgate Cemetery, which Gustave and his mother visited, was not far from Upper Holloway across open country. The cemetery was far too clean and tidy – 'these people seem to have died in white gloves' he told Louise Colet[46] – for Flaubert's taste in scenery, which exactly coincided with what Rose Macaulay called 'ruin pleasure'. He loved above all vegetation pushing through ruins, 'this invasion by nature which suddenly happens to the work of man when his hand is no longer there to defend it'.[47] He detested the little gardens round the tombs with their raked beds and faded flowers, and of course the travesties of Egyptian and Etruscan architecture.

While they were in London, Gustave visited Harriet Collier, then living in Upper Grosvenor Street. After he had returned to Croisset he told her that he would long remember their walk in Hyde Park and the foggy Sunday afternoon when he said goodbye to her and 'had more fog in his heart than there was over London'.[48] He and his mother and little Caroline visited the Great Exhibition on 30 September in an atrocious fog, and they went to a Chinese exhibition at Albert Gate and to the East India Company's museum in Leadenhall Street – visits fascinatingly described and documented by Professor Jean Seznec.[49] But the main object of coming to London was to find the governess.

Flaubert's niece, in the memoirs already quoted, described how one afternoon she was taken to a pensionnat where girls paraded before her grandmother. These were governesses. Mme Flaubert chose 'Miss Isabelle Hetton [*sic*]', described by Caroline as quite a pretty brunette although scarred by smallpox. It was arranged that she would go to Croisset.[50] (From this description she seems to have been the model for the governess employed for M. Dambreuse's 'niece' in *L'Éducation sentimentale*, described as 'an Englishwoman strongly marked by smallpox'.)[51] Unfortunately Isabel Hutton (as her name was), who was described as the 'devout' governess, and who arrived at Croisset early in November 1851, was not a good choice. She was severe and the piano lessons were stormy.[52] Little Caroline's sole idea was to flee from her and take refuge with Julie in the kitchen.[53] In April 1852 Flaubert told Harriet that she was teaching Caroline well and did not spoil her but sometimes even slapped her. '*She is very proud*', he wrote in English, and said that she detested France and the French[54] – perhaps not unlike Charlotte Brontë detesting the Catholics of Brussels. Mme Flaubert had to put up with Isabel Hutton for some months, but on 2 July 1853 Gustave told 'the Muse' that this governess had 'an arrogant, capricious, and brutal character and maltreated the child so much that they had dismissed her and she was going.'[55]

This letter is important in establishing the date of Isabel Hutton's departure, since it has been stated that it was not this governess but Juliet Herbert who was mentioned in Gustave's letter to Louise Colet of 27 March 1853 discussing the Farmer cover-up for Hugo's letters.[56] In that letter Gustave told Louise that Mrs Farmer was by far the best person to be the intermediary, because 'who knew if the governess's acquaintances might not talk?' and because the Colliers knew Nieuwekerke, who was Princess Mathilde's lover.[57] If the statement about the governess had referred to Juliet Herbert, it would be an interesting crumb of evidence regarding the background of the Herbert family, but it clearly referred to Isabel Hutton.

IV Juliet Herbert at Croisset

Virgile a fait la femme amoureuse, Shakespeare la jeune fille amoureuse, toutes les autres amoureuses sont des copies plus ou moins éloignées de Didon et Juliette.
FLAUBERT, quoted by his niece, Caroline Commanville, in her *Souvenirs.*

The Herbert Family

On 2 May 1829 a christening service was held in the then newly built All Souls Church, Langham Place, which John Nash had designed as the terminal feature of the long, at that date low, curved sweep of Regent Street. With its columnar porch and 'witty' conical spire rising out of a second colonnade,[1] this church was at the time vigorously assaulted as an outrage against stylistic propriety. Its congregation mirrored the heterogeneous population of St. Marylebone south district. Cavendish Square abounded in dukes, earls, viscounts, a countess, and several lords and knights,[2] but the streets leading into the square and much of the rest of the region, including Oxford Street, were inhabited by a socially mixed population, among them those who provided the goods and services required by the upper classes. The christening ceremony in May 1829 must have chiefly consisted of the latter group, for the baby's father was a master builder who lived in Old Cavendish Street and had room for workshops adjacent to his house.

The baby, who was christened Juliet, was the daughter of Richard and Caroline Herbert, and she was born on 27 April 1829.[3] Her mother, the daughter of Joseph and Mary Harris, was born in October 1802,[4] and married Richard Herbert at St Marylebone Parish Church on 16 October 1824.[5] Juliet had two elder sisters: Marianne Eliza, who was three years older, and Augusta Louisa, two years older.[6] The choice of romantic names for two of their daughters is perhaps an indication of a little originality. Very few girls were christened Juliet at that time.

It has been seen that Richard Herbert was a brother of William Herbert,[7] a large builder, at that date living in Farm Street, just off

Berkeley Square,[8] who was born in Warwickshire and married a Marylebone girl.[9] It is not known precisely when he and his brother Richard and their sisters came to London, but in 1823–4 a John Herbert, Surveyor and Builder, was living in Farm Street and is likely to have been a kinsman, since there is much contemporary evidence for family specialization in one trade. The enormous expansion of London in the period 1816–20 and the building boom of 1822 in particular were causing builders to flock to London.

William and Richard had another brother, Edward, and four sisters.[10] One sister, Eliza, married Witherden Young, an architect – a marriage which (as will appear) seems to have been helpful in William's career. In 1825 William became one of the three developers of the Pimlico region of the immense Grosvenor Estates in London, taking three acres between Vauxhall Bridge Road and the Grosvenor Basin, although in the same year he had to write to Thomas Cundy, the architect and surveyor of the London estates of the Marquess of Westminster, then Lord Grosvenor, about raising the marshy, ill-drained ground.[11] (It was filled in.) He also established sawmills at Grosvenor Basin, a large basin surrounded by wharves and warehouses with locks large enough to allow the entrance of barges and coasting vessels, connected with the Thames by the Grosvenor Canal, which was constructed in 1823–5.[12] Other Pimlico tenants were Thomas Cubitt, the large-scale speculative builder, and Thomas and his brother Joseph Cundy. In the London directories William Herbert is usually listed as 'builder and sawmills, Grosvenor basin, Pimlico', but in three deeds (of 13, 14, and 15 June 1826)[13] he appears as occupier of ground and a 'messuage' (dwelling house with out-buildings) 'open on the south side of Gillingham Street', and his address is given as 15 Gillingham Street in the 1843 directories (when he also had premises in King William Street, Strand, which he himself developed, evidently together with Witherden Young).[14]

Only through the detail of these title-deeds is it possible to trace anything of the history of William's much more obscure brother Richard, for the 1826 deeds show that the Gillingham Street property was leased by Lord Grosvenor and William Herbert to Richard Herbert's father-in-law, Joseph Harris, a poulterer of Duke Street, Manchester Square, and Gillingham Street is given as Richard Herbert's address in the lease he took for 17a[15] Old Cavendish Street on 31 October 1826.[16] Richard agreed to pay the quite high rent of £100 p.a. for this 'parcel of ground', on the west side of Old Cavendish Street and the east side of Henrietta Passage, from 24 December 1826.

When the Richard Herberts moved to Old Cavendish Street it had a mixed population, including a physician, three tailors, a bookseller, a cabinet-maker, a firm of ladies' shoemakers, an upholsterer, a fishmonger, and a tallow chandler.[17] (This last occupation was considered socially undesirable, and when the Grosvenor Mayfair estate was developed, surcharges and restrictive clauses were designed to keep out tallow chandlers but were unsuccessful in so doing, even as late as the 1870s.)[18] But however Richard fared before 1830, that year witnessed the start of a severe slump in the building industry, and Richard (a small, independent builder) was one of its victims. On 7 January 1832 his house and workshops were assigned to J. C. Purling in a deed in which Richard, 'late of Old Cavendish Street', was described as a bankrupt.[19] Bankruptcies listed in *The Times* indexes in 1831 occupy as much as 6½ columns in one quarter, and in the first quarter of 1832 no less than 7½ columns, giving some indication of the severity of a depression which coincided also with very bad harvests. And small builders were especially vulnerable since they had no guild or union until 1832, when the Operative Builders' Union was formed.[20]

The Richard Herberts do not appear to have actually moved out of the Old Cavendish Street house until 1832 or 1833,[21] and in 1831, when they had another baby girl, christened Adelaide Wilhelmina at All Souls on 15 July (commemorating the coronation of William IV), her father's address still appeared as 16½ Old Cavendish Street.[22]

When Richard Herbert was declared a bankrupt, the Bankruptcy Act of 1831 had just come into force. It established a special court of commissioners, with four judges and a review court, and official assignees attached to the court for the purpose of distributing the bankrupt's assets. Bankrupt traders (as opposed to non-traders) were discharged if an arrangement could be arrived at with the creditors. The file of *Examinations, Depositions and other Proceedings*[23] for Richard Herbert's bankruptcy shows that this is precisely what happened, and it also throws much light on the amount of capital required by an independent builder who was not a member of a powerful city company.[24]

Richard's bankruptcy was precipitated by his timber merchant who, on 16 August 1831, was told that his bill could not be met, Richard was declared bankrupt on 25 August, and on 25 October that year the *London Gazette* announced that a meeting would be held on 15 November between the creditors and assignees to arrange a settlement of his debts. His principal debts were to his timber merchant, the suppliers of tiles, cement, bricks, lead, slate, and lime, and to the carman, glasscutter, and colour manufacturer; his chief domestic debts were to the upholsterer, milkman, cheesemonger, coal merchant, and butcher – the last being owed no less than £50. The proceedings reveal that the creditors agreed to settle for 11*s*. 11¼*d*. in the pound. Among the creditors was William Herbert. According to a fiat of 11 January 1833, Richard owed John Warren and Mary Harris, coexecutors of Joseph Harris deceased, the sum of £1,341, this sum having been advanced to him by Joseph Harris. According to the memorandum of a meeting of the creditors, the assignees were empowered to compound the debt due to John Warren and Mary Harris, for which they held two leases of houses in Gillingham Street, Pimlico, deposited by Richard as security. These were evidently the 1826 leases. In January 1833, when the final dividend was declared, debts totalled a little over £3,296 and the sum of £1,026 was in the hands of the assignees. The amounts were confirmed in the audit of 24 March 1840.

It is possible that by this time Richard had already died, since his death does not appear to be registered in the national registers, which start in September 1837. Without knowing the parish to which the Herberts moved when they lost the Old Cavendish Street house, it is not possible to trace his death, which may be recorded in any of the innumerable London parish registers. Since he was not a trader, if he was still living, he would at least have escaped the Dickensian fate of the Debtors' Prison.

After Joseph Harris's death, his business seems to have been taken over by his son Henry, who is listed at the Duke Street address in the 1841 census.[25] Neither Mrs Harris nor Richard (if still alive) nor his wife Caroline appears in the directories after 1833, since they had no business premises. There is thus no means of tracing the Richard Herbert family at the very time when it would be of especial interest to know how the four little girls were brought up and educated. It seems most probable that Mary Harris would have moved into leasehold property and taken in Mrs Herbert and her young family.

Juliet's uncle William, no doubt partly because he had diversified into sawmilling, prospered despite the slump, and early in 1832 he had moved from Farm Street to Cavendish House, Clapham Park, which he had built for Thomas Cubitt and now rented from him.[26] The 1841 census return for Cavendish House,[27] in which he is described as 'retired builder and architect', aged 45, shows that he was then living with his father (Juliet's grandfather), William Herbert senior (aged 64), his wife Mary, and his daughter Elizabeth Mary (aged 20). They had many servants. William junior evidently did not provide a home for his sister-in-law Caroline and her children. His son George William went to Exeter College, Oxford, and read divinity,[28] and his daughter married James Hopgood, Cubitt's lawyer, which linked him still more closely with Cubitt. William built their house next door to Cavendish House on the Common. From 1844 (possibly earlier) he subscribed to the Art-Union of London and was on its Council from 1855 till 1862.[29] He collected 'pictures, water-colours, drawings and sculpture',[30] and after his retirement his offices in King William Street were taken over by his brother-in-law, Witherden Young, the architect, and by James Hopgood.[31] He died in September 1863, bequeathing an estate worth nearly £70,000 to his son and daughter, but his daughter was free 'to appoint' her 'portion' among descendants of her paternal and maternal grandparents, including children of Richard Herbert.[32]

There is a gap of some fifteen years in the evidence concerning the Richard Herbert family, for it is not until 1848 that Mrs Caroline Herbert began to insert her name in the directories. As has been seen, she kept a 'ladies' school' at 13 Milman's Row, a short street between Beaufort and Blantyre Streets, extending from the King's Road to the present Cheyne Walk in Chelsea. At this period Milman's Row had small, late eighteenth-century terraced houses on the east side, one of which Mrs Herbert rented. (Caroline Commanville described it as 'une minuscule maison'.)[33] It was named after Sir William Milman, who had bought Gorges House (an Elizabethan gabled mansion) just north of Lindsey House at the end of the seventeenth century. In 1726 his four nieces leased the property for building 'a new row of buildings intended to be called Milman's Row'.[34] At the end of the terrace, which was demolished some time after World War II, were three mid-seventeenth-century two-storey cottages, and on the west side was Strewan House (long since swallowed up by development) and its gardens. The riverside between Milman's Row and Beaufort Street was then known as Lindsey Row, after Lindsey House (the former headquarters of the Moravian sect in London), where Whistler lived in 1866–78.[35]

In 1851, when Mrs Herbert first appears in the census returns (see p. 5) with her daughter Adelaide, they had only one domestic servant. There is no evidence to show how Mrs Herbert acquired sufficient business and administrative acumen to run a school in which, as has been seen, she did not necessarily do any teaching herself. She must have been unusually competent, since her school appears in the directories until 1871, this date coinciding with the evidence of the 1871 census return[36] showing that she had retired. It was very uncommon for such small schools to last for over twenty years. The fact that she was to die penniless in 1881[37] is a sad commentary on the age; at the same time it does not seem to reflect well on the wealthy and prosperous William. As the 1871 census return for Milman's Row shows, all four of Caroline's daughters, including poor Adelaide whom Flaubert's niece described as 'weak and hunchbacked',[38] were compelled to spend their lives in 'governess drudgery', for William's daughter, Elizabeth Hopgood, lived until 1890,[39] and it was only after her death that the children of Richard Herbert could benefit from the reversionary clause in William's will.

Thanks to the memoirs of Flaubert's niece, *Heures d'autrefois*, it is possible to learn where Marianne was in 1851, and this knowledge seems to indicate that the Herbert girls were given an education and acquired accomplishments which were manifestly of a higher standard than the common run of the mill, for Marianne spent twenty years in the service of 'le marquis de Westminster', whose children she taught.[40] This marquess was Richard Grosvenor, who became second Marquess in 1845 and had married Elizabeth Mary, daughter of the second Marquess of Stafford, in 1819. They had thirteen children, only one dying in infancy; consequently, as has already been mentioned (p. 46), until the older children grew up, they had two governesses. According to Flaubert's niece, Marianne had retired by 1870 (and is described as 'retired governess' in the 1871 census), so that she may have gone to the Grosvenors in say 1845 (the year Richard Belgrave became second Marquess of Westminster) when she was 19, and is likely to have had some experience, if only in her mother's school. In that year the three youngest Grosvenor children must have needed a governess.[41] It is not inconceivable that Marianne may have been recommended by her uncle William, for Lord Grosvenor took a keen interest in the development of his Pimlico estate and used to inspect it with Cundy and sometimes Thomas Cubitt, when he must have met William.[42] In any event, Marianne gave satisfaction or she would not have remained in the Marquess's service for twenty years. (It is possible that the former head governess had retired and that the Grosvenors only needed one governess.)

Nothing is known of Juliet's posts. Her absence from the 1851 Milman's Row census return suggests that she was governessing elsewhere. She may (but of course this must be purely speculative), like Mrs Gaskell's Cynthia Kirkpatrick in *Wives and Daughters*, have been sent to school in Boulogne, or possibly in Dieppe or – like Charlotte Brontë – may have been a pupil and then a teacher in Brussels. A message she asked Gustave to give his niece when he was visiting London in 1865 might lend a little substance to the supposition that she may have been in Dieppe at some time, for she then asked him to thank Caroline, who was living in Dieppe, for going to see 'Mlle Émilie' (see p. 73). All the evidence (see pp. 64–5) points to her having a far better knowledge of French than she could have acquired in an English school; indeed, schoolmistresses who gave evidence to the Schools Inquiry Commission complained of the difficulty of finding qualified French teachers.[43]

Juliet goes to Croisset

In the nature of the case, there can be no hard evidence of the precise date when Juliet went to Croisset; nor, alas, is there any indication of how Mme Flaubert found her, for Mme Flaubert did not visit England again after the departure of Isabel Hutton. She may have consulted Jane Farmer, but since the Herberts lived in south London and the Farmers in north London, on the face of it, contact would seem unlikely. The possibility that the Herbert family may have lived in north London before they went to Chelsea is too speculative to be taken into account. She may even have discovered that Juliet was already governessing in France, but that would be an even more speculative hypothesis.

The first mention of another governess does not occur in the correspondence until May 1855; in fact Juliet is not mentioned by name until Gustave, writing from Paris (where he was occupied with the publication of *Madame Bovary*), in April 1857, asks how Caroline is getting on with her. However, there is important evidence to show that she must already have been at Croisset for at least a year or longer. This (as will appear) is that while she was there, she and Gustave together translated Byron's 'Prisoner of Chillon' and Juliet not only translated *Madame Bovary* but was all the time going over this translation with Gustave – and this must have taken a very considerable time. Yet she could only have been working on this translation and (as will also appear) have been giving English lessons to Gustave when she was not teaching or looking after Caroline, i.e. occasionally during the day but most often during the evenings. But Juliet left Croisset about May 1857 (see p. 65). For it to have been possible for her to make these two translations, it is thus self-evident that by then she must already have been at Croisset for a quite extensive period of time.

There is also important negative evidence. In the first place, there is no mention in the correspondence of any other governess who followed Isabel Hutton but preceded Juliet, but in 1853 and the first half of 1854 Gustave was writing frequently to 'the Muse' and from November of that year, when Bouilhet moved to Paris, and throughout 1854, he was writing frequently to Bouilhet. On the evidence of what Gustave had to say about Isabel Hutton when she was at Croisset, had there been not only an intermediary governess but also the departure of that governess, it seems most unlikely that he would not have mentioned this in his letters. After the experience of Isabel Hutton and the fact that Mme Flaubert had felt compelled to keep her on after she had proved so unsuitable, it also seems highly improbable that she would have wished to arrange for another governess to come out from England unless this time she could be satisfied that she had a more sympathetic nature and would fit in better at Croisset.

Taking both the positive and negative evidence into consideration, we believe that the governess mentioned by Gustave in his letter to Bouilhet of 9 May 1855 (when he had broken with 'the Muse') was Juliet Herbert, and that the negative evidence for any other successor to Isabel Hutton suggests that she may have gone to Croisset in 1854, when she was 25. It is important to bear in mind that she was no girl of 18 or 19, or she could not have interested Gustave mentally or attracted him physically.

In May 1855 Flaubert told Bouilhet: 'Since I saw you excited by (and for) the governess, I was excited too: at table my eyes willingly follow the gentle slope of her breast. I believe she perceives this. For she blushes five or six times during the meal.'[44] In October that year he told Bouilhet that the former headmaster of the Collège de Rouen, now retired, had travelled in the same train as the governess and was *most* amiable, even to the extent of carrying her bags and running to fetch her a cab. They sat face to face and he paid her court. They had a literary conversation about Flaubert.[45] Since this must have been the governess's own description, it argues that they were on friendly and familiar terms by that date. On 11 August 1856, telling Bouilhet how he was working like an ox on the second version of the *Tentation de saint Antoine*, he mentioned that his mother was going to Dieppe for a few days: 'I will remain alone with the governess. If I were as a young man should be! . . . But . . .'.[46]

The next three letters to Bouilhet show that Gustave was having English lessons with this governess whom he found so attractive, presumably in the study in the evenings after the others had gone to bed. In the first letter of 24 August 1856 he said 'I am doing English with the governess.'[47] On 31 August he said 'I am still doing English with the governess; we are reading *Macbeth* . . . and I will soon understand all Shakespeare.'[48] The governess was beginning to enter Flaubert's life at the level of the intellect and imagination, and the mixture of Shakespeare, whom he much admired,[49] and Juliet, whom he much desired, was evidently heady, for on 21 September 1856 he told Bouilhet: 'I am still doing English with the governess (who excites me immeasurably; I hold myself back on the stairs so as not to grab her behind). If I go on, in six months I will read Shakespeare as an open book.'[50] Then, and only on 24 April 1857, comes the first mention of Juliet by name, in a letter to Caroline asking 'Are you getting on well with Miss Juliet?'[51] It was probably in the preceding January that Juliet gave Caroline a copy of the Routledge 1856 edition of Hans Andersen (now in Flaubert's library at the Canteleu-Croisset Mairie) which she inscribed 'With best wishes for the New Year, from her affect Juliet H.'

Before considering Juliet's stay at Croisset, a brief résumé of Flaubert's main preoccupations in the period 1855–7 is necessary. He was continuing to write *Madame Bovary*, which he did not complete until 30 April 1856, when he immediately started work on the second *Tentation*. From 1 October until 15 December a bowdlerized version (cut and 'corrected' without Flaubert's consent) of *Madame Bovary* appeared in the *Revue de Paris*, and on 18 October Flaubert took a flat in Paris at 42 boulevard du Temple, henceforth dividing his time between Croisset and Paris. In January and February 1857 fragments of the rewritten *Tentation* appeared in *L'Artiste*, coinciding with the *Bovary* trial (29 January–7 February). After Flaubert's acquittal on 7 February, Michel Lévy immediately put in hand the first edition of *Madame Bovary*, which appeared in April 1857. Thus Gustave was in Paris from January until the end of April 1857, and this is why he was writing to his niece on 24 April. On 1 September that year he started to write *Salammbô*; he had been doing preliminary work on it during that summer.

The copy of the translation he and Juliet made of the 'Prisoner of Chillon' was listed in the *Catalogue de la vente Franklin-Grout* (Antibes, 28–30 avril 1931, no. 15) as '*Le Prisonnier de Chillon*, traduit par Gustave Flaubert et Juliet Herbert, dédié à leur petite amie Caroline Hamard, Croisset, 1857'.[52] Byron had been a seminal author for Flaubert. In February 1847 he told 'the Muse' that he had just finished 'Cain': 'What a poet!',[53] and 'Cain' was one of his sources for his youthful work *Smarh*.[54] It cannot have been easy to translate 'The Prisoner of Chillon', presumably in rhymed verse, but it must have been infinitely more difficult to translate *Madame Bovary* (the translation was evidently made from a fair copy of the MS). Flaubert wrote to Michel Lévy about it on 8 or 9 May 1857, saying:

> An English translation which *fully* satisfies me is being made under my eyes. If one is going to appear in England, I want it to be this one and not any other one.
>
> My translator is a woman who has no relations with any London publisher, but who should be returning to England in about a fortnight. Can you fix her up with (sounds indecent) one of your trans-Channel colleagues?[55]
>
> It seems to me that it would go down well in England.
>
> Would it be better to wait in the interests of the French edition? That is your affair. In any case, I lay claim to its priority. Have I not the right to give my opinion? Do something for my protégée and that will oblige me from all points of view.

The letter enclosed a corrected copy of *Bovary* and Flaubert added: 'My translator has written to M. Bentley'.[56]

The publishers Richard Bentley & Sons were bought by Macmillan in 1898, and in 1948 the British Library acquired the Bentley Papers.[57] We searched these papers (in particular the volume of incoming correspondence for 14 May 1849 to 8 March 1858 and the daybooks) but we found no reference whatsoever to Flaubert or to anyone calling with a translation. (This at least proves that there was no other translator, or alternatively, that the translator *was* Juliet.) There are references in the Bentley Papers to other works which Lévy published (e.g. Guizot's memoirs). We can only conclude that in fact no letter was received by Bentley and that Flaubert's statement 'My translator has written to M. Bentley' meant what it said but that the letter was never sent, possibly because Lévy objected. That Lévy did not proceed with this translation is known from Flaubert's letter of June 1862 to the lawyer Ernest Duplan (brother of Jules) saying that the famous 'translation rights reserved' appearing in all modern books seemed to him 'a bitter joke', 'a piece of pure humbug'. 'I had one of *Bovary* (in English) made under my eyes which was a masterpiece. I had asked Lévy to arrange to have it published with a London publisher. Nothing doing!'[58]

Though Juliet must have been disappointed to lose the fee and to learn that all that hard work came to nothing, to judge from Gertrude Tennant's letter acknowledging an inscribed copy of *Bovary* (see p. 35) and from the reception in England of the first published translation (by Eleanor Aveling, Karl Marx's daughter, in 1886), the non-appearance of her translation may have spared her feelings. (The contemporary English view of *all* French novels was such that when in 1860 Swinburne lent his hostess a Balzac volume her husband, Sir Walter Trevelyan, threw the book in the fire and made Swinburne leave the house.)[51] The statement in Flaubert's letter to Lévy that the translator was leaving for England in about a fortnight's time may have referred to Juliet's return home for a June holiday or, as will be seen, to her leaving Croisset as governess. In a letter Bouilhet wrote to Flaubert from Paris, including also a useful note for *Salammbô*, in May or June 1857 there is a reference to a pair of her slippers: 'If you are writing to Mme Flaubert, tell her that she will receive Mlle Juliette's slippers at the end of the week.'[60] Whether these slippers were left behind when Juliet had visited Paris with Mme Flaubert (who had a flat above Gustave's) or not, and the whereabouts of Mme Flaubert when the letter was written (she was evidently not at Croisset) are unexplained.

It is Bouilhet's next mention of Juliet which provides the only evidence of the date when she left the Flauberts. The letter has been dated 8 September 1857, and he wrote: 'One other piece of news here – the departure of the governess disturbs me a little too – she was a charming girl, and I am afraid she will leave a great void for your mother – they seemed to get on very well together.'[61] This letter is important not only in giving the date when Juliet left Croisset but in demonstrating that she charmed Bouilhet and Mme Flaubert (who was not easy to please) as well as Gustave. There was clearly no question of her leaving because the Flauberts were dissatisfied with her, for she had become (in that respect like Miss Taylor in *Emma*) less a governess than a friend. However, it is from that date that Mme Flaubert began to take Caroline to Paris every winter for her to go to some kind of finishing school,[62] so that despite the void left by Juliet's absence, the decision seems to have been made to discontinue having a permanent governess at Croisset.

Professor Bart's reading of Bouilhet's letter referring to the departure of the governess was that a governess who may have preceded Juliet left in 1857 but was then replaced by another one (who may have been Juliet), but what the evidence suggests is that Mme Flaubert made an arrangement to continue to employ Juliet as a governess, although only during the summers. This seems to be the purport of several of Bouilhet's letters mentioning Juliet's presence at Croisset, and of one in particular referring to 'the work' of Juliet and Caroline.

In 1858 there is no mention of a governess either in Gustave's letters from Algeria and Tunisia, which he visited in April–May of that year (returning to Paris on 6 June) or in Bouilhet's letters to Gustave, when he was seeing Mme Flaubert at Croisset and in Paris. However, if the catalogue description and date of a letter from Gustave to Ernest Feydeau can be relied on, Gustave told Feydeau that he must come to Croisset before 1 September 1858 if he wished to see the governess (who was described in excited terms). Where the actual letter is does not appear to be known (it is not in the Lovenjoul library, as stated by Professor Bart).[63]

In a letter by Bouilhet assigned to January 1859 there occurs another reference to Juliet's slippers, apparently (again?) left behind in Paris; if the letter is dated correctly, Juliet seems to have revisited Mme Flaubert in Paris. Bouilhet said that Mme Flaubert should by then have learned that he had asked 'Mulot' to return Mlle Juliet's slippers.[64] Then on 29 July and 13 August that year, two letters of

Bouilhet's confirm Juliet's presence at Croisset that summer; the first letter ends 'Adieu – présente mes bons souvenirs à Miss Juliette et mon respect à Mme Flaubert'[65] and the second states that Gustave had done well to give Juliet a volume, concluding with remembrances to 'Miss Juliette' and 'Lilinne', to whom he intended to dedicate a poem in his next volume, since she loved poetry so much.[66] That this was only a summer visit is confirmed by the fact that when Bouilhet next wrote, in the second half of September, he sent respects to Mme Flaubert and Caroline but did not mention Juliet.[67]

Professor Bart's supposition that Juliet had 'probably become' Flaubert's mistress by the summer of 1859[68] can be no more than a supposition; if she did become his mistress while she was at Croisset, this could have occurred in any of the years she was there, but it is at least likely that Gustave may have felt some constraint on his behaviour in his mother's house.

Bouilhet's letters show how often he thought of Juliet. On 14 June 1860 he mentioned the 'gracieux souvenir de mlle Juliette',[69] and in July that year said that he had ordered a copy of *Melænis* which he had inscribed for 'Miss Juliette'.[70] It is a letter he wrote later that month which seems to indicate that Juliet was not just spending summer holidays at Croisset, for this letter ends 'Rappelle-moi au travail de Caroline et de miss Juliette'.[71] (It is on the recto of the folio of this letter that Bouilhet wrote 'Milman Row 13, Chelsea, S.W.7' – see p. 5.) Again next year, 1861, at the end of July or early in August Bouilhet sent remembrances to 'Mlle Juliette'.[72]

There are no other references to Juliet in Bouilhet's or Flaubert's letters that year until on 15 December Flaubert wrote to Caroline telling her that he had promised during the holidays to give 'miss Juliet' as a New Year present the *Grammaire des grammaires*, and asked Caroline to include this, together with a copy of Du Camp's *L'Expédition dans le royaume des deux Siciles* (published by Calmann-Lévy that year) in the package she was sending Juliet.[73] The gift of the *Grammaire des grammaires*, compiled by Charles-Pierre Girault-Duvivier (1765–1832), first published in 1811 and containing everything said by 'les meilleurs grammairiens et par l'Académie sur les questions les plus délicates de la langue française',[74] paid a signal compliment to Juliet's linguistic attainments and interests. Flaubert himself told the Goncourts in September 1862 that he was going to bed with this volume (and the Academy dictionary).[75]

July 1861 was the last of Juliet's summer visits to Croisset, because Gustave and his mother had to spend the next two summers at Vichy for the sake of Mme Flaubert's health. The next year, 1864, was the year when (in April) Caroline unwillingly married Ernest Commanville, a timber merchant who had a sawmill in Dieppe, urged to do so by her grandmother, fearing that after her death she might be left alone, and by her uncle, who warned her that the kind of man who would be more attractive to her was likely to be a bohemian. The Commanvilles spent the summer at Neuville, near Dieppe, and Juliet was invited to visit them there that July. Hence her reappearance in Flaubert's correspondence in two letters to Caroline of that month. The first discusses the trains Juliet would catch to Rouen, where he or he and his mother would meet her, and the second (written when Juliet was at Croisset) asks Caroline to try to come a day earlier.[76] They are important in showing that Juliet revisited Croisset in 1864.

V Gustave's First Visit to Juliet, 1865

'In Paris you have become a legendary figure', Edmond de Goncourt told Flaubert in December 1861.[1] The court case had made *Madame Bovary* a *succès de scandale* as well as a literary success; a second printing was put in hand in May 1857, but, as has been mentioned, Flaubert did not reap the profits, though this book brought him many new friends, including Sainte-Beuve, the Goncourt brothers, and Baudelaire.[2] His next novel, *Salammbô*, set in Punic Carthage, was an immediate success when it appeared in 1862, and brought George Sand into Flaubert's circle of friends. In January 1863 he was invited to dine with the daughter of Napoleon I's youngest brother Jérôme, Princess Mathilde, who, after separating from her husband, had settled in Paris where she became a famous hostess – among the writers who frequented her salons were Sainte-Beuve, Renan, Mérimée, Gautier, the Goncourt brothers, and much later the young Proust. Her friendship was important to Flaubert since he became deeply attached to her and through her he was taken up at court. He was invited to a soirée at the Tuileries in April 1864 and in February that year had been to a George Sand première in Prince Napoleon's box. (Prince Napoleon, another Jérôme, was Princess Mathilde's brother.) In November Flaubert was to visit the Emperor at Compiègne. Flaubert had been transformed from the all-but-unknown provincial writer buried at Croisset into a literary lion, who attended the celebrated Magny dinners. (The first dîner-Magny took place on 22 November 1862; Flaubert was invited very soon afterwards, possibly to the second one.)[3] It was of the essence of his character that neither his new friends – from 1863 to include the much-loved Turgenev – nor royal patronage in any way affected his relationship with an obscure English governess.

Since the beginning of 1864 Flaubert had been almost totally preoccupied by *L'Éducation sentimentale*, the novel he started to write on 1 September that year: 'I think ceaselessly of my novel. . . . I relate everything I see and think to this work (according to my habit)', he told his niece in January that year, when he was planning this novel.[4] (The new version bore little resemblance to the youthful work with the same title which he did not try to publish.) The core of this 'tale of modern manners' set in Paris ('I want to write the moral history of the men of my generation'),[5] which opens in December 1840 and encompasses the 1848 revolution, was Frédéric Moreau's love of Mme Arnoux: 'it is a story of love, of passion as it can be nowadays; that is to say, inactive passion'.[6] Here Flaubert drew on his love of Mme Schlésinger, but in this, and throughout *L'Éducation*, he was far from writing a *roman à clef*. He was using his own experience in precisely the same way as he had told Louise in August 1853: 'I will write about all that I see, not as it is, but transfigured.'[7] It was already 'my terrible novel' in March 1864.[8] In the summer he was hard at work reading the French socialists – the Saint-Simonians, Fourier, Proudhon, and Lamennais ('They are all up to the neck in the middle ages; they all . . . believe in biblical revelation').[9] In the late autumn he was 'crushed by the difficulties of my book' and asking had he aged? was he spent?[10] Like *Madame Bovary*, it was a very difficult book for him to write, and one which required exhaustive study and preparation.

In May 1865 he told Princess Mathilde that he was becoming a hypochondriac and was ordered some distraction. His niece, who was with him to cheer him up, would remain with him till the end of July and he would probably spend the rest of the summer in Dieppe.[11] But he was either making polite excuses for not visiting the Princess's house at Saint-Gratien, where she spent the summer, or he had changed his plans by the time Bouilhet wrote to him, it is believed in June or July. Wishing him *bon voyage*, Bouilhet said: 'You are very lucky to have decided to go and take the air in a beautiful country.'[12] Then in a later letter Bouilhet said: 'I am very surprised by your journey to England seeing that it was not in your programme, and I am racking my brains to divine the motive.' Flaubert had seemingly been entirely discreet about Juliet, but that this unannounced visit to England was not occasioned by a 'cheque' resembling the one which featured in Bergerat's novel *Le Chèque* is shown in Appendix II. Bouilhet added 'Goodbye old man, and enjoy your various peregrinations.'[13]

Since in 1865 Flaubert went from London to Baden-Baden, as is amply documented in the Baden *Badeblatt* (which recorded his arrival in its issue of 15 July) and in his letters, the 'beautiful country' of Bouilhet's first letter can, surely, only have been Germany?[14] Flaubert had an invitation from Du Camp to stay at the

Allee-Haus, in the middle of the town, where Maxime and the Husson ménage had arrived on 23 June that year and where also the popular novelist Amedée Achard was staying. Jean-Christophe-Armand Husson was Directeur Général de l'Assistance Publique in the 1860s[15] and Du Camp, who had a liaison with his wife Adèle, wanted Gustave to get to know the Hussons better.[16] The Schlésingers' house was scarcely ten minutes away from the Allee-Haus, and the Viardot villa was about 200 metres distant, while Turgenev had furnished rooms at 277 Schillerstrasse, just round the corner from the Viardots. Although Flaubert did not meet the celebrated singer Pauline Viardot until 1872, he had twice heard her in her 'sublime' performance in Gluck's *Orfeo* in 1860,[17] and as a friend of Turgenev's since 1863, he must have been interested in her, since all Europe knew of Turgenev's lifelong passion for her. (In 1865 she had retired as a singer but gave her first concert performance as a pianist in Baden that year.) This was also the epoch when Baden was most subject to French influence – Berlioz had gone there to open the theatre and there were numerous distinguished French and foreign visitors.[18] Baden would therefore have had several attractions for Flaubert in 1865, although it is likely that the main one would have been the presumed presence there of Mme Schlésinger, for to see her again at the time he was going to write about Mme Arnoux strongly resembles his habit of documenting himself before using that documentation as the starting-point for his writing. However, it cannot be known for certain if she was there by the time Flaubert arrived in Baden, because the postscript of an unpublished letter by Bouilhet of September 1865 states 'Mme Maurice Schlésinger *est encore à Mantes*'.[19] An old school friend of hers lived at Mantes, whom Mme Schlésinger visited from time to time. Professor Bruneau's reading of this postscript is that Flaubert may have discovered when he got to Baden that Mme Schlésinger was in Mantes, but it is not impossible that she was still in Baden in the second part of July and then in Mantes in August and part of September. Bouilhet's belief that the Baden visit was in Flaubert's programme seems to suggest that he thought Flaubert would be visiting her there for the book. There is, of course, no proof that he actually did see her either in Baden or in Mantes.

Bouilhet's next letter was written while Flaubert was in England: he refers to 'the marvellous beer you are drinking in a heretical country, while here it is detestable', tells Flaubert to 'cock a snook at

John Bull for me' and to try not to spoil his catholicism through contact with 'the hideous Reformation – this is the final prayer of your archbishop, Monseigneur'.[20] ('Monseigneur' was Bouilhet's nickname, and Flaubert was his 'Vicaire Général'.)

Only one letter Flaubert wrote from London in 1865 has survived (it was wrongly dated August 1866 in the Conard edition). It lacks an address and the sole indication of when it was written is 'mardi, 8 heures du soir'. The date ascribed to it is 4(?) July, but as will be seen, that is a week out, for it must have been written on 11 July. Flaubert said he did not want to leave London without sending Caroline a line; he was leaving the next evening at half-past six. He would take the train to Paris, where he would go to the Strasbourg station, and he would be in Baden the same evening, at 10 p.m. He had seen many very curious things in London and several which would be very useful for his novel. He asked her to write to him c/o M. Du Camp, Allée Haus, Baden-Baden. He said 'Mlle Juliet embraces you and is going to write soon' and added in a postscript 'Juliet, who is with me now, embraces you. She thanks you very much for going to see Mlle Émilie. She asks me to tell you that she is very happy to see France again.'[21] There is no explanation of who Mlle Émilie was but, as has been mentioned, she seems to have been a French acquaintance of Juliet's.

The date of the diary

What was it that Flaubert saw in London in 1865 that was useful for *L'Éducation*? We can only know what he saw (whether or not it was useful for his novel) if it can be established that the skeleton diary of a visit to London included in *Carnet de voyage 13* (preserved in the Bibliothèque historique de la ville de Paris) described the 1865 visit and not the return visit to London which he made in 1866. At first sight it seems that the skeleton diary must belong to 1866 and not to 1865, since it is headed '1866, lundi 26 juin' (in fact in 1866 26 June was not a Monday),[22] but before returning to this date, it is necessary to discuss the whole of *Carnet 13* and also to make the very important point that the library numbered the folios from back to front (at that repeating the number 36). The notebook itself shuts with a clasp, and there can be no doubt that the true beginning comes at the very end of the numbered folios.

If one reads the notebook in the order in which Flaubert must have started writing it (in inverse order according to the numbering of the folios), it begins with notes on the British Museum, the Royal Gallery, Kensington, the Bridgewater Collection, Grosvenor House, Westminster, Hampton Court, the National Gallery (ff. 63–49 verso). But the next sequence of notes cannot be read in the same order – this is a description of Chartres, which has to be read from back to front. The heading 'Chartres' occurs on f. 48^{v}, and the description continues down to f. 40, so clearly it belongs with other notes written when Flaubert started making notes at the back of the notebook (as he often did in the other *carnets*). At the end of the Chartres sequence there are two wholly blank leaves (ff. 38–9) and then a leaf which is blank on one side but has one word, 'Euston', on the other (f. 37 and verso). Following these blank leaves is another sequence which has to be read, like the first sequence, in inverse order according to the numbering of the folios, and this sequence consists of a skeleton diary of a visit to London. It starts on f. 36^{v}, which describes the train journey to Dieppe and part of the Channel crossing, but then Flaubert turned over two leaves (one of these was the second f. 36), so that the voyage ends on the recto of f. 35 and the arrival at Victoria comes on f. 34. The diary then continues down to f. 32 verso. It is again followed by a series of blank leaves (f. 32 recto to f. 29).

The sequences which start from the back of the notebook, and which therefore follow the numerical order of the folio numbering, are: a pencil sketch (f. 1), a Latin quotation and (turning the folio upside-down) 'Campaing ami de Regimbart', which is clearly a note for *L'Éducation* (f. 2, verso blank), and another pencil plan (f. 3, verso blank). After these, three folios have been torn out. On the fourth folio (verso again blank) is a reminder to ask Taine about Ruskin as art critic, and this is followed by notes on the role of lawyers' clerks (ff. 5–6^{v}). Then, with the notebook turned the other way round, comes a description of what Frédéric Moreau saw from his window on the Quai Napoléon (f. 7); the verso is blank. On f. 8 occurs the phrase 'les bains Deligny disposés en Allambra [*sic*]', which is discussed on pp. 158–9, and on its verso are some notes clearly relating to *L'Éducation* which end with a mention of the death of Mme Lenormand on 23 June. (This refers to the famous fortune-teller, Marie–Anne Adélaide Lenormand, 1772–1843. The Empress Josephine contributed much to the vogue she enjoyed.)[23] On the next folio a sequence of notes on costume continues until

f. 10^v. Then there is a sequence of notes on ceramics (ff. 11–14), which is followed by a description of the route into Paris terminating at the Jardin des Plantes followed by Frédéric on his return to Paris at the beginning of Part II of the novel. That sequence ends on f. 17, the verso being blank, followed by another blank folio, which in turn is followed by a description of some ceramics and a painting seen in Kensington (18–19^v), after which come notes from newspapers, notably *La Quotidienne*, for 1847, this sequence in turn being followed by notes on Saint Simonians and socialists (20–8).

This analysis demonstrates that the notes in *carnet 13* were emphatically not written in one chronological sequence. The sequence at the back appears to have been written from some time in the autumn of 1865 (i.e. after the London and Baden visits), for the notes on lawyers' clerks, the view from the Quai Napoléon, and the costume notes were for chapters 4 and 5 of Part I of *L'Éducation*, which Flaubert was working on in the late summer of 1865 after these visits. (It was his custom to make notes for various parts of a book shortly before writing the relevant chapters.)[24] In respect of this study, the most important of these notes is the one about 'les bains Deligny', which occurs between the view from the Quai Napoléon and the mention of the death of Mme Lenormand (a note he did not use) and just before the costume notes, showing that it was a note for chapter 5, and it will be seen (p. 158) that it was used in that chapter. But the notes on ceramics and the description of the route into Paris belong to 1866 – it was in February that year that Flaubert told his niece that he was 'lost in porcelain factories' and was reading treatises on pottery; he had been visited by the driver of a *diligence* and was going with him to the Gare d'Ivry.[25] Hence the Kensington notes in this section of the *carnet* cannot be earlier in date than 1866, the year of the return visit to London, after which Flaubert returned to Paris and visited Chartres. But what of the sequence which starts at the true beginning of the *carnet*?

The visits to London museums and galleries and to Hampton Court might have occurred in 1866 or 1865, and at first sight the skeleton diary (which significantly follows and does not precede these notes) must refer to the 1866 visit because of the date heading. If, however, the year is carefully examined (see plate 7a), it appears that Flaubert originally wrote '1856' (reversing the last two figures of 1865), and then corrected the third figure to 6 but overlooked the last one. That hypothesis is clinched by the fact that 26 June 1865 was a Monday whereas it was not a Monday in 1866. As will also be shown in the next chapter, the return visit in 1866 was made in the second half of July.

In case it may be believed that Flaubert made a mistake in the day and the month but not in the year, it is to be noted first that immediately he arrived at Victoria, he telegraphed (naturally to his ever-anxious mother), whereas he could not telegraph her in 1866 (see p. 92). Second, the diary records a visit of seventeen days, so that if it belonged to 1866 instead of 1865, even if he had made some slip in writing the day and the month, he could not have left London until some time in August, but writing to his niece from London on 18 July 1866, he told her that he would be back in Paris 'dimanche en huit'.[26] Since 18 July was a Wednesday, that brings the date to 29 July. There is, on the other hand, a good deal of evidence to corroborate a seventeen-day visit starting on 26 June and ending on 12 July 1865, when he left for Baden. There is above all the testimony of the postmark on the envelope of a letter Bouilhet wrote to Flaubert and addressed 'chez Monsieur Maxime Du Camp, allée Hauss [*sic*], Baden-Baden';[27] the date of the postmark is 14 July 1865. And Flaubert wrote two letters from Baden, one to Jules Duplan, probably on 20 July,[28] and one to the Goncourts on 27 July,[29] telling them that he had had a month's holiday divided between London and Baden. There is, finally, a most remarkable coincidence between the weather reported in the diary and the meteorological evidence for 1865. The first weather record in the diary is for Friday 30 June, which notes abominable rain and then cold, so that it was necessary to light a fire. On that day the minimum temperature was 54.9°F. and the maximum only 61.8°F. The next diary record is for Tuesday 4 July, which records 'magnificent weather'; on that day the maximum temperature was 80°F. For Thursday 6 July the diary records 'storm, heat'. Here the accuracy of Flaubert's notes receives striking confirmation in G. J. Symons's *British Rainfall 1865*, which records that on that day 'storms had been coasting about all day' and the heat in Hertfordshire and in London was intense. A 'violent storm' passed from the south-west to the north-east. The maximum temperature was 80.3°F. The last diary record, for 10 July, of rain and a cold wind, coincides with a minimum temperature of 53.9°F. and a maximum of 63.7°F.[30]

There remains one unsolved problem – the fact that *Carnet 13* has a label inside it showing that it was purchased from 'J. Limbird, Stationer, Printer & Engraver, 344, Strand, Opposite Waterloo Bridge'.[31] Since the diary opens with the railway journey to Dieppe, it can only be supposed that Flaubert made the notes of his journey to London on a loose leaf (he quite often tore leaves out of notebooks – see also p. 5) or elsewhere and then copied them in the new notebook which, in fact, he had the opportunity of buying on the first day in London, recorded in the diary as 'Mardi, Westminster'. That conjecture would be rash if not supported by so much evidence to show that the diary cannot have been written in 1866. It is notable that, as will be seen, the description of the journey to London is far more detailed than the day-to-day chronicle of the stay in London, which is so laconic as at times to be cryptic. Here the frequent cancellations and additions, as well as the omission of one day, demonstrate that the London diary was written retrospectively, when Flaubert often misremembered and then made corrections. The location of the entire diary (i.e. the journey to London and the stay in London) shows that it can only have been written *after* the notes on museums, galleries, etc. which come at the true beginning of the notebook, and the handwriting gives the impression of having been done rapidly and in motion, i.e. in the train or on the boat on the return journey. Clearly, Flaubert began by copying out his record of the journey to London (the handwriting of this section does not differ materially from that of the London section) and then jotted down mnemonics of his stay in London, often beginning by confusing the days on which he went to various places or institutions. It is important to note that Flaubert himself, on a slip of paper he inserted in the pocket beneath the cover flap, entitled this notebook 'Notes diverses pour L'Éducation, Chartres, Émaux'. He did not add a date, and the CHH title 'Notes pour l'année 1866', which might be supposed to be Flaubert's own title, is very misleading.

Other London notes in *Carnet 13*

The question arises whether the other notes in the *carnet*, on museums and galleries and Hampton Court, belong to 1865 or 1866. Clearly, if this sequence of notes coincides with the sequence in the diary which mentions, though it does not describe, the same museums and galleries and Hampton Court, then these notes too must *ipso facto* belong to the 1865 visit.

The following table shows how the order coincides.

Diary		*Detailed description*
Wed.	British Museum	British Museum
Thurs.	—	Royal Gallery
Fri.	Kensington	Kensington
Sat.	Bridgewater Collection. National Gallery	Bridgewater Collection
Mon.	Grosvenor House. Kensington.	Grosvenor House.
Tue.	Hampton Court	Hampton Court
Sat.	National Gallery	National Gallery

The omission of Thursday from the diary (the most probable day for the visit to the Royal Gallery) suggests that Flaubert forgot this; it is, of course, very easy to omit one day when retrospectively writing up a diary. The omission of the second visit to Kensington from the detailed descriptions may perhaps be accounted for by the fact that the diary records Flaubert's looking at Flemish tapestries on that occasion, and he may (for once) have felt that he did not need detailed notes on them.

Milman's Row at the time of Flaubert's visit

The 1861 census return for Milman's Row admirably conveys the social composition of this street at about the time when Flaubert visited Juliet. It indicates that Chelsea was not only sought after by artists of note but by those whose names have not come down to us as well. There was a portrait painter at no. 10 whose name, Edward Havell, suggests kinship with the early nineteenth-century engravers David and Robert Havell, whose *Picturesque Views of the Thames* appeared in 1812.[32] At no. 4 was an 'artist in oil painting' and next door was a draughtsman. At no. 19 a lodger taught 'pianoforte, singing, and harp' and another piano teacher lived at 3a. Craftsmen and artisans were prominent; they include a carpenter, a shoemaker, a pipe-trimmer, a millwright and a wheelwright, an iron turner and a leather cutter. The professions were represented by an inspector of police, a clerk to the Education Department, an engineer and a civil engineer, a dentist's assistant and two accountants, but labourers lived in the row too: bricklayers, a plasterer and jobber, and a nurserymen's labourer and a woodcutter. There were several needlewomen and dressmakers, a nurse and some charwomen, a costermonger, carman, ostler, and the collector at the steamboat pier, who lived at no. 2. The occupations of the Herberts' immediate neighbours, at nos 12 and 14, were on the one side the civil servant and his wife and two daughters, and on the other a woman with her son who was a designer, a shopman, grocer, and cheesemonger, and a lodging-house keeper (perhaps helpful to Juliet in the matter of finding lodgings for Gustave?).

The houses seem, at least by present-day standards, not to have been as 'minuscule' as Caroline described them. The portrait painter lived with his wife, mother-in-law, six children, and a servant. At no. 17 a house-painter and his wife had three lodgers and a boarder, besides their own son and daughter.[33]

The diary of the visit

Immediately after Flaubert's customary start of travel notes with 'the railway' comes the puzzling name Fontanelle or Fontanille, which does not seem to have any connection with the 'thin gentleman' fellow-passenger he described. (When a stranger resembled someone he knew, Flaubert used an equals sign or the word 'ressemble'.) But no such place-name exists or existed on or near the Rouen–Dieppe line and, so far as we can discover, the name Fontanelle occurs only in Murray's 1847 *Hand-Book for Travellers in France* as the *former* name of the undistinguished monastic ruin St Wandrille, near Caudebec. Since this is in the opposite direction from the Rouen–Dieppe line, it does not seem relevant, even though twenty years earlier Flaubert had visited St Wandrille. (His letter of July 1845 recalling how he used to fetch his sister from her pension, quoted on p. 50, mentions their outings with Ernest Chevalier to la Maillerie and St Wandrille, and he no doubt knew its former name.) Fontanille does not appear in any gazetteer or guidebook. The writer Bernard Le Bovier de Fontanelle – Flaubert often misspelled names – seems even less relevant.[34] Possibly those with greater local knowledge can find the explanation for this mention of Fontanelle or Fontanille.

Shortly after this comes an indisputable indication of a relationship with Juliet that was more emotional than one of friendship: 'battement de cœur', followed almost immediately by a description of the wait at Dieppe not as annoying but as 'agonizing'. (It must have been occasioned by the fact that before the harbour was deepened, the cross-Channel packets could only sail at high tide.)[35] The notes on the two fellow-travellers in the train and the other passengers on the boat (see p. 148) strikingly illustrate the way in which the creative process was always at work for, preoccupied though Flaubert was by the meeting with Juliet and by *L'Éducation*, these sharp-eyed observations resemble notes for unwritten works. As the later notebooks show, Flaubert's mind teemed with projects which he did not live long enough to execute. Two of the boat passengers suggested people – the '*types*' so often mentioned in the notebooks – he knew: M. Stroehlin (he omitted the h), a Rouen textile mill owner,[36] and – of fascinating interest – 'Mme de Baulaincourt'. Mme de Beaulaincourt (the correct spelling), daughter of the maréchal de Castellane, who first married the marquis de Contades, forfeited her social position because of her innumerable lovers and an illegitimate son whom she acknowledged until, in 1859, she married the comte de Beaulaincourt. Of special interest to Flaubert may have been the fact that when she was a girl Chateaubriand, one of her mother's lovers, was a frequent visitor to the house. Mérimée wrote numerous letters to her and she was later the model for Proust's Mme de Villeparisis. She reappeared in Flaubert's notes five years later (still misspelled) – in *Carnet 20* of 1870, which he called 'Expansions'. In this later note, made for a novel about the Second Empire, she is depicted as a woman who is the victim of having been 'a type' in her youth, so that she is compelled to dress and wear her hair in a certain way, even if it no longer becomes her.[37]

The crossing seemed very long. The Sussex cliffs reminded him of Normandy, but he thought the grass had a more raked appearance. At Newhaven he had soup and roast beef, served by a very fresh-looking English girl. He thought the country between Newhaven and London was 'magnificent' and very well cultivated, and he noted a few insignificant stations with posters, like those outside Paris. He was unable to see London when he arrived at 'Vittoria', where 'Juliette' met him. He recorded: 'Cab, telegraphs[,] her house[,] her mother – evening in the salon – my lodgings' (f. 34). It is of some importance to reproduce Flaubert's punctuation (sometimes lack of it) here, and especially the dashes which, as Professor Bruneau points out, 'express the movement of his thought more than full stops or commas'.[38] In particular, the insertion of a comma instead of a dash ('Le soir au salon, mon logement') in the CHH transcription of this passage make it seem as if Flaubert was put up in what Caroline later termed the Herberts' parlour. Leaving aside Flaubert's height, weight, and addiction to tobacco, it cannot be seriously believed that he spent the night on Mrs Herbert's sofa, or even in her 'ladies' school'. It seems clear that Juliet found him lodgings, probably in the King's Road (where he lodged in 1866).

The diary's laconic, 'shorthand' notes of the places and galleries visited make no mention of Juliet, though this does not necessarily mean that she did not accompany Gustave; indeed, the record of a 'delightful return' after one of the dinners in London must surely indicate her presence? It may thus be a reasonable hypothesis to suppose that at least on the three other occasions when the diary records that Flaubert dined in London, and also when he went to Cremorne, Juliet was with him, although there is no evidence either way.

As has been seen, the first day recorded 'Tuesday. Westminster', but Gustave originally wrote 'British Museum' and crossed it out. He probably went by omnibus – there were several buses linking Chelsea and Piccadilly.[39] After Westminster, the diary notes a visit to a firm of opticians and cutlers and then 'Farrence', meaning Thomas Farrance, confectioners and pastry-cooks of 66 and 67 Charing Cross, listed in Baedeker's 1866 London guide as opposite the National Gallery. (It was at 'a pastry-cook's shop in Charing Cross' that George Osborne, in *Vanity Fair*, ate ices when he left Amelia with his sisters, ostensibly to transact business.) Flaubert then recorded walking up Regent Street.

Wednesday (28 June) noted a visit to the zoo and the British Museum, followed by dinner at 'the hotel near a railway' (probably Charing Cross). The separate notes on the British Museum visit (at the beginning of the *carnet*) describe 'the Assyrian room' – it was then known as the Kouyunjik Gallery, where the yield of Layard's excavations in 1847–50 at 'Kouyunjik, the ancient Nineveh' was exhibited.[40] Flaubert described in particular three attendants leading three horses which he thought marvellous in movement and in execution, above all the first horse, which was slightly bending its left leg – at that date a frieze of fourteen horses held by grooms was displayed in that gallery. There is no record for Thursday, when the notes suggest a visit to the Royal Gallery. (We have not succeeded in finding a gallery of that name corresponding with his notes but only a Royal Gallery of Illustrations.) The notes describe 'an Indian princess, blue background, pectoral of pearls and sapphires . . .' and 'Colisée, the empress in red in the centre, impassive . . .'

Friday (30 June) was the day when it rained abominably and he went to Kensington, probably with Juliet. It was cold and a coal fire was lit in the evening. The Kensington notes show that they visited the 'National Gallery of British Art' in the South Kensington Museum, the forerunner of the Victoria and Albert Museum, which at that date contained one heterogeneous collection of arts and sciences. Among the paintings described in the notes (which correspond with most of those listed in contemporary Baedekers) were Gainsborough's portrait of 'mrs Siddans [*sic*]', Reynolds's 'Lord Ligonier'[41] and 'Infant Samuel', a Lawrence painting of a woman in white which 'makes one think of portraits of Mme Récamier', Hoppner's 'William Pitt' ('resembles Philippe Égalité'), a Joseph Wright depicting an air-pump, Hogarth's 'Marriage à la Mode' series of engravings and a self-portrait, and two Landseers. (He thought the Hogarth self-portrait was like the alleged Le Nain belonging to the Goncourt brothers.)

Saturday (1 July) records a visit to the Bridgewater Collection 'in sight of St James's Park'[42] and the National Gallery, but Flaubert first wrote 'Kensington', which he crossed out. The Bridgewater Collection was the collection of pictures originally left – with Cleveland, later Bridgewater House (now Stafford House) facing Green Park – by Francis Egerton, the third and last duke, a canal developer, to his nephew, Lord Gower.[43] It was still called Bridgewater House in 1914.

> It housed one of the greatest collections of pictures in England. . . . The core derived from the collection of the Duke of Orleans, Regent of France from 1714 to 1723, who had acquired his pictures from the collection of Queen Christina of Sweden and Cardinals Richelieu and Mazarin, whose collections had been enriched by some of the finest works which King Charles I had gathered with such loving care.[44]

The collection included four Raphaels and four Titians, no less than six Rembrandts and three Rubenses, Turner's 'Gale at Sea' and various other Italian, Flemish, and Dutch paintings.[45] Flaubert singled out Rembrandt's 'portrait of a woman – very ugly – a marvellous lace collar – very blonde hair with the hair on the forehead cut like a cantor's', and a self-portrait. He thought Titian's 'The Three Ages' was the masterpiece of the collection and also described paintings by Lely, Cuyp, Vandermeer, Stuyversandt, the two Ostades, Teniers, etc. As already shown, the notes on the National Gallery at the back of the *carnet* relate not to this visit but to one made a week later – another indication that the diary was written retrospectively. The record of dinner at 'the hotel' on the same day (probably again the Charing Cross Hotel) suggests that Juliet may have been with him.

On Sunday (2 July) the diary records all day spent in the garden, i.e. the Milman's Row garden, with dinner *en famille* at 2 o'clock with champagne (undoubtedly provided by Flaubert), then the garden again, and then the 'salon'. The entry for later that evening is of exceptional interest: 'At 8 p.m. walk on the bridge and on the quai as far as Camorne=*bastringue* – the evening. Moonlight.' By 'Camorne' Flaubert meant Cremorne Gardens. At 8 p.m. in July it was still daylight. The moon rose during or after the visit to Cremorne.

The bridge was still the wooden Battersea Bridge, built in 1771 and from 1824 lit by gas. Its beautiful and complicated timber structure attracted Turner, de Wint, and Whistler[46] (whose painting depicting the lights of Cremorne from the bridge is now in the Tate Gallery). A 'bastringue' denoted a *bal populaire*: Galignani's *New Paris Guide* for 1860 described it as 'a popular and rather contemptuous name given to the lower sort of balls which take place in gardens or eating-houses on the exterior boulevards' but noted that some of them 'have since been patronised by a better class'. Flaubert used the term here in respect of Cremorne Gardens, between the Thames and World's End Tavern in the King's Road, which had been a pleasure ground since 1843 and from 1861 was managed by Edward Tyrell Smith, a former landlord of Drury Lane, lessee of the Lyceum, founder of the Alhambra in Leicester Square, and at one time (among other things) proprietor of the *Sunday Times*. The twelve acres of its gardens, surrounded by magnificent trees, were enlarged from 1850 by the acquisition of the grounds of Ashburnham House. It had the usual pleasure-ground equipment of fountains and statuary, refreshment bars, etc., but its most conspicuous feature was a great Chinese-style pagoda, built in 1857, which housed the orchestra and was brilliantly lit by hundreds of coloured lamps. It was surrounded by a circular platform, known as the Chinese Platform, said to have been capable of accommodating 4,000 dancers. Round it tall lampholders supported arches from which hung lustres, gas jets, and various coloured devices. Chinese lanterns hung from trees. In the centre of the gardens was an American bowling saloon, on the west side a circus, on the south a theatre; there was a maze and a marionette theatre too. Dancing started at 8.30 and went on till 11 or later, but the smart set did not come until after fireworks (the subject of another Whistler painting in the Tate Gallery). A half-crown supper could be had at the Cremorne House dining room or in supper boxes (those 'twinkling boxes' described by Thackeray at Vauxhall), and there was Cremorne sherry 'if you aspired no higher'.[47] On summer evenings 'shoals of company came by steamer, for the gardens had all the delights of Vauxhall, without the costliness'.[48] Though the men, at any rate the dancers, wore silk hats (and were so depicted in the prints by P. Levin – shown in plate 4 – and by Walter Greaves), Cremorne was a favourite place for 'familles de petits bourgeois' and artisans, as the *Guide-Chaix* pointed out.[49]

It may not be too speculative to suppose that this visit made an impression on Flaubert, and that a man who (as Professor Seznec shows) had visited a special Chinese exhibition in London as well as the China section of the Great Exhibition in 1851 would have been struck by the pagoda.[50]

On Monday (3 July) Flaubert noted a visit to Grosvenor House to see 'the Duke of Westminster's gallery' (he was in fact not a duke but a marquess).[51] This was the handsome gallery designed by Thomas Cundy which was added to Grosvenor House in 1827 for the second Earl Grosvenor's world-famous collection, which included eleven Rubens, ten Claudes, and paintings by Titian, Rembrandt, Velasquez, and Murillo.[52] According to Baedeker's 1866 London guide, Grosvenor House was open to the public on Thursday afternoons in May and June. It is therefore possible that Marianne got permission for Flaubert to visit the gallery on this Monday in July. His notes describe paintings by Canaletto, Salvator Rosa, Rubens, Carlo Dolci, and Raphael, as well as Gainsborough's 'Blue Boy' and Rembrandt's 'Woman with a Fan'. Then he recorded a walk in Hyde Park and sitting near the 'Achille-Wellington statue', which he thought 'resembled the entrance to the Champs-Élysées'. There was a mad old woman. He bought a railway guide (to study trains for the journey to Baden?) and returned to Kensington, where he looked at Flemish tapestries. He dined at the Herberts' ('chez Juliet').

On Tuesday (4 July) he described 'magnificent weather' and he, with or without Juliet, went to Hampton Court. As the 1853 *Illustrated Hand-book to London* put it, one of the first acts of 'our gentle Queen' had been to open the palace and its artistic treasures 'to the humblest of her subjects', and it was open every day except Friday. In his interesting notes, Flaubert describes sitting on a bench in an avenue planted with yews opposite the palace. (Like the *Guide-Chaix*, he termed it a 'château'.) He was clearly in the fountain garden. Someone (very officiously) forbade him to smoke. There was a 'Louis XIV' small garden on the south side of the palace and a long walk covered with elms ('une longue allée couverte d'ormes'). However, it was not elms that formerly covered the pleached alley he so clearly described but hornbeams. He noted the vine under glass. He must have been reminded of the Hampton Court gardens, and especially the planting of the yews, when he visited Fontainebleau (for *L'Éducation*) in 1868, for, as Pevsner states, despite later alterations, the present appearance of the gardens and both parks is late seventeenth or very early eighteenth century, 'that is the period of the greatest influence on all Europe of Versailles and Le Nôtre's immortal work'.[53] The gardener in charge of Hampton Court seems to have been a pupil of Le Nôtre and two other French pupils of his are also mentioned. Any visitor to Fontainebleau cannot fail to be struck by the resemblance between the planting of its yews and the three avenues of yews planted by William III's gardeners in the Hampton Court fountain garden, and Flaubert's description of the 'larges allées jaunes' and the 'ifs en pyramides' at Fontainebleau at once recalls Hampton Court as well.[54]

The pictures Flaubert noted in Hampton Court palace were many full-length portraits of court ladies of William III, a painting by Ricci of Christ curing the paralytic, Bassano's 'Bear Hunt', Zucchero's portrait of Queen Elizabeth, and two large Holbeins.

In Bushy ('Buschey') Park children were playing under the enormous chestnuts. 'Soldiers' daughters' in red skirts and white caps filled three omnibuses, some on the top deck. (This may perhaps have been an orphanage outing.) A little carriage came bringing provisions and the children fell on it. They sat in a circle on the grass with hampers and white-metal milk churns in the middle. There was a hymn before they were given the food by under-mistresses: 'nothing prettier or more touching than that'. At the same time (so he puzzlingly says) the soldiers' daughters were passing in the omnibus singing 'God Save the Queen' (he gave it its English title) and Scottish airs.[55] He spent the night at the Mitre Hotel and recorded the view from the second floor.[56]

I see a meadow divided by frequent lines of bushes; they are more numerous on the horizon and form woods – in the foreground a haystack – on the right the railway station – by the bank rowing boats – at the gate opposite unharnessed private carriages[57] – the river seen foreshortened colour of pale steel – boats on it like flies – small white clouds, the sky is pale blue satin, the moon rises.[58]

Next day (Wednesday, 5 July) the diary records a visit to Kew ('Kiew') Gardens.[59] The words following 'Kiew' are illegible additions – they might read 'le tavernier [illegible] et sa femme'. It would have been of some interest to have had Flaubert's comments on Sir William Temple's pagoda. On Thursday (6 July) he recorded a visit to the Crystal Palace at Sydenham and described the stony road (it was necessary to climb the hill from the railway station), a storm, and heat. The Crystal Palace still had its palm house (destroyed by fire in December 1866) and it had Egyptian, Roman, 'Alhambra', Byzantine, and Romanesque courts, the last with reproductions of the Fontevrault effigies; it also had medieval and Italian courts.[60] It seems that Juliet must have been with him for, returning to town, he recorded dining 'in the corner room near the open window' – perhaps again at the Charing Cross Hotel – and a 'délicieux retour', possibly in a cab. If this assumption is right, this too can surely only indicate a relationship that was something other than friendship. The word 'chapeau' follows 'délicieux retour'.

Friday (7 July) notes a visit to the Farmers by underground – then something of a novelty. What the CHH edition describes as an illegible word is clearly 'hornesey' for Hornesey, followed by 'Mrs Farmer, garden – the grass is being cut and rolled'. (Coming from Flaubert, this would not be a compliment.) Back in London he again called at Farrance (this time spelled 'Farrens') and after changing money went to 'Charring-Cross' for information (probably for the journey to Baden). He dined at the Herberts ('à la maison'). Saturday (8 July) records another dinner in London, suggesting that Juliet may have been with him. If so, they went by boat to the Palace of Westminster, walked on the bridge (the one completed in 1862), and then visited the National Gallery. In his notes on the gallery Flaubert singled out Turner's 'Calais Pier', Rubens's 'Judgement of Paris', and Van Eyck's 'Arnolfini Marriage' and portrait of a man in a red turban. His unerring eye observed that Arnolfini's wife appears to be pregnant. The dinner recorded that evening was at Verrey's in Regent Street (it is still there). According to the *Illustrated Handbook*, Verrey's 'does the *cuisine* in the style of the Palais Royal'. No doubt the experience of English cookery heightened Flaubert's enjoyment of this meal. The diary recorded an early return, at 8.30 p.m.

All Sunday (9 July) was spent at Milman's Row, where there was a long conversation; there was rain and sun in the norning. Adelaide cut up cucumbers and they dined at 2 o'clock again. This vignette is followed by an illegible addition enclosed in parentheses. (We are unable to endorse the CHH reading 'chancelière = crinoline', for the second word cannot be read as 'crinoline', and the first word may begin 'chand', on the analogy of the d in Adelaide – see plate 7b.) On Monday morning (10 July) there was rain and a cold wind; he warmed himself up at the house, wrote letters (the letter to Caroline quoted on p. 73), and read Octave Feuillet's *Rédemption* while 'J.' slept. There is no mention of the others. (The CHH editors have inserted two words which do not exist in the manuscript after the title of Feuillet's novel, so that their version reads 'foutu embêtement pendant que Juliette [*sic*] dormait'.)[61] Flaubert then wrote 'mardi', which he crossed out but without writing in another day; it must therefore have likewise been on Monday that he visited 'horticultural garden – Kensington Gardens'. The Horticultural Gardens were then in South Kensington, where the Society had hired the ground from the commissioners of the 1851 Exhibition. Baedeker described the gardens as 'tastefully laid out in terraces', embellished with fountains, miniature cascades, and bronze and terracotta figures.

On Tuesday the 11th the diary notes a visit by boat to London Bridge (built by the Rennie family in 1832) and the Temple gardens ('Temple's garden'), and watching water-jousting on the Thames. Next day (12 July) it records a walk on the Bridge (it must have been Battersea Bridge) and the departure from the house at 7(?) o'clock. We may suspect that this was a sad parting for Juliet, but she evidently spared him the kind of parting scene he had endured from 'the Muse', or he would not have returned to London to visit her the following year.

It seems a justifiable question to ask what the eminently respectable Mrs Herbert and Juliet's governess sisters thought of her relationship with Gustave. He may have appeared to have been her fiancée (by agreement between them?). It is just possible, or at least not inconceivable, that he even sometimes believed that he might marry her and they would both live at Croisset, since Mme Flaubert was fond of Juliet and may even have encouraged such a marriage. However, the claim by Edmond Ledoux (reported by Philip Spencer) to have seen a copy of the *Tentation de saint Antoine* that had been 'sent' to Juliet and was inscribed 'À ma fiancée' must arouse scepticism.[62] Such an inscription, especially in 1874 (the book was published that March), is completely out of character. It was also Ledoux who claimed, against all the indications, that Flaubert committed suicide, but was unable to produce the evidence he maintained he eventually could produce, and, all else apart, this must cast doubt on his reliability as a witness.

Flaubert arrived in Baden either late on Thursday the 13th or on Friday the 14th, and the letters referred to on p. 76 and the *Badeblatt* of 23 July suggest that he stayed there until the 23rd. When he returned to Croisset he found his mother seriously ill, as he told the Princess on the 27th.[63] Very soon afterwards the Flaubert family suffered another of the disasters to which they seemed extraordinarily prone, for on 3 August Achille's son-in-law, Adolphe Rocquigny, committed suicide. To say the least, Flaubert's composition of *L'Éducation* was delayed, although on 14 August he was able to tell his niece that her grandmother was having fairly good nights.[64]

The question of whether any of the 'curious things' seen in London were in fact useful for Flaubert's *L'Éducation* or any other of his novels will be considered in Appendix III.

VI The Second Visit to Juliet

'I have written a piece of verse *pro Amoribus*, or better *de Amoribus – vel Elegantius ob amores* – unless I revise it *amorum causa*, which is all the same to me.'[1] Following Gustave's visits to London and Baden in 1865 it is, at the very least, of exceptional interest that Bouilhet should have written such a poem which, alas, has not come down to us. No corresponding poem, by any other title, appeared in his *Dernières chansons*,[2] the volume which Flaubert brought out in 1872 after his death; nor does it appear in the collection of unpublished poems which Letellier included in his book on Bouilhet.[3] At least, however, Bouilhet's letter telling Flaubert that he had written this poem can be dated with some precision because, echoing the phrase so often repeated in the daily press, 'the political horizon is darkening',[4] Bouilhet added: 'war seems more and more imminent.' That was the Austro-Prussian war, and since Austria declared war on 17 June 1866, the letter must have been written in May or early June – even though Bismarck had secured French neutrality by visiting Napoleon III at Biarritz in October 1865, Bouilhet feared that France would be drawn in. He later told Flaubert that he was not sending *de Amoribus* because he wanted to retouch it a little.[5]

By May or the first half of June 1866 Bouilhet must have had some account of the 1865 visits to London and Baden – if he did not see Flaubert at Croisset after his return from Baden, he certainly saw him in Paris in March 1866,[6] and it is inconceivable that he did not ask about both visits. From what Gustave said about Juliet, Bouilhet may have divined that the relationship went beyond friendship, or it is possible that Gustave dropped the veil of his previous reticence and spoke openly. (He had spoken openly about his love affair with Louise Colet to the Goncourts in February 1862,[7] and in 1864 had told them that all the women he had possessed had been no more than substitutes for another woman.)[8] As will be seen, Bouilhet also knew that Flaubert intended to visit Juliet again that summer and therefore that she had clearly become very important to him. There was certainly nothing in Bouilhet's own life then to inspire a poem about love (singular or plural). He had left Paris in 1857 and was living at Mantes with Léonie Leparfait, his humble common-law wife and her illegitimate son Philippe, whose father had abandoned her. There may thus be some grounds for thinking that the poem could have been inspired by Flaubert's love life (as Flaubert's description of the dancing girl with whom he spent a night at Esneh in 1850 had inspired Bouilhet's poem 'Kuchiuk-Hanem, Souvenir'). Bouilhet may have been thinking on the lines of Gustave's amours with Juliet, or – just possibly – he may have noticed that Gustave's 'recherche du temps perdu' for *L'Éducation* had fanned the embers of his first love into a renewed fire – not a reawakened passion for the grey-haired Mme Schlésinger of 1865 (if indeed he did see her that year) but for the Mme Schlésinger of Trouville, whose apparent reappearance fourteen years later in Rome, wearing almost identical clothing (see p. 26) had momentarily reawakened the full intensity of that passion. This can be no more than conjectural, but if it is at all legitimate to believe that Bouilhet had come to think that Gustave had fallen in love with Juliet, this poem is one of the key pieces in the design we have likened to the fragments of a mosaic.

The 1866 visit

That Bouilhet knew that Gustave had decided to return to England in 1866 we know from a letter in a sequence he wrote before Gustave's departure – a departure that was in fact later than intended, for Gustave was much put out by a visit to Croisset by Dr Cloquet and his wife which, from his point of view, went wrong. (The Cloquets were very old friends; Dr Jules Cloquet had been a pupil of Dr Flaubert's, and in 1840 Gustave had visited the Pyrenees with him, his sister, and a friend of theirs who was an Italian priest.) The Cloquets had been expected on Tuesday, 10 July, but on Wednesday Dr Cloquet arrived alone, announcing that his wife would not be coming until Thursday, whereas Gustave had planned to leave with both of them on that Thursday, sailing for Newhaven the same day. This unannounced change in the dates of the visit much upset Mme Flaubert (now aged 73) as well as Gustave's plans – the more so because he and Mme Flaubert had counted on Caroline coming to Croisset to help entertain them.[9] Since she did not come, Gustave told her on 11 July, he and Mme Flaubert did not know how to amuse them, and the fact that they were staying until Saturday had thrown out all his little plans: 'I am obliged to cancel my rendez-vous'.[10] That rendez-vous was assuredly one with Juliet to meet him at Victoria. The protracted Cloquet visit also meant that Mme Flaubert would not be able to go to Dieppe with Gustave, as originally planned, because she would now need more time to pack, after their departure.

Bouilhet's letters were, as usual, undated, but since he originally believed that Gustave was leaving on the 12th, and since one letter in the sequence mentions a historical occurrence, it is possible to date them a little more precisely than has been done by the Lovenjoul library and to point to one letter that has been misplaced in the sequence. Bouilhet first wrote on a Saturday which must have been 30 June. He asked to be remembered to a charming person in London and expressed no surprise that Gustave was going to England but advised him firmly to complete his 'plan' before setting out.[11] The 'plan' was the synopsis of Part II of *L'Éducation*, for Gustave had finished Part I on 23 January that year,[12] and early in February, while wintering in Paris, he was visiting porcelain factories and reading treatises on pottery – pots took precedence over a Tuileries ball,[13] because in Part II of the novel Jacques Arnoux (Mme Arnoux's husband) starts a pottery factory at Creil, near Paris. Bouilhet significantly added that Gustave would travel more happily if he had completed the plan. Then he wrote, again on a Saturday (which must have been 7 July), saying 'You are quite right not to set out before finally preparing your Chapter III – you will only travel with more pleasure'.[14] The last letter in the sequence was written on a Tuesday, which must have been 10 July, because this letter mentions that Cialdini had crossed the Po, an event which occurred on 8 July – after the battle of Sadowa on the 3rd, General Enrico Cialdini, commander of several divisions of the Italian regular army, crossed the Po into Venetia.[15] It appears from this letter that Gustave had invited Bouilhet to travel with him, for Bouilhet said that he was doing without this journey, and all other distraction, on economic grounds.[16]

If Gustave did leave with the Cloquets on Saturday 14 July, they seem to have left too late for him to catch the boat. Since the packet (still an English concern and not an Anglo-French one until 1872) did not sail on Sundays,[17] he was unable to arrive in London until Monday, 16 July. He then immediately wrote to his mother. This was the first of the two letters written from 311 King's Road where, evidently, Gustave lodged in 1866. In this letter he said that he would have sent word by telegraph 'if I knew exactly where you are' – he did not know whether she would still be at Croisset or in Dieppe. He added that he had had a magnificent crossing but was exhausted by the heat; he would be back in Paris in a fortnight's time and hoped to be at Croisset on about 19 August.[18] Two days later he wrote to Caroline saying that Mme Flaubert should by then be with her, and that Caroline could tell her that he was very well though he had scarcely recovered from the terrible heat of last Saturday and Sunday (the maximum temperature in London on Sunday was 85°F).

> It is still so hot that we have not been able to go out. We will begin our promenades this evening. . . . Juliet asks me to embrace you and also to tell you that you owe her a letter. We speak much of you and of the old days. I will be back in Paris on Sunday week. I want to be back in Croisset on the 19th.[19]

The evening promenades with Juliet cannot but be suggestive of Battersea Bridge and of the 'retour délicieux' of 1865. Between 16 and 30 July that year the temperature was consistently in the 70s or 80s, falling to 69.6°F. on only one day, 19 July.

These two letters are the only ones relating to this visit that appear to have survived. We can, however, learn just a little more about it by turning back to *Carnet de voyage 13* since, as has already been noted, the visit to Kensington described in the notes written at the back of that *carnet* can only belong to 1866. As might be expected from Flaubert's preoccupation with ceramics and pottery in that year, this time in the South Kensington Museum he was making notes on 'coloured Minton tiles' from 'Stroke-upon-Trend [Stoke-on-Trent]' which he thought were like those made by 'Jean (Paris)'. He noted other Minton products and terracotta vases by Boni in Milan, and described in some detail a great Italian platter depicting a procession of Leo X in a litter, a man on an elephant, mounted Cardinals and foot-soldiers, the Medici banner behind – from the factory of Caffagiolo, near Florence. He was also interested in a painting by Thomas Stothard (he wrote 'Strothard') depicting 'the intemperance of Antony and Cleopatra', which he thought so like a Delacroix that one could mistake it for one.[20]

It seems to have been this year too that Gustave (and Juliet?) went to Greenwich, since no visit to Greenwich was recorded in 1865. Writing to Caroline when she was in London in 1870 (see p. 109), he told her that 'the place I like best in London is the green sward of Greenwich'.[21]

Flaubert was back in Paris early in August. On the 6th he told Caroline that she had written a charming letter to him while he was in London,[22] and on the 16th, in a letter written from Caude-Côte, near Dieppe, he told the Goncourts that he had been to England to see friends, had returned to Paris and had been to Chartres (the notes of that visit appear in *Carnet 13*).[23] On 20 August he told Amélie Bosquet that he had spent a fortnight in England and a fortnight in Paris and its environs.[24] On the 15th, at the instance of Princess Mathilde, he had been made a Chevalier of the Légion d'Honneur.

A projected visit

It is very striking that although Gustave had now seen Juliet three years running (since she had visited Croisset in 1864), and although he was still plunged in the work he was doing for *L'Éducation*, he intended to visit her again in 1867.

Early that year – the year of the great Exposition universelle in Paris – he was again reading 1848 newspapers,[25] and in mid-April he told Bouilhet that he had had to go to Sèvres and Creil (in connection with Arnoux's pottery) and had taken notes from twenty-seven volumes in six weeks.[26] On 6 May he had decided to hasten his return to Croisset because his mother had had a 'petite attaque' a week earlier and wanted him to be there.[27] On 7 June he told his niece that he had been invited to a soirée at the Tuileries, the Sovereigns desiring to see him as 'one of the most splendid curiosities of France'.[28] (The sovereigns, who had been invited to the opening of the Exposition, were Tsar Alexander II, King Leopold of the Belgians, William I of Prussia, the king of Sweden, the Emperor Franz-Joseph, and the Sultan.[29] Queen Victoria was still in mourning for the Prince Consort.) On 10 June Flaubert was one of only 600 guests invited to the Tuileries ball, and he told Princess Mathilde that it remained in his memory as a 'chose féerique', like a dream.[30] He returned to Croisset next day, but on 19 July he told her that he was going to bring his mother to Paris at the beginning of August to show her the Exposition.[31] On 12 August – the year of this letter has been wrongly given in all the editions of the correspondence published so far – he told Caroline that he was going to spend twelve days in London and would then go to Nogent and perhaps to Saint-Gratien,[32] but on the 19th he told her that in fact he had not gone because '*entre nous*', he had had too severe an attack of colic to permit him to travel, '*but I ask you to say nothing to your grandmother* . . . I think it is the effect of the heat.'[33] This was a return of the dysentery he had got in the Near East, and on 4 August he told the Princess that he was still tormented by this 'grotesque indisposition'.[34] Some time in September, as has already been mentioned (p. 52), the Farmer family paid a visit to Croisset, very likely coming on from the Exposition, which Flaubert himself had revisited probably on the 4th, after which he had had to return to Croisset because of the dysentery.[35] He was then so hard at work again that he told George Sand that he hoped to finish Part II by February 1868, though that meant that he could not visit Nohant.[36]

The year 1867 was crucial for Gustave financially. He was again in debt, and in May he made a characteristic and ruinous mistake. Since he detested money matters, he told Ernest Commanville to keep his modest capital, after sending him 5,000 francs to pay his debts, and then pay him the interest on his investments. He (again characteristically) asked his nephew not to tell his mother: 'She will imagine that I am ruining myself.'[37] Unfortunately Mme Flaubert would not have been wrong. Flaubert's financial position was, as will be seen, another reason he himself later gave for the impossibility of his marrying anyone.

Juliet must have been very disappointed in the summer of 1867, when she had expected that Gustave would come to London. There is no evidence that he intended to visit London in 1868, a year that was (even for him) an exceptionally busy one, and above all it was the year when he was writing so intensively that he told George Sand in March that he hoped she would come to Croisset, for he would be lost if he were to go to Nohant before the book was finished: 'Your friend is a man of wax; everything is imprinted on it. . . . When I got back from your house, I would only think of you and yours'.[38] Nothing was now to distract him from the inner reality of the characters he was creating. In a letter he wrote to her on 24 November that year, which is even more revealing of his creative life, he told her that if he visited her 'real figures would replace . . . the imaginary figures I am composing with much difficulty. My entire castle of cards would collapse.'[39] A visit to

England would surely have been even more undermining to his card castle, and he needed time in the summer to go to Fontainebleau, which he had chosen as the setting of an important part of the story of *L'Éducation*. He paid two visits to Fontainebleau, one in July and another in August, and after two days in Paris, he spent August and September first with his niece in Dieppe and then at Croisset, where he expected Turgenev. (In fact Turgenev was not able to visit Croisset until November that year.)

A novel by Miss Braddon

On 28 October 1868 Flaubert wrote to Henri Harrisse, the American writer and authority on the history of the Americas, who had translated Renan's *Vie de Jésus* and attended the Magny dinners: 'As for the novel of mistress Braddon, I know the thing, someone sent me an analysis and extracts from England. Pay no attention to such a misery. That is what I know from our friends.'[40] The novel was *Charlotte's Inheritance*, published that year by Mary Elizabeth Braddon (1827–1915), writer of best-sellers whose *Lady Audley's Secret* (1862) and *Aurora Floyd* (1863) were all the rage. The father of the hero of the new novel was called Gustave Lenoble; he was tall, with a Scandinavian appearance, lived in a ruined château near Rouen with a farmyard to one side and an orchard behind, as a law student in Paris he lodged near the Luxembourg, and he married an Englishwoman. For good measure, the sub-plot featured arsenical poisoning for monetary gain. The question raised in the *Supplément* to the Conard edition of Flaubert's *Correspondance* was did Miss Braddon meet Flaubert?[41] There is the further question of who sent him the analysis and extracts.

It is impossible to imagine that the immensely successful Miss Braddon (she married her publisher John Maxwell in 1874) can have met Flaubert, who was all but totally unknown in England in 1868, but the superficial coincidences in *Charlotte's Inheritance* may not entirely be accounted for by the strong probability that Miss Braddon, in common with hundreds of her countrymen, spent holidays in Dieppe and so may have known some other isolated Norman château or manor with a farm and orchard. She may have, indeed she is likely to have, met Hamilton Aïdé; the author of his obituary in *The Times* said that his novels were not even then – December 1906 – forgotten by people with a taste for the mid-Victorian type of story. And Aïdé, after meeting Gustave at Trouville in 1842, had visited Croisset in August 1859.[42] It is therefore quite possible that he may have described Flaubert and Croisset to Miss Braddon, but there is no proof that he did. What, however, does seem virtually certain is that Miss Braddon (who admired Balzac and must have heard of *Madame Bovary*)[43] was the 'English authoress' at a dinner party in Paris described by Taine in a series of Parisian sketches, at which an attaché of the embassy was also present. As a contributor to *Le Figaro*, whose own novels were being translated into French from 1863 onwards, she is the sole English woman author likely to have attended such a dinner (it could not have been George Eliot; Mrs Gaskell and the Brontës were dead). On this occasion the attaché defended the French novel which the 'authoress Miss Mathews' was accusing of corrupting morals. The attaché counter-accused her of not reading these novels, and said he was going to send her a recent one which was 'the most celebrated, the most profound, and the most useful of all the moral works of the day. It was written by a kind of monk, a true Benedictine', who had been to the Holy Land and had even been shot at by infidels. He lived 'in a hermitage near Rouen, shut in day and night and working without respite'. His object was to put young girls on guard against laziness, idle curiosity, and the danger of immoral books. 'His name is Gustave Flaubert and his book is entitled *Madame Bovary ou les suites de l'inconduite* [*sic*]'. 'Miss Mathews' is reported to have asked the name of the publisher and to have said that she would translate the book as soon as she returned to London, and have it distributed by the Wesleyan Society for the propagation of right principles – possibly a dinner-party quip.[44]

If Miss Braddon did in fact take what she heard about Flaubert either from Aïdé or at that Paris dinner party, and no doubt other conversations in France, as the point of departure for *Charlotte's Inheritance*, any resemblances are totally superficial: her Gustave Lenoble is a stock pasteboard figure, who died of starvation after being disowned by his family for marrying an Englishwoman who had been 'ruined' because she ran off with a man who promised to marry her but abandoned her.

There can be no proof of the identity of the 'someone' in England who sent Flaubert the analysis and extracts. It cannot have been Gertrude Tennant, for they were out of touch; they were in fact still out of touch in 1871 when Gustave visited England without telling her or visiting her. It cannot have been her brother, Herbert Collier, who had been commissioned in the 8th Dragoons in 1858 and had transferred to the Bengal Staff Corps in November 1863, remaining in India until at least 1871.[45] But, again, it may well have been Aïdé who, in May 1857, had written to Gustave from Manchester to thank him for an inscribed copy of *Madame Bovary*.[46] (Aïdé seems to have gone to Manchester to see the exhibition of 'The Art Treasures of the United Kingdom' which included paintings lent by Christ Church, Oxford, Liverpool, Dulwich, and by Prince Albert of Belgium and other private collectors, as well as ornamental art and photographs.) Gustave replied in June, asking for Gertrude's address and regretting that he could not visit Manchester;[47] in fact they were in touch with each other. In 1868 Aïdé was living with his widowed mother at Lyndhurst in the New Forest, where they had lived since 1853.[48] As a writer of novels himself, he is bound to have followed contemporary fiction, and press notices would have drawn his attention to *Charlotte's Inheritance.* He could certainly have passed on the news and probably extracts to Gustave, curious as it seems to be that no such letter from him apparently survived, whereas his letter about *Madame Bovary* did survive, and (see p. 143) except for some letters deliberately destroyed, Gustave kept even the most insignificant ones.

Of course there was another person, equally if not even more likely to have read reports of this novel and then no doubt to have borrowed a copy from Mudie's – Juliet. If it was she who made the analysis and extracts, the absence of proof in the survival of a covering letter is readily explainable for, as has been seen, no letter from her appears to have survived. The 'our friends' in the last sentence of Gustave's letter to Henri Harrisse may have referred to 'our friends' in Paris – including Taine? – or, alternatively, perhaps both Aïdé and Juliet sent the information to Gustave and for some unexplained reason Aïdé's letter was lost. If so, 'our friends' referred to both of them.

The Calves' Head Club dossier

Another case of an English friend sending Gustave information occurred the very next year, for although he finished writing *L'Éducation* in May 1869, as late as February that year he got someone in England to insert a query on the Calves' Head Club (founded to ridicule the cult of the martyrdom of Charles I) in *Notes and Queries*.[49] Presumably Flaubert had come across some reference to this club in the books he had been reading. He wanted this information for Part III of his novel, in which some time in March or April 1848 Frédéric Moreau tries to be adopted as a candidate in the Assembly elections that year. In the 'Notices to Correspondents' which appeared in this periodical on 27 February 1869, 'G. F.' was referred to eight articles on the Calves' Head Club which had been published in earlier issues. His informant seems to have translated these articles and certainly one which appeared in *The Book of Days*, edited by R. Chambers.[50] It has been seen (p. 9) that the manuscript of this last translation was reproduced photographically in René Dumesnil's pictorial anthology, *Flaubert et L'Éducation sentimentale*, published by the Société les Belles Lettres in 1943; in his edition of the novel, Dumesnil gave a fuller account of the notes and extracts which were sent, drawing attention to some grammatical slips and to the translator's use of 'tu' in the phrase 'les détails des dîners sont à peu près les mêmes que ceux que je t'ai déjà envoyés'.[51] Dumesnil believed that this 'tutoiement' indicated that the dossier was made 'by a member of the Collier family, doubtless Herbert', but in this he was influenced by the then widely held erroneous belief that in 1866 Flaubert stayed with Gertrude and Harriet when he visited England.

But Herbert was in India and both Gertrude and Harriet (in Scotland) were out of touch with Gustave. In any case, neither Gertrude nor Harriet would have addressed him as 'tu'. The full significance of the 'tu' in this single, tantalizing fragment of the covering letter quoted by Dumesnil may best be appreciated when we know that in December 1886 Caroline Commanville told Edmond de Goncourt that she had permission (from Louise Colet's daughter, Mme Bissieu) to publish Flaubert's love letters to 'the Muse' (i.e. the copies of them she had procured) on one condition, that throughout the *tu* would be replaced by *vous*.[52] Few even of Gustave's men friends addressed him as 'tu', and those who did were very old friends, friends of his youth like Du Camp and Bouilhet. Turgenev addressed him as 'vous', and so did Aïdé in the letter thanking him for *Madame Bovary*. But in order to make doubly sure that it was not Aïdé who sent the Calves' Head Club dossier to Gustave, we examined his signature, which appears on his agreement with Richard Bentley in 1858 to publish his novel *Rita*.[53]

Even so small a specimen of Aïdé's handwriting as his signature makes it clear beyond doubt that the dossier is not in his hand, because he wrote an entirely distinctive copy-book copper-plate hand which was merely ornamented with a flourish or two – it is a hand with very little character, but the capital H is unmistakable because he began writing the two uprights as if they were to be a capital N, joining them at the top, and then brought the base of the second upright upwards so as to make a cross-stroke which he prolonged by extending it in a flourish below the entire letter. The capital A is a copy-book A with a more pronounced scroll at the top. It will be seen at once that the handwriting reproduced by Dumesnil is quite different.

However, anyone turning to Dumesnil's photographs will notice distinct differences between the writing on his pages 49 and 50 (compare, for example, the capital C, D, and H in both), but in both hands the capital H ('History' on p. 49 and 'Head' on p. 50) differs entirely from Aïdé's idiosyncratic one. Continuing the comparison with the writing on Dumesnil's p. 50, a striking characteristic of that hand is the pronounced cross-stroke of the lower-case t – that of 'tenant' extends over the following e and n, that of 'différentes' extends well beyond the final s, that of 'Street' as far as the second e, but the t of Hamilton in Aïdé's signature does not extend beyond the o. Moreover, an entirely different impression is given by the two hands since that in which the extracts are written is emphatically not copy-book copper-plate, and the letters do not rise as far above the line as do Aïdé's.

Thus the extracts were not sent by Aïdé or any other member of the Collier family. Since Gustave did not have any other close friends in England except the Herberts, it seems that they must have been made by a member or more than one member of the Herbert family.[54] In fact the difference between the two hands on Dumesnil's pages 49 and 50 has one eminently feasible explanation. On p. 49 there appears only a transcription of the title-page of *The Book of Days*, but there is a clear trace of another line beneath the imprint, which was cut through. Surely the explanation is that the person who copied the title-page then also copied – in English – the extract, which the person who actually sent the dossier then translated into French? The Herbert sister best equipped to do that was undeniably Juliet, and she was also the sole sister who could have addressed Gustave as 'tu'. If it can indeed be proved that it was

Juliet who wrote the covering letter, the use of 'tu' is itself highly indicative.

Thanks to the inscription in the copy of Hans Andersen which Juliet gave to Caroline (see plate 6a), it is possible to compare her handwriting with that in the extract. There is, first, a general resemblance in style, with an absence in both of the more fussy capital letters shown on Dumesnil's p. 49, and in respect of height and depth of most letters above and below the line, as well as in the liaisons between letters. There are also many similarities. For example, taking first each letter in 'Caroline', the C corresponds with that in 'Club', the a with that in 'attribue', the r with that in 'Street', the o with that in Suffolk, the i (with the dot over the succeeding letter) with that in 'tyrannie', the n with that in 'fondement', the e (with its terminal up-turn) with that in 'attribue'. The l in Caroline and in Juliet seems taller than that in 'affistolèrent' but does not otherwise differ. There are two capital H's in the inscription – not identical with each other. They do not precisely agree with that in 'Head' in the extract, but the m in Hamard agrees with that in 'acclamation' and the d with that in 'Head'. No w appears in the inscription. The t's in it (in 'with' and 'the') correspond with those in 'assistants', and there is a marked resemblance between the long cross-stroke of the t in 'the' and those in the extract. There is a particularly marked resemblance between the f in 'from' and that in 'froidement'. But the most striking difference occurs in the J of 'Janvier' in the extract and that in Juliet, although the first J is curiously like the Y in the 'Year' in the inscription. Another, rather eccentric, similarity is the use of dashes – in the inscription after Hamard and the final H, and in the extract after 'Club' and the last word (as well as after the "Book of Days").

It may or may not be considered that the resemblances between the handwriting of the extract and the inscription outweigh the differences (which may reflect a tendency to inconsistency shown in two different r's, which appear also in the signature of Juliet's will). But two further important details seem to argue strongly in favour of Juliet as the translator of the extract. These are the 'tutoiement' in the covering letter, in conjunction with the consistent use of 'pr' for 'pour' – an abbreviation always used by Gustave himself – in the extract. There can unfortunately be no proof unless the covering letter can be rediscovered. The careful Dumesnil did not state where he found the letter or the extracts, still less where they were to be found at the time he prepared his pictorial anthology, but – as Mme Durry mentioned –[55] he clearly had access to the 'Renseignements pour l'éducation sentimentale' which were sold at the Hôtel Drouot in 1931 at the same time as the great collection of 'brouillons, plans, esquisses de l'Education sentimentale' (2,355 folios). The catalogue of that sale shows that the 'Renseignements' were listed as item 184, one of the items under this heading being 'Le Calve[*sic*] Head Club'; the collection of brouillons etc. was item 183, which was purchased by Sacha Guitry and some time after his death in 1957 was acquired by the Bibliothèque nationale, but the BN did not acquire item 184 (which was not in Guitry's collection). This item may therefore be presumed to be still in private ownership if it was not a casualty of World War II, so that it is to be hoped (if it still exists) either that it will come up for sale again or that its owner may allow access to it, for it would then be possible to prove that it was (or was not) Juliet who translated the extracts and was on terms of intimacy with Gustave by 1866. This is, of course, a matter of some importance since it would afford proof that Gustave was writing to Juliet about his novels and probably explaining them step by step, as he had formerly to 'the Muse'.

As will be seen, Juliet was almost certainly governessing for the Conant family in February 1869. They lived in Rutland and also had a London house, but may not have been in London at that time of the year. There is no copy of *The Book of Days* in the carefully preserved library at Lyndon Hall, but what more natural than for Juliet to have asked Marianne to get the information for her? (Marianne seems by far the most likely sister because of her Westminster connections, because Adelaide was worn out by travel to and from the class she held, and because nothing is known of Augusta.) This, surely, is the explanation for the two different hands in the documents reproduced by Dumesnil?

Bouilhet's death

Gustave may have planned another holiday in England in 1869, for in March 1868 he told George Sand that that summer or autumn, when he would have finished *L'Éducation*, 'you will see what a pretty commercial traveller I will make'.[56] In fact, events were to rule out any holiday in 1869.

He finished the novel on 16 May 1869: 'Finished! old man! Yes, my book is finished,' he told Duplan.[57] But there were several reasons why it was difficult to make arrangements for a holiday. First, Caroline was going to Norway and Sweden on business with her husband, and they left in June, but before they went, Gustave had asked Caroline if she was going to the Pyrenees in August. He said he would be greatly obliged if she could forgo this; otherwise he would have no holiday, since he had to be in Paris from the beginning of September to see his book through the press. He was also much preoccupied by the need to move from the boulevard du Temple, as it was too dear and ran him into the expense of too many carriages, but the move would cost the earth and he had no time to look for another flat; he hardly had the time to recopy *L'Éducation*. He now had to ask Ernest to send him 1,000 francs.[58]

On 9 June, when he was working on the third and final version of the *Tentation de saint Antoine*, Flaubert got back to Croisset with a bad attack of influenza, worn out and needing a long rest, but he believed that he would be back in Paris shortly, when he and Bouilhet together would be working on a phrase-by-phrase revision of *L'Éducation*. He had signed the lease for his new flat in the rue Murillo, overlooking the Parc Monceau.[59] On about 23 June he told Caroline that Bouilhet, who had gone to Paris to revise his play *Aïssé* with the director of the Odéon, who had agreed to stage it, would be returning that day; in a week's time they would be correcting *L'Éducation* and then he only awaited Caroline's return, when he would be off to Paris for the little holiday he much needed.[60] It seems probable that he thought of visiting Juliet, but as it turned out, that became impossible.

Bouilhet who, partly thanks to Princess Mathilde, had become librarian of the Rouen municipal library in 1867, was already seriously ill with a kidney disease when he went to Paris; at the beginning of July he went to Vichy on medical advice. Flaubert then told Caroline that if Bouilhet did not return by the beginning of August, he would have to go back to Croisset in September: 'All that throws my holiday off the rails'.[61] But the Vichy authorities sent Bouilhet back to Rouen because they could do nothing for him. Bouilhet then summoned Achille Flaubert – he had not done so before because he feared to learn the truth, which Achille now pronounced: the illness was incurable. Flaubert visited Bouilhet every second day, and when he believed that there was some improvement, he left him so as to move into the rue Murillo, but on

Sunday 18 July Bouilhet died, aged 49, and Flaubert received a dispatch in telegraphic style announcing his death. 'I have just buried part of myself, an old friend, whose loss is irreparable,' he told the Princess,[62] and he asked Duplan what was the good of writing now that Bouilhet was not there?[63] Flaubert at once became president of the committee formed to raise funds for a memorial, and from now on was to devote an extraordinary amount of time and energy to preparing an edition of Bouilhet's last poems and writing an introduction for it, to making arrangements to stage *Aïssé* (which were frustrated time and again), and trying to get *Le Château des cœurs* staged. (This was a fairy play which he and Bouilhet, in collaboration with the Count d'Osmoy, had written in 1862–3. What Flaubert had tried to do was to inject a satirical content into the popular dramatic form based on magic, but he wrote his *féerie* in such a way that things had to materialize at their mention. Hence it was impossible to stage.) It is noteworthy that Juliet, to whom he must have written immediately, subscribed 20 francs to the memorial fund in August 1869.[64] Flaubert was now far too busy to go to England; in addition to the other ventures, he was collecting material for an article on Bouilhet for *Le Moniteur* and had also to deal with a list of 251 corrections that Du Camp (in lieu of Bouilhet) submitted for *L'Éducation*.[65] Then there were the proofs to read. As he told Caroline on 31 August, 'all my travel plans except for Dieppe have been abandoned'.[66] Added to all else, the move to the rue Murillo cost much time and energy – in September he was having to deal with painters, carpeting, and the move. This sad year, when his work on the *Tentation* was held up indefinitely, Flaubert was still more saddened by the death of Sainte-Beuve on 13 October. 'The little band is diminishing,' he told Du Camp the same day. 'Who is there to talk to about literature now?'[67]

Fragments of *L'Éducation* were published in various newspapers on 16 November and the book appeared on the 17th. As Flaubert told Caroline, the timing was unfortunate because of the political situation: 'Rochefort has been completely demonetized . . . the opposition has fallen in public opinion'.[68] Henri Rochefort had edited the notorious *La Lanterne*, which ran a campaign of insult and calumny against the Bonaparte establishment after the 1868 press law had relaxed the previous tight censorship. The scandal of his election as deputy for Paris five days after the publication of *L'Éducation* and the fact that the country was in the grip of a kind of revolutionary agitation preoccupied public attention.[69] Not only for political reasons but also because they failed to understand the book, and particularly its end, the reviewers were hostile, and there was no Sainte-Beuve to defend it. One hostile reviewer was Amélie Bosquet, who believed that she was portrayed in it, and Flaubert was so much hurt by her publishing this unfavourable review that this ended their friendship. The 'little band' was indeed diminishing, for Jules de Goncourt was already mortally ill.

VII 1870–1872

Mon cœur est assez large pour contenir tous les genres de tendresse: l'une n'empêche pas l'autre, ni les autres.

FLAUBERT to his niece Caroline, 24 September 1872.

France declared war on Prussia on 19 July 1870. As Flaubert said on the 22nd, 'the good Frenchman wants to fight: (1) because he believes he has been provoked by Prussia; (2) because savagery is the natural state of man; (3) because war has a mystical element which transports the masses.'[1]

Caroline Commanville was then at Neuville, but although trainloads of Parisians fleeing from the possibility of a siege soon began to arrive in Dieppe, the Dieppois showed no signs of panic. In August, after news of the unfavourable battles of Forbach and Wissenberg in Alsace, Dieppe began to organize its National Guard.[2] The disaster of Sedan and the surrender of the Emperor (with no less than 2,700 officers and 39 generals)[3] occurred on 1 September; the Second Empire was succeeded by a Provisional Government of National Defence. Despite Flaubert's hatred of politics, the brusque overthrow of the regime profoundly shocked him for, as Zola perceived, he believed in the hierarchy.[4] Writing to his niece on 22 September, he said one did not receive such shocks to the brain with impunity; he regarded himself as a man who was finished. 'The society which is going to emerge from our ruins will be a military and a republican one, that is to say antipathetic to all my instincts.'[5] And Flaubert had to endure the war and the occupation without the company of Caroline and without her help in looking after Mme Flaubert, now not only extremely deaf but so frail that she was unable to walk across a room without holding on to the furniture.[6]

On 4 September a republic was proclaimed in Dieppe. The Prussians were nowhere near it and did not in fact arrive until December, but before the third week of September Caroline, her maid, and her King Charles spaniel called Putzel had left for England. She did not leave Dieppe because she feared the arrival of the Prussians; still less because Normandy was occupied by them.[7]

When Gustave and Mme Flaubert together had induced the pretty, well-educated and artistic Caroline to marry Ernest Commanville, Gustave had argued in his favour 'one knows his character, his origins, and his connections'; one could not know those of a Parisian.[8] The irony of this is that he and Mme Flaubert were to discover, when it was too late to withdraw, that neither of Ernest's parents were Rouennais and that, according to French law, he himself was not even entitled to the name Commanville because his grandfather had been illegitimate.[9] (He had impressed the Flaubert family because he had paid his father's debts.) Caroline acceded to the pressure of her uncle and her grandmother on condition that Mme Flaubert made it clear to Ernest that the marriage would not be consumated. Since, not unnaturally, Mme Flaubert did not pass this on to Ernest, Caroline felt duped.[10] From the start, this marriage boded ill for the family.

The Commanvilles had a summer villa at Neuville, Dieppe, and spent the winters in Rouen. With a total illogicality, considering that he himself had urged Caroline to marry a Rouennais bourgeois, less than a year later, in February 1865, Gustave was writing to her disparagingly about the Rouen social circles in which Ernest and Caroline were now moving especially the ball of 'M. le Préfet'.[11] The same month Gustave was asking Caroline if she was continuing to be the delight of the Rouen salons and that of 'M. le Préfet' in particular, adding: 'The said Préfet appears to me to be enraptured by your person' and 'It seems to me that you are degrading yourself a little in frequenting my unspeakable compatriots so much'.[12] 'M. le Préfet' was in fact far more distinguished than Ernest Commanville. He was the intelligent and artistic Baron Ernest-Hilaire Leroy.[13]

Unfortunately for Caroline, what began as a flirtation turned into passionate love. This was the tragic development for her, for she resembled her uncle in her romantic and passionate temperament and her longing for love.[14] She had been sacrificed on the altar of bourgeois respectability, for which, ironically, her rancorously anti-bourgeois uncle was equally responsible with her grandmother, since the disastrous Commanville marriage had been precipitated by a youthful infatuation for her drawing master, Johanny Maisiat (apparently not regarded as having a settled income). As she had been duped into marrying against her will, her uncle at least would have been in no position to blame her if she had run off with the Baron. Caroline herself recorded that it was not social conscience or conventional morality which prevented her from doing so, but solely the thought of causing suffering to 'the three people I judged myself to belong to – my husband, my uncle, and my grandmother'.[15] The cost of this self-sacrifice is reflected in the prolonged impact on her never very robust health and in the acute depression and misery she had to endure.

Considering Gustave's comments (in February 1866 he was asking her to write 'if the adorations of M. le Préfet leave you any leisure' and in September 1867, referring to her visit to the Dieppe races, 'Was M. le sénateur Préfet most agreeable? Did you shine?'),[16] it is not surprising that Ernest became suspicious. He decided that it was necessary to leave Rouen and set up in Paris and also that travel abroad was the best cure. He therefore took Caroline with him to Scandinavia in June 1869 and to East Prussia in November that year, giving her Putzel when they were in Germany. But as the meetings with the Baron became increasingly difficult, Caroline's health began to suffer and she was advised to go to Bagnères de Luchon for a cure in June 1870. Gustave's letters to her make it clear how profoundly unhappy she was there.

After the declaration of war the Baron joined the volunteers, and in the sole interview he had with Caroline, he told her of his decision to do so. When the disastrous war went from bad to worse, Caroline feared that internal communications in France might be cut by enemy lines. To quote her own memoirs, in going abroad she saw 'the possibility of receiving news of him . . . the thought of whom obsessed her'.[17]

Caroline in England

The first news of Caroline in London comes in the letter Gustave wrote to her from Croisset on 22 September, already quoted – one revealing his utter devotion to Caroline as well as the things he had himself most disliked in London. It conjures up the cut-off-the-joint-and-two-veg. style of English cookery and states that London terrified him; it also mentions Juliet's current post as governess, which will be described later.

> Your second letter (that of today) is less sad than the first, but when Juliet has returned to Lyndon, I fear that you will be very bored in London where, besides, the climate is not healthy. I have always been unwell there. It is a town which frightens me: and then I doubt that the food will be good for

you: no *pot-au-feu*! nor a thousand little things we are accustomed to. The good ladies with whom you are having your meals do not have your style of cuisine. And I fear that you may fall ill in London. I believe you would do better, in a few days time, to go and live in Brighton; you could take a small flat and Marguerite could cook for you. . . . Stay in England until further notice. Embrace Juliet and give my greetings to all her family.[18]

Flaubert has been criticized for fussing about the food Caroline was getting 'at a moment when the siege of Paris was in full swing and the people were starving',[19] but in fact the Paris siege had hardly begun – the city's last links with the outside world were not cut until a day later and food supplies had not yet run down.

From Caroline's own account of this visit, one might conclude that she was staying at Milman's Row, but, as Mme Chevalley-Sabatier wrote, it is difficult to visualize Caroline, always accompanied by her maid, in this 'more than modest interior'.[20] It is not for nothing that Gustave's letter referred to 'the good ladies with whom you are having your meals', for there cannot have been room for Caroline and her maid at the little Milman's Row house, which was still accommodating the school (presumably on the ground floor) and at the same time (as will appear) Mrs Herbert, Juliet, Marianne, and Adelaide, and possibly Augusta too. The Herberts must have arranged lodgings for Caroline and her maid but have given them meals. In her unpublished memoirs Caroline left an invaluable description of the Herbert household, which Mme Chevalley-Sabatier quoted in her book on Flaubert and Caroline, but she made a few small changes and omissions. Caroline wrote:

I visited the house belonging to the mother of my former governess, Juliet Herbert. She lived in a minute house in Chelsea and never went out. Sitting in the window corner of the parlour, she did needlework or read edifying books.[21] Very deaf, she put a kind of tin saucepan up to her ear when she asked a question and wanted to hear the answer. Two of her daughters were living with her. The eldest, Marianne, had returned home after spending twenty years with the Marquess of Westminster,[22] whose children she educated. She too had become very deaf, and had several metres of rubber wound round her waist and when she wanted to talk to anyone she unwound her waistband and gave you the end of it which was topped with a hearing device. She was a very well-educated person who having frequented the English aristocracy, was interesting on account of all she could tell me about it.

The other daughter, weak and hunchbacked, but with a charming expression, held a little class[23] in a distant quarter; she came back late in the evening, worn out, and often went to bed without 'supper'.

Mrs Herbert had two other daughters as well, both governesses. One of them was Juliet – at that moment she was educating the Miss Conants.[24] I was invited to pay a visit to Lyndon Hall, the Conants' residence. This was how I experienced English country life, which I liked very much.[25]

This account is incidentally very revealing of the extent to which, in this respect totally unlike her uncle, Caroline was a snob. It is also the sole source which gives the name of Juliet's employers, which is the more important because the place has been misspelt, while the CHH edition states that Lyndon is 'near Cardiff'.[26]

Mrs Herbert was then aged 68, and this was the last year in which her school continued. Marianne's deafness had seemingly made it necessary for her to retire at the age of 45. She probably received a small pension from the Grosvenors. We know that she was still invited as a visitor, for the Dowager Marchioness's biographer tells us that she, Lady Elizabeth, spent the last years of her life in Somerset, herself increasingly deaf and preferring to stay in her room rather than dine downstairs when there were visitors, and have to see 'the yellow face across the table of even deafer Miss Herbert, with a black tube round her (like an Indian faquir and his snake) with a horrible brass mouth'.[27] (There is no explanation of who Miss Herbert was, and she is omitted from the index.) The second daughter whom Caroline described (without naming her) was Adelaide. We know nothing of Augusta, for she is not mentioned in any of the records. One regrets that there is no description of how Juliet's appearance struck Caroline, for they had not met since 1864.

Gustave next wrote on 27 September, saying that he now felt bucked up and resigned to anything: 'I say to *anything*'. This was because the Prussian armistice conditions had caused a general revulsion: now it was a case of do or die. He was starting night patrols (he had enlisted as a lieutenant in the National Guard). If the Loire or Lyon army could cut the Prussian railways 'we are saved'. He told her how he longed to see her; that Juliet had written to say that she (Caroline) was settling down in London, and he insisted on her spending long sessions at the British Museum and in the National Gallery. Since he was still out of touch with Gertrude Tennant, he did not advise Caroline to call on her in Richmond Terrace.[28] He asked if Caroline did not find the walks along the Thames charming (as, evidently, he had), and it was in this letter that he told her that Greenwich was his favourite place in London.

Despite the tramp of armies, he reminded her that she had not sent him news of Putzel, and asked if she was a great success, and he told her that it would be impossible for him and Mme Flaubert to join her, since emigration for fit men had been stopped.[29] (His mother was in Rouen.) Then, in reply to a letter he seems to have received from her on 4 October (when he told Ernest that she did not seem madly gay), he wrote next day to say that Rouen was not going to resist: 'I know nothing more ignoble than Normandy.' The republic seemed to him to exceed the empire in stupidity – soldiers were taken from one province to another and that was all. He thought Paris would continue to hold out for a little longer but it was being said that it would soon be short of food. In a month's time the first act of the drama would be over: 'the second will be civil war.' Saying that she seemed very reasonable and very stoic, he said he felt *broken* because he saw the abyss so clearly. 'Whatever happens, the world to which I belonged has had its day.' That Caroline was now staying with the Farmers is clear from his saying that she did not seem enchanted with the Farmer family: 'It is too bourgeois. What a pity Juliet has not remained in London. . . . Be sure to give my greetings to Mme Herbert and her daughters. Do you know Adelaide? (the one who is hunchbacked and has the most charming eyes in the world).'[30]

Writing next on 24 October, he told her that the Prussians were not yet at Rouen. He was glad that Caroline had met Frankline Grout – she was Caroline's best friend, the daughter of Dr Parfait Grout, a pupil of Dr Flaubert's, whose brother Franklin (they were both named after Benjamin Franklin) Caroline was eventually to marry.[31] Gustave was concerned for his niece about chilly weather in London, telling her to arrange to have a room with a fireplace and to take care not to fall ill in the bad climate of London. If she felt unwell, she must return: 'It seems to me that if you were with us, I would suffer less than half the torment'.[32] Then, in the last of the letters he wrote to her that month (on 28 October), he said that before leaving for Lyndon, she had told him that she would send him her new London address: 'I have not got it yet (your grandmother and I have not been able to *read* the one got from you the day before yesterday)'. He was therefore sending that letter c/o Mrs Herbert. He then believed that Rouen would not be attacked until after an important engagement in the Loire and a sortie by General Trochu – the fate of Normandy and of France would depend on that double action. He regretted that he had not sent Mme Flaubert to England with her, for he could then have gone to Paris, where at least he might have done something: 'Why did you leave, my poor Caro! Your charming company would have buoyed us up.' But he added that it was egotistical to say this because she was better off in London than in Dieppe.

One phrase in this letter reflects a deep emotional tie with Juliet: 'My life has not been funny these last eighteen months. Think of all those I have lost. Now I have no one but you and poor Juliet. And you are not, either of you, there.' It appears later (see p. 118) that Caroline was not pleased to be equated with Juliet in her uncle's affections.[33]

Gustave's later letters, describing the, for him, inexpressibly detestable occupation of Croisset by the Prussians, do not allude to Juliet.

Lyndon Hall in Rutland is a rectangular, stone-built, two storey building without wings or projections and with tall, two-light windows with mullions and transoms. It was begun in 1665 and completed in 1675, but considerable additions were made later. Except for these additions, it is described as 'an excellent example of the transition between the Jacobean and the more pure classical style of architecture which was then being gradually adopted'. The manor was believed to have been granted by William the Conqueror to the first Earl of Warwick, and the garden with its trees is mentioned early in the fourteenth century.[34] It is just outside the village of Lyndon, near Oakham, a part of the country that can scarcely have changed since 1870.

The Conant family which employed Juliet did not live at Lyndon Hall until 1862, when Edward Nathaniel Conant (1820–1901) succeeded his uncle, the Reverend Edward Brown, who had purchased the estate in 1846 on the death of the last of the Hambleton family (who had themselves purchased the manor in 1662). Edward Nathaniel, educated at Rugby and St. John's College, Oxford (B.A. 1842), in 1844 married Gertrude Mary Proby, daughter of the Reverend Charles Proby, vicar of Twickenham and a canon of Windsor. They had eleven surviving children, but only two of them were boys, and on the death of Mrs Conant in March 1866, the care of the youngest children must largely have devolved on Gertrude Catherine, the eldest girl (1845–1930), who was then 21 and who never married. The other children and their names and ages in 1866 were: Frances Ann (b. 1846), 20; Edward Henry (b. 1847) 19; Emily Agnes (b. 1849), 17; Amy Louise Emily (b. 1850), 16; Ernest William Proby (b. 1852), 14; Eleanor Mary (b. 1854), 12; Cecilia Eva (b. 1856), 10; Catherine Agnes (b. 1859), 7; Beatrice Alice (b. 1860), 6; and Grace Mary (b. 1862), 4.[35] Both boys were educated at Eton. It was at least for the younger girls that the Conants needed a governess.

Once more, just when evidence is most needed, it cannot be found. The Leicester Archives, which hold the earlier records of Lyndon Hall, have no nineteenth-century material and there are no letters or photographs at Lyndon Hall itself which record a family governess. However, it seems at least probable that Juliet became the Conants' governess some time in the 1860s, since Gustave wrote of her 'returning' to Lyndon in 1870, and the fact that she was allowed to invite Caroline to stay there argues that she was well established with the family by then. Especially after the death of Mrs Conant, the role of governess in that family was a particularly responsible one, and it must have required tact and understanding not to clash with Gertrude (for her father did not remarry and she must have been the châtelaine of Lyndon Hall). With so many young people and children, including a dashing lieutenant in the 5th Dragoon Guards (Edward Henry), there were no doubt gay parties and outings.

Unfortunately we know nothing more of Juliet's sojourn at Lyndon than the little vignette of life there recorded by Caroline and then summarized by her niece. At Lyndon, she says, Caroline

> appreciated the old Elizabethan manor in the middle of a park with century-old trees and the customary way of life of the period: elegant costumes, changed according to the time of the day, excursions in the carriage or on horseback, the freedom allowed to visitors, games of all kinds and evening prayers presided over by the head of the family, in the presence of a large domestic staff.[36]

Thanks to the publication of a letter Caroline wrote from London on 4 December 1870,[37] we know that the new London address Gustave was asking her for was 49 Oakley Street, Chelsea, and the 1871 census return reveals that this house belonged to an Italian sculptor, Francesco Caecarini. Here she had the company of several fellow Rouennais who were refugees. She told her friend she had left France because her husband had wanted her to. It must have been additionally galling to Gustave that she was learning German while she was in England,[38] for after the end of the occupation of Croisset by ten Prussians (when Gustave and his mother took refuge in Rouen), at first he could not bear to enter the house. He told George Sand that he had buried 'a great box full of letters'[39] – letters which must have included Louise Colet's and Juliet's. (Du Camp's statement that he took his papers, letters, notes, and books 'by armfulls' and threw them on the fire is manifestly wrong.)[40] Caroline did not return to Neuville until mid-February 1871, when Ernest invited Mme Flaubert and Gustave to join them.

After Sedan Princess Mathilde had gone to Brussels, where Flaubert and Alexandre Dumas *fils* decided to visit her in March 1871, but since the Rouen–Amiens line was blocked by the Prussians, they went through Paris, where Gustave visualized the Prussians' triumphal march. When he got to Brussels he heard of the Commune insurrection and asked Caroline to let him know immediately (via England) if all was quiet in Rouen, since he counted on leaving for London next day.[41] He then wrote (on 21 March) saying that if he had not positively promised to go to London, he would return to Dieppe immediately, without staying in England, since he so much wanted to know what was happening. That this was a visit to Juliet we know, because he asked Caroline to write care of Juliet.[42] He wrote again on the 23rd to say that he had arrived in London, 'not without difficulty', and asked Caroline to try to reply immediately to Hatchett's Hotel, Dover Street. (This must have been a very expensive visit.) He sent the usual message – 'Juliet embraces you'.[43] Two days later he thanked Caroline for a very reassuring letter, saying that Juliet sent 'mille tendresses' and everyone at Milman's Row had spoken of Putzel with admiration and love.[44] We know no more of this visit, except that it lasted a day longer than Gustave had intended because the boat did not sail on a Sunday.[45]

Since this visit was not in holiday time, it is pertinent to ask how Gustave was able to see Juliet. As has been seen, the Conant family was not at Lyndon Hall in 1871, and their whereabouts was described as unknown.[46] However, since the three eldest girls were of an age to be launched in society and the next in age, Eleanor, was already 17, it seemed possible that they might have come to London. Although they are absent from the usual directories, they are fortunately listed, from 1868, at 14 Grosvenor Gardens, S.W., and Lyndon Hall, in *Boyle's Court Guide*. In 1871 they were at Grosvenor Gardens, and the census return[47] lists Edward Nathaniel as magistrate and landowner, then aged 50, while the five youngest girls are all described as 'scholars'. The domestic staff consisted of a butler, two footmen, a cook-housekeeper, three housemaids and two lady's maids, and a kitchen maid, but since there was no resident governess and since the 1871 Milman's Row census return shows that Juliet was living there, it seems a reasonable assumption that she continued to be the Conants' governess but that she went daily from Chelsea. (Communications were very good; she could also have walked that distance.) On this visit she may only have been able to see Gustave in the evenings and at the weekend. She had not seen him for over four years and must have found him much changed, since when she returned to France, Caroline maintained that he had aged far more than Mme Flaubert.

According to Mme Chevalley-Sabatier, when Gustave got back to Neuville in March, he found Caroline prostrated with grief after a last meeting with the Baron, who died soon afterwards.[48] In reality, however, this last meeting did not occur shortly before the Baron's death but before (like many office-holders of the former regime) he went to Belgium. The Baron had fought gallantly in the Loire army and had been decorated, but his health suffered severely and he died at Fleurus in Belgium a little more than a year later, on 9 July 1872.[49]

Sickert's daughter Nelly, then aged eight, who was at school at Neuville, recorded that she often 'watched a gentleman strolling about in his dressing-gown' at the house next door, which belonged to a 'Madame de Commenville [*sic*]'. She learned that his name was Gustave Flaubert.[50]

Juliet was to crop up once more in 1871. During the war all contact between Flaubert and Turgenev was broken, while Turgenev was in Germany, Russia, Belgium, and England, but Gustave succeeded in renewing relations after a false report of the death of Pauline Viardot. Turgenev replied from London, and they arranged that he would visit Croisset between 15 and 20 August, but when Gustave got no reply to two reminders asking which day he could expect Turgenev, he told Caroline on 9 August that he had asked Juliet to 'passer chez lui', i.e. to call at his London address.[51] (The note in the CHH edition stating that Juliet was in Paris with him on that date needs correction; Gustave was in Paris but Juliet was in

London and Turgenev was in Scotland.) Turgenev's London address was 16 Beaumont Street, Marylebone, but Juliet must have gone for nothing, since Turgenev had not answered because he had extended his visit to Scotland for the grouse shooting, after attending the Walter Scott centenary celebrations in Edinburgh.[52]

Gustave saw Juliet and Mme Schlésinger that year, for in November Mme Schlésinger spent a night at Croisset. She had had to visit Trouville in connection with winding up her husband's estate (Maurice had died that April) and she asked Gustave to visit her there, but he could not leave Mme Flaubert. She therefore visited Croisset on 8 November.

The crucial year 1872

On the evening of 6 or 7 April 1872 Mme Flaubert died.[53] However much he had expected it, however much he had felt the burden of looking after her in her old age, her death shocked and grieved Gustave profoundly. 'Will I have the strength to live absolutely alone, in solitude? I doubt it', he told George Sand on 16 April.[54] He found meals, 'tête-à-tête' with himself at the empty table, hard.[55] And Croisset now belonged to Caroline – '*ton* Croisset', as he was to write to her on 29 April.[56] So many of his friends were dead (and Gautier, after enduring the privations of the siege of Paris, was dying) that he thought of giving up his Paris flat. But by 25 April he was at work again on the *Tentation* and advising Caroline to occupy her mind.[57] And towards the end of May he was asking Mme Schlésinger – his 'toujours aimée' – how she could suppose that he had forgotten her; he had simply not had the strength to write.[58] He asked her to try to remain in Paris until 20 June when he counted on being there. However, she must have been unable to do so, because although Flaubert was in Paris before 20 June, he did not see her. He finished the *Tentation* on 20 June and described it as the work of his whole life because he had first had the idea of writing it in 1845.[59]

On 5 June he had told the Princess that he would perhaps be spending July at Luchon with his niece, whose health was causing anxiety.[60] On the 13th, writing to Caroline from Paris, he said: 'Our journey really is fixed for around the 8th, is it not? The sooner you can go will suit me best, because of Juliet'.[61] This is the first we learn of an arrangement for Juliet to visit France that year, but since

Ernest was unable to go, Gustave had to accompany Caroline to Luchon. Then, on returning to Croisset from Paris, he found an angry letter from Juliet – a unique instance of a governess taking her former employer to task? If, as seems probable, Juliet was still the Conants' governess, it must have been very difficult all round to make a sudden change in the date of her holiday, and it is surprising that she was able to visit France in September, as in fact she did. Gustave told Caroline that Juliet was indignant because he had said he would be staying at Luchon until early August. 'I try to please everyone and everyone gets cross with me.' Therefore Ernest would have to fetch her at the very beginning of August.[62]

According to Caroline's niece, while Gustave and Caroline were at Luchon, Caroline told him how repugnant her marriage had been and how she had felt duped by Mme Flaubert. She also told him about the Baron and what it had been to be understood, appreciated, loved, and respected.[63] Gustave possibly reciprocated with some confidences, although it would be strange if by then Caroline was not aware of the nature of his relations with Juliet – the 1871 visit was surely indicative? He was still at Luchon on 5 August (a Monday) when he wrote to Turgenev saying he would be back in Paris that Friday and three or four days later would be at Croisset, when he expected him, though 'I must absent myself in the first days of September'.[64] Mme Chevalley-Sabatier's statement that Gustave returned to Croisset at the end of July to find Juliet waiting for him there[65] must be erroneous. He was not back in Croisset until August, when he spent a fortnight there waiting for Turgenev who, as so often, was unable to come. Flaubert wrote to Turgenev on the 29th asking if he had had another attack of gout and telling him that he must be away '*pour mes affaires*' until about 20 September.[66] On 1 September he told Caroline that he would rather see her (in Dieppe) 'when Juliet will have returned to England. I do not know if she will go to Dieppe before or after her visit to Paris. . . . I think she will be in Paris this Sunday. I will therefore leave here on Saturday, telling everyone that I am going to the Princess. I will stay at the rue Murillo.'[67] Caroline's niece believed that this letter indicated that Juliet's stay in France was extended, but this too seems to be mistaken. Apart from the expected visit of Turgenev, it is really out of the question that Flaubert would have had Juliet staying with him alone at Croisset – there had been sufficient talk when George Sand visited Croisset when Mme Flaubert was still alive. What is remarkable is his overt statement to Caroline that he was bamboozling 'everyone' and meeting Juliet in secret in Paris.

Gustave was still at Croisset on 5 September, when he told Caroline 'Juliet will visit you when you have left Paris, where she is arriving on Sunday. I will leave here on Saturday morning.'[68] Since this letter was written on Thursday, he must have got to Paris on the 7th for the first of his Paris meetings with Juliet, about which we known nothing more than the fact that it occurred, except for one or two not unimportant details.

Before he went to Paris Edmond Laporte, who became the closest friend of his later years, offered to give him a greyhound. (Laporte, introduced to Gustave by Jules Duplan, lived at Grand-Couronne, opposite Croisset, and was manager of a lace factory.) On 1 September Gustave had told Caroline that he hesitated to accept the greyhound, the more so because he feared rabies.[69] But it seems that Juliet persuaded him to have it, because the day after he met her in Paris he wrote to Laporte asking him to call the dog Julio and to bring it to Croisset in three weeks' time,[70] and – as he told Caroline on the 14th – Juliet gave him a 'superb collar' for it.[71] He said that he called it Julio for a host of mystic reasons;[72] her name was undoubtedly one of them.

On the same day that he wrote to Laporte he told Caroline that when 'la pauvre Juliet' would have left him ('pauvre' was almost always a term of endearment – his mother had always been his 'pauvre vieille') he would spend three or four days at Saint-Gratien (to which the Princess had returned in 1871) and would then go back to his 'hermitage', but 'in spite of the company I now have', he wanted to see his poor niece, whom he much missed: 'We talk of you more than twenty times a day'.[73] On the 14th he told her, less than tactfully, that he thought that in a week's time 'my dear companion (I am not speaking of you) will go and see you in your "delightful villa" '[74] (It is significant that Gustave should have used the ambiguous term 'compagne' in this letter to Caroline, who already knew that he was concealing this meeting with Juliet by telling 'everyone' that he was to be at Saint-Gratien.) In his next letter to Caroline (not precisely dated) he said that on Saturday, when Juliet would no longer be there, he would go to Saint-Gratien and then would be back at Croisset on the Thursday.[75] Writing from Croisset on the 24th, he hoped that Juliet had not embarked if the sea was too rough and that she did not have a bad crossing.[76]

Earlier in this letter there occurs the sentence quoted at the head of this chapter – surely the key to his fugal relations with Juliet, with Caroline, and with Mme Schlésinger? This reply strongly suggests that Caroline was jealous and reproached him.

If it was Juliet who prevailed on Flaubert to accept the greyhound, she had been right in believing that the dog would be some company for him. On 27 September he told his niece that his sole distraction was to embrace his 'pauvre chien', to whom he talked. 'His calm and beauty make one jealous.'[77] On 5 October he told Mme Roger des Genettes and Mme Schlésinger that he had walked with Julio looking at the effects of the sun on yellowing leaves, thinking of his future books and ruminating on the past. Among beloved ghosts, Mme Schlésinger's shone out the most splendidly of all; she was 'Ma vieille Amie, ma vieille Tendresse'.[78] How did he sign himself to Juliet? All we know is that by this date he had no idea of marrying her, if indeed he ever had had such an idea. When George Sand asked why he did not marry ('To be alone is odious, it is deadly, it is also cruel to those who love you')[79] Flaubert replied:

> As for living with a woman, for marrying, as you advise me to, it is a prospect I find unreal. Why? I do not know, but it is so . . . The female being has never been dovetailed into my existence, and then I am not rich enough, and then, and then . . . I am too old . . . and then too scrupulous to inflict my person on another in perpetuity.[80]

In further explanation, he later said he did not despise 'feminine feeling' but that, materially speaking, a woman had never been 'dans mes habitudes':

> I have *loved* more than anyone, a presumptuous phrase which means 'like anyone else', and perhaps more than the average man. I know all the tendernesses; the storms of the heart have rained down on me. And then chance, the force of events made solitude little by little increase around me, and now I am alone, absolutely alone. My income is not sufficient to take a woman into my life, or even to live in Paris for six months a year; so it is impossible for me to change my existence.[81]

Here is the evidence which seems to dispose of the alleged 1874 inscription 'À ma fiancée' (see p. 88).

VIII The Last Years, 1873–80

J'aime les passions longues et qui traversent patiemment et en droite ligne tous les courants de la vie, comme de bons nageurs, sans dévier.
FLAUBERT on Victor Hugo's liaison with Juliette Drouet, letter of 21–2 May 1853.

During the last years of Flaubert's life the great work that was claiming most, but by no means all, of his time and energy was *Bouvard et Pécuchet*. It would be out of place here to attempt to summarize its genesis, very early in Flaubert's life, or its substance, but he himself gave a brief idea of it to Mme Roger des Genettes in August 1872 when he told her: 'It is the history of two good fellows who are clerks, a kind of farcical critical encyclopedia'.[1] For this 'frightful tome',[2] planned to occupy two volumes of which all but one chapter of the first was completed before his death, prodigious documentation and note-taking were required.

In January 1873 Flaubert noted that George Sand and Turgenev were the only literary friends he now had (Gautier had died the previous October): 'Those two are worth a crowd, it is true, but something nearer the heart would do no harm.'[3] If Juliet was nearer the heart, as by now it cannot be doubted that she was, this was another year when he seems not to have planned to meet her, probably because Caroline spent six weeks with him in the summer, after which he visited Paris (to conduct research for his novel and read proofs), Dieppe, Saint-Gratien, and Brie and Beauce (the last for *Bouvard et Pécuchet*). Turgenev, who stayed with him at Croisset in early October, tried to arrange for a Russian translation of the *Tentation*, which Flaubert sold to Charpentier in December of that year, but the Tsar prohibited publication and Flaubert lost the 2,000–3,000 francs it would have earned him.

In February 1874, after another attack of influenza, he was saying 'je me roule dans le noir' and asked if this was the result of over-doing it for the past eight months or the radical absence of a feminine element in his life. Why had he not dear little ones? 'I was cowardly in my youth and afraid of life.'[4] It was a bad year. In March his play, *Le Candidat*, which he had written in 1873 but without any of the care, preparation, or art of the novels, was staged, but it was a total failure – an originally sympathetic audience found nothing of the Flaubert they had come for.[5] He withdrew it after the third performance to spare the actors from being hissed. Then, although George Sand declared that it was 'a masterpiece, a magnificent book',[6] there were vitriolic attacks on the *Tentation* after its publication in April. In May Flaubert's doctor ordered him to go to Switzerland to 'décongestionner' (his face had become redder) and 'dénévropathiser' (he was described as 'une vieille femme hystérique'),[7] and in July his friend Edmond Laporte took him to Kaltbad-Rigi, where he was bored 'd'une façon gigantesque' in the company of over-fed tourists whose absence of looks or charm he vividly described. It was there he had the idea of a great book in three parts, *Sous Napoléon III*,[8] which we must greatly regret that he did not have time to write, and there also he confessed how much he had taken to heart the failure to understand *L'Éducation sentimentale*.[9]

After a brief visit to Paris and Dieppe, he was back at Croisset in August, with no other company than Julio ('morganatically united' with 'a young person' in the neighbourhood),[10] but on the 21st he told Caroline that he was going to Paris next week for a fortnight. 'There I will see dear Juliet and I will go to Saint-Gratien.'[11] He was in Paris from the 28th. It thus seems difficult to conclude that the letter he wrote to Laporte from Croisset on 19 September, boasting of his sexual exploits during 'twenty days',[12] can have referred to anyone other than Juliet, for it is not really credible to visualize Flaubert spending his days with her and his nights with actresses or 'les filles'. And, as will be seen, in later years much points not only to similar meetings in Paris with Juliet, but in those years (although not in 1874)[13] there is evidence that he was taking quite elaborate steps to conceal these meetings. But it is clear that there would have been no need for a cover story had he merely been indulging in casual relations with actresses or prostitutes. The more elaborate webs of deception spun in later years and the pointers then to Juliet's presence in Paris, as well as Flaubert's thought in sending her his own copies of the last publication to appear in his lifetime, all seem to confirm that it was Juliet who was his mistress for those twenty days in 1874 and again in 1876, 1877, and 1878.

As is of course well known, Flaubert – a man of prodigious physical and mental energy – was highly sexed, as he was also (when occasion offered) a *bon vivant*. The contradictions in his nature which he himself had so clearly discerned embraced the monkish anchorite chained to his desk at Croisset and the man who loved good company, as well as the sensualist who had explored and dissected 'carnal love'[14] in much the same way as, for the *Tentation*, he explored the heresies of the third-century Alexandrian world. Is this not akin to what Luxury said to St Antony in the 1856 version of the *Tentation*: 'love women; embrace Nature through every desire of your being and roll yourself, enamoured, on her vast breast'?[15] In considering the sensualist, one should never lose sight of the Flaubert who devoted most of his life to gargantuan feats of scholarship partly because, as has been seen, he recognized that he was far less universal than a Shakespeare, and partly (as Professor Seznec so convincingly shows) because of that love of antiquity which became 'his refuge from the ugliness and mediocrities of his age', to the study of which he devoted himself with a kind of 'heroic joy'.[16] It was surely his sensual and emotional nature which put him at the opposite end of the scale from the aridly cerebral Mr Casaubon portrayed in George Eliot's *Middlemarch*? Philip Spencer's dictum that he 'turned fornication into an infrequent and trivial pastime for which he found occasion when he happened to be in Paris'[17] seems a misunderstanding. If as a younger man Flaubert had married, it would not have been possible for him to have become the kind of writer he was. When he was no longer young, habit and poverty put marriage out of the question. His sexual adventures could not, of course, have taken place at Croisset, where it was as impossible to prevent talk as on a small Greek island. But the words 'trivial pastime' seem strangely inappropriate. Flaubert did not trivialize sex; on the contrary, it was highly important for him. And if in 1864 he had thought it imperative to prove his virility (see p. 30), ten years later he no doubt rejoiced in his continuing sexual potency. In fact, the life of abstinence and, after Mme Flaubert's death, of trappist solitude must obviously have intensified a longing for its opposite. As he put it to Caroline in December 1876, when he had decided to remain at Croisset until the end of January 1877, 'but . . . when I do appear in the capital, what champagne! what actresses!'[18] (However, as will be seen, by then he could not have afforded champagne or the *douceurs* required by actresses.)

If, in 1874 and some later years, his mistress was Juliet, that does not mean to say that his relationship with her was no more than or even mainly a sensual one. Naturally all Laporte heard about was the Norman-Gascon boast of his sexual potency, for it cannot be believed that Flaubert, so well aware that 'the least love affairs may cost a woman, however low, her position, her fortune, even her life',[19] would have mentioned Juliet by name, but it is by now impossible to doubt the emotional nature of their relationship. It may be appropriate to recall that, in the first phase of their passionate affair, he had said to 'the Muse': 'Where the devil have you ever found that I said anything analogous to this: "that I have never loved any woman I have possessed and that those I have loved have accorded me nothing?" '[20] That could perhaps go hand in hand with the essence of 'the flaubertian theory of desire that satisfaction destroys it'[21] because the meetings with Juliet were perforce to be so infrequent. In any case, if their relations included sexual satisfaction, this can only have strengthened the bonds between them.

As for Juliet, we must first, surely, disabuse ourselves of any tendency to think of her in terms of a stereotype of the middle-aged English governess (she was 45 in 1874). She was, as she had always been, a woman who strongly attracted Flaubert, who even as a young man had preferred mature women. One cannot, alas, know from written evidence what her feelings were for him, but the factual evidence indicates that Flaubert's charm and magnetism, his warmth and, perhaps for her especially, the paternal side of his character, his dazzling mental gifts, possibly also the *mystique* of his travels and exotic tastes had bound him to her. Otherwise, although it was evidently a deep emotional bond, she could have broken it – if, for instance, she had felt betrayed because she had once believed that he would marry her. That she must have suffered anguish, ' the torment of love unsatisfied', seems undeniable, but she returned to Paris of her own volition. We can only hope and suspect that she too received the kind of letter that in 1858 he had written to another woman whose beauty moved him:

> Since my departure from you, have you not sometimes felt something like a breath passing over you? It was something of me which, escaping from my heart, crossed space invisibly. . . . I have lived for five weeks with this memory, which is also a desire. Your image has incessantly kept me company in my solitude.[22]

It as at least probable that it was his letters, the hope of future meetings, and the remembrance of past ones that may have sweetened the at times unenviable governess drudgery.

There were pressing reasons why Flaubert could not see her in 1875, a year when he felt 'old, used up, disgusted with everything. It seems to me that I am crossing an endless solitude, to go heaven knows where.'[23] He had not even the counterpoise of belief in his writing – in April he told Mme Roger des Genettes that he no longer believed in *Bouvard et Pécuchet*: 'the perspective of its difficulties crushes me in advance',[24] and in May he told George Sand that he had grave doubts over this book, and money worries, and an invincible melancholy.[25]

Since 1871, because Commanville's Norwegian operations had been financially disastrous,[26] his business had been going from bad to worse. Although in that year Flaubert had, with predictable loyalty, done his utmost to help his nephew by enlisting the Princess to try to raise a loan from Rothschild, the attempt was frustrated by her lawyer.[27] Between then and 1875 Commanville gave Flaubert no information on what was going on, although it was becoming more and more difficult for Flaubert to extract any of his own money out of his nephew, even to pay for necessities. Matters came to a head in 1875. By May Flaubert knew that they were desperate, by July that Commanville was insolvent and even Croisset might have to be sold. 'I have lived a laborious and austere existence. . . . I can do no more! I feel at the end of my tether. . . . And then the idea of no more having a roof over my head, a *home* [he used the English word] is intolerable.'[28] Again George Sand perceived that what was still harder for him to endure was the suffering 'of this young woman who is a daughter to you'.[29] His worry and anxiety were such that he was unable to write anything for three months, and on 13 August he told Zola that his nephew was completely ruined. To stave off bankruptcy he sold a farm at Deauville which he had inherited, giving all the proceeds to Commanville, but it had also been necessary for Caroline to agree to pay 2,500 francs a year for ten years to clear a debt of 50,000 with Faucon, a businessman of Sotteville who was among the principal creditors. (Flaubert in jest sometimes referred to 'Faucon, Pécuchet & Cie'.) Because these payments came out of her dowry settlement, there had to be two guarantors, who were the lawyer-politician Raoul Duval and Laporte, but they also seem to have advanced 25,000 francs each.[30] Flaubert told the Princess on 3 October that honour was saved, but that was all – the worry of how to continue to live remained.[31] It was then that the warm-hearted and generous

George Sand told him that if it were not beyond her means, she would buy Croisset for him to spend the rest of his life there – she did not, of course, know that it belonged to Caroline. 'I have no money but I will try to invest a little capital.'[32]

Overwhelmed by these anxieties, in mid-September 1875 Flaubert had gone to stay with an old friend at Concarneau, Georges Pouchet, a scientist who was conducting experiments on fish. Unable to continue the vast *Bouvard et Pécuchet*, on 25 September he decided to begin 'something short'. This was *La Légende de saint Julien l'hospitalier*, the first of the *Trois Contes*. At least the Commanville disaster had one positive, one unexpectedly fortunate outcome: Flaubert would not otherwise have written 'something short', which had to be followed by another short work (written in response to George Sand's plea that he should write something less depressing, which would appeal to everyone),[33] and then, to make up a volume, by one more.

Not since his youthful writings had Flaubert attempted a 'short work' before. The decision he now took was one which acted as a forcing house for his greatest gifts as a writer: he combined the observant, at times almost clinical, eye – one might say his scientific inheritance – with the cast of mind of a poet who naturally thinks in images (he was totally uninterested in rhyme and metre). Through the wounding rejection of the first *Tentation*, he had learned the hard way to write with concision and concentration – he himself used the metaphor of the horse being submitted to dressage.[34] Such discipline became quintessential in short works, in which not only every word must tell but so too its exact placing in the sentence.[35] All three of the *contes* (in that respect like *Madame Bovary*) were not tales but character studies. As Maupassant put it, Flaubert gave no psychological explanations; all had to appear through the actions of the characters.[36] Although Flaubert certainly did not know Turgenev's precept that 'the writer must be a psychologist, but a secret one',[37] he had independently arrived at exactly the same method. The secret was perhaps the sense expressed by Keats when he wrote 'if a Sparrow come before my Window I take part in its existince [*sic*] and pick about the Gravel.'[38] As Flaubert himself had noted years earlier, it was necessary to transport oneself into one's characters.[39] Hence in the *Trois Contes* the physical setting, the world in which the characters live, is as integral to them as are the emblems of their calling in Holbein's paintings of 'The Ambassadors'. But the necessary feats of concentration can only be suggested by the despoiling of acres of flowers for the manufacture of a phial of attar of roses. As he himself said when he began *Un cœur simple*, his descriptions were too long: 'I take out charming things; literature is the art of sacrifices.'[40] It perhaps needs saying that without the luxuriance he had to curb, the end-result would never had its intensity. Exuberance can be cured, but there is no cure for vacuity.

Returning to Paris for the winter Flaubert finished *Saint Julien* in February 1876 and almost immediately started *Un cœur simple*. On 8 March Louise Colet died and the news moved him – it made him go back on the course of his life, as he told Mme Roger des Genettes.[41] 'Am I old, mon Dieu, am I old' he exclaimed on 20 April, yet there was no sign whatsoever of any hardening of the creative arteries: already he had decided to write 'the history of St John the Baptist', which was to become *Hérodias*. George Sand's death on 7 June affected him profoundly; he wrote of her funeral that 'it seemed as if I were burying my mother for the second time',[42] yet he also significantly said: 'My heart is becoming a necropolis, but there is room for the living. It seems to me that the earth is becoming unpeopled. All the more reason to cleave to those who remain, to love still more those one loves.'[43] His frequent protestations about old age (he was the same age as George Sand's son Maurice) need to be taken with a grain of salt. Only forty-eight hours after the funeral, writing of the greenness, trees, and silence of 'mon Croisset', he announced that he would start *Hérodias* as soon as he finished *Un cœur simple* at the end of August.[44] He was swimming in the Seine every day and telling Caroline (who had gone to Eaux-Bonnes) not to become exalted at Lourdes but to continue to reserve her faith for 'choses plus élevées'.[45] He believed that his nephew's affairs were taking a good turn, and now that he was writing so intensively, he decided not to return to Paris before New Year. He finished *Un cœur simple* on 17 August and on the 23rd, writing to Caroline, he enclosed a letter from Juliet saying that she asked Caroline, when she wrote, to send him her letters, Juliet 'not knowing in advance where she will be.'[46] The most probable interpretation of this is that Juliet had just left the Conants – the youngest girl was now 14. Needless to say, on this and on any subsequent post or posts she had, there is no evidence we have been able to discover.

It looks very much as if the letter enclosing one for Caroline confirmed arrangements with Juliet for another secret meeting in Paris for that September, and then, at much the same time of the year in 1877 and 1878, Flaubert devised a quite elaborate pattern of deception, deliberately exploiting the fact that it was generally known that he customarily spent some time at Saint-Gratien in September. To avoid repetition, all the summer meetings in Paris, including those when he apparently did not spin webs of deception, will be considered here.

If the 1876 series of letters (CHH nos. 2816–22) is studied, it will be noticed, for example, that after telling Caroline on 2 September that he was to lunch at Saint-Gratien and spend some days there from the 3rd, he asked Mme Brainne (widow of a journalist, a close friend of Gustave's later years)[47] to come to his Paris lodging on the 3rd, and on the 6th, in a letter which did not come to light until 1972, he told Laporte that he was supposed to be at Saint-Gratien but in fact was in Paris 'where I am de-rusting my weapon'.[48] Again on the 12th he told Laporte 'For the common herd I am supposed to be at Saint-Gratien'.[49] (He did go there, but later.) For a man described by Du Camp as easily duped because he could not imagine anyone practising deception (see p. 30), Flaubert showed considerable virtuosity. This time the pointer to Juliet is the letter enclosing one to Caroline. Again, such deception would not have been necessary for a casual sexual spree. It is perhaps relevant too to point out that Flaubert was chronically short of money. On 7 August he had asked if Ernest could let him have 500 francs for the month of September,[50] and on the 10th he told Caroline that he *must have* 500 francs or at least 300 by 26 or 28 August.[51] Whether he got 300 or 500 francs, he clearly had nothing to spare for frills.

There is a very definite pointer to Juliet in 1877, when in August and September in Paris Flaubert practised exactly the same deceptions as he had the previous summer. The letters to Caroline and to various friends (CHH nos. 3001–15) show that he was telling Laporte the truth on 6 September, when he again said that he was supposed to be at Saint-Gratien but in fact was in Paris, 'where . . .'.[52] This time (though of course he gave not the slightest hint of the identity of the woman in question), he also let Goncourt and Turgenev into the secret. He told Goncourt on the 5th that he had left the Princess eight days ago but had given her to believe that he was no longer in Paris, while *vis-à-vis* people he knew in Paris, he was still at Saint-Gratien: 'The object of these machiavellian contrivances . . . is to be free in my *secret* activities. You are notified. Do not betray me.'[53] And after boasting of his sexual prowess to Laporte on the 11th,[54] next day he told Turgenev not to be astonished by his long stay in the capital – he had been '(*inter nos*)' detained '*Veneris causa*!!!'[55] The pointer to Juliet is that when he got back to Croisset, he told Caroline on the 17th that Julio's new collar became him superbly.[56] Since it was Juliet who had given Flaubert the first collar, there is strong presumptive evidence that it was she who gave him the new one, and it was another holiday with her that he was concealing – the sequence of letters shows that he had something like a fortnight free of other meetings.

In 1878 Flaubert was again in Paris on 3 September – he had told Maupassant on 15 August that he was likely to 'embellish the capital' with his presence from 10 to 25 September, 'but do not tell anyone.'[57] As it turned out, this time 'everyone' must have known that he was in Paris, for he met Turgenev, Mme Brainne, Pouchet, Goncourt, his two publishers (Charpentier and Lemerre), and Agénor Bardoux, who was Minister of Public Instruction from 1877 until January 1879. In fact Flaubert had a very full programme, including winding up arrangements for the Commanvilles to let their apartment and share his, using his influence with Bardoux to try to get Laporte a job, making another attempt to get his *féerie* produced, and visiting an exhibition. Nevertheless, a letter to Laporte of 11 September makes it clear that his time was not entirely taken up by these meetings and arrangements.[58] But nothing other than what seems to have become an established custom indicates that Juliet may have been with him that year too.

Again in 1879 Flaubert was back in Paris at the end of August, once more with a very full programme – he was correcting proofs for the Charpentier edition of *L'Éducation* and the Lemerre edition of *Salammbô* as well as proofs of a Turgenev story that was to appear in the *Nouvelle revue*; he was also putting in hand an edition of Bouilhet's *Poésies complètes* and meeting the composer and critic Ernest Reyer about the scenario for a *Salammbô* opera, and he paid a brief visit to Saint-Gratien. Even so, on 16 September, boasting to Laporte of further sexual exploits during the past fortnight, he said: 'I find it exigent of you to ask me if I have been writing in Paris, Frankly, I write enough the whole year long to have the right to a little rest.'[59] Once more, there is nothing other than past experience to link this with Juliet.

Returning to 1876 (after the interruption of the summer meetings in Paris), on 19 October that year he at last heard again with delight from Gertrude Tennant, who was to bring two of her daughters, Dolly and Evelyn, to France, and he told her that he would be returning to Paris that winter.[60] He had finished *Hérodias* by 9 December, and on Christmas Day he told her that he was completely alone so as to be able to publish his *Trois Contes* in the spring. It is not surprising that in the spring of 1877 the pressure of work that winter and too much coffee had made Flaubert's heart beat too fast and caused trembling fits; yet, as he told Mme Roger des Genettes on 2 April, he wanted to write a tale about the battle of Thermopylae,[61] an idea that was to obsess him in 1879. In May he asked Charpentier to send to England two works published by his firm.[62] One was the *Trois Contes* (published that April), which we know Gertrude must have received because he told her he was going to send her a copy earlier that year.[63] He had probably sent Juliet a copy himself, so that the second work may have been the *Tentation*, also for Gertrude. Flaubert was in better spirits, as he told Mme Brainne on 4 July, saying (as indeed everything was to show) that his morale was still good and 'the heart does not age'.[64] His morale must have been sustained by the admiration he had now aroused among younger writers who, when *Un cœur simple* was published in *Le Moniteur* in April, had invited him, Zola, and Edmond de Goncourt to a banquet in his honour. (On the menu were *Potage purée Bovary*, *Poularde truffée à la saint Antoine*, and *Artichaut au cœur simple*.) The younger writers were Maupassant, Huysmans, Henry Céard, Paul Alexis, and Octave Mirbeau.

Early in 1878 Flaubert was working in 'gigantic proportions' on *Bouvard et Pécuchet*. On 4 May (from Paris) he thanked Gertrude Tennant for sending a portrait of one of her daughters which reminded him of everything best in his youth,[65] and then on 1 September he told her of his forthcoming Paris visit, saying that he would be returning to Croisset on the 22nd or 23rd, when he counted on seeing her; she must know his true home, 'mon *antre*'.[66] However, in October he told her that he had spent all September in Paris and had vainly expected her every day, so now he asked her to come to Rouen.[67]

In the meanwhile the Commanville affairs were rapidly sliding into the ultimate crisis of 1879. There had been fresh disturbing news in 1877, when Flaubert again saved the day by personally enlisting Raoul Duval's renewed help and also visiting the wealthy Mme Pelouze, then proprietor of the château de Chenonceaux (which he had previously visited), and who helped to the extent of 50,000 francs. Laporte was by that time himself in difficulties, in part because of his previous guarantees to Commanville and in part because of the failure of the lace factory he ran. (Hence Flaubert's attempts to get him a job.) But the reprieve Flaubert won for the Commanvilles was only temporary. Nor, it seems, did the Commanvilles so much as sympathize with the man who had handed over his whole fortune and had made such heroic efforts to prevent their ruin, for as Flaubert wrote to Caroline from Paris in September 1878:

> If Ernest continues to give me nothing at all, as he has for the last two years, I do not know I will be able to spend three months in Paris this winter – and you find me unjust when a little murmur escapes me! Your privations, my dear Caroline, do not prevent mine. On the contrary, they aggravate them.[68]

Back at Croisset after the Paris visit, as the rain poured down and the river roared under 'a black sky with sapphire bands',[69] all the worries crowded in again, aggravated by the rejection of the *féerie* by the *Moniteur universel.* Early in December he told Mme Brainne that they were now at the bottom of the abyss; the sawmill would be sold for a song. It was not the lack of money and the resulting privations and complete absence of liberty that enraged him, 'but I feel mentally polluted by these petty preoccupations, by these commercial dialogues'.[70] And in December he told the Princess 'when one is at the bottom of the abyss, there is nothing more to fear . . . I have steered my boat badly through too much idealism.'[71]

In the penultimate year of Flaubert's life, 1879, almost everything went disastrously wrong. The continuing long-drawn-out financial worries would have been crushing enough. Then, on 27 January, he slipped on ice, breaking a bone in his leg and severely spraining his ankle. Laporte immediately came to his help. Though in much pain and discomfort, Flaubert told the Princess in February that his accident was a bagatelle beside his other troubles – the 'maudites *affaires*'.[72] When the sawmill was sold in March Flaubert, the chief creditor, received nothing because he had no guarantee. He insisted that, 'coûte que coûte', the Commanvilles must pay their friends and significantly asked on the 25th why they had not paid Raoul Duval and Laporte. That same month the treasurer of the Bouilhet memorial committee went mad and this too fell on Flaubert, who was responsible for 10,000 francs subscribed for the monument which could not be found. But nothing could more reflect an indomitable spirit than the letter he wrote to the Princess in March telling her of the signs of spring, 'so beaten as I am by fate, so damaged as I feel I am', and continuing 'But I am calumniating myself. . . . Yes, laugh at me, I am as much of a *troubadour* as I was at 18.'[73] And in April, noticing the lilac in bud, he told Caroline 'in spite of everything, something of spring comes into your heart'[74] – this despite painful rheumatism and a swollen foot. At the end of the month, telling her that he had nothing left after paying his housekeeper with what in any case he owed on the Bouilhet subscriptions, he said 'You talk of my next journey to Paris, but what would I live on?'[75] His poor Julio too became so ill that he was not expected to live ('He is exactly like a person; he makes little gestures that are profoundly human').[76] However much Caroline may have felt at the end of her tether, she seems to have been chillingly lacking in sympathy. Far from being a misanthropist, Flaubert suffered keenly and increasingly from the loneliness of Croisset, 'when I see no human being and when I am not cheered up by a letter . . . . *d'affaires*',[77] but to judge from his bitter, ironic apology to her on 16 May, she must have reproached him for complaining:

I went from your house yesterday *tormented by remorse*. For some time I have been really unpleasant in person and in my letters but, in my excuse, you must imagine that I have been suffering immeasurably, that I keep back a hundred times more than I say. . . . I do not satisfy any need of my heart and my solitude is complete. I am quite sure that not one of the people I know could live as I am living. Never mind, poor child, I was too egotistical . . . and ask forgiveness.[78]

Others were more sympathetic. In April Flaubert's 'three angels', the beautiful Mme Brainne and her sister Mme Lapierre (wife of the editor of the *Nouvelliste de Rouen*) and their friend Mme Pasquier, the actress (her stage name was Mme Pasca) had arranged a dinner to celebrate Flaubert's patron saint, Saint Polycarp, adopted for the appropriateness of his saying 'Lord, what a century you have caused me to be born in.' And although Flaubert's pride made him at first refuse an honorary position his friends were attempting to obtain for him, such proof of their solicitude must have touched him. Characteristically, when in February he was prevailed on to accept a position which in fact never materialized because of a change of ministry, his reason for accepting it was, as he told Caroline, 'the idea that I would cost you less'.[79] The contrast with the Commanvilles' attitude to Flaubert, to whom they referred as 'the consumer',[80] could not be more absolute. At the end of May Maupassant did prevail on Flaubert to accept a government pension which gave him an income of 3,000 francs, but it was not until October Flaubert heard of this officially.

Though still very lame, he spent three weeks in Paris in June, still hoping for a production of his *féerie*, but by 3 July he was compelled to renounce this dream. He again expressed his longing to write *The Battle of Thermopylae*, and the continuing extraordinary fertility of his imagination is strikingly revealed by Goncourt's record of his visit to Saint-Gratien that September, when Flaubert told him that he was tormented by two or three ideas for further *contes*, then he planned a study of two or three Rouen families before and up to the revolution; then there was to be his great novel on the empire (*Sous Napoléon III*), but he was above all 'obsessed' by Thermopylae and said he intended to return to Greece to write it.[81] None of this sounds like a tired, dispirited old man. Indeed, he was even more hopeful about the Commanville affairs – he told Turgenev in August that Ernest had succeeded in setting up a sawmill and told Mme des Genettes that he had made an arrangement for Caucasian oak timber to be sawn, at Rouen.[82] (But he had let the interest on his debts accumulate.)[83]

In reality the Commanville affairs were rapidly deteriorating because their payments on the guarantee were in arrears, and at the same time Laporte's difficulties were increasing, while Faucon was demanding a renewal of the guarantee. By September Faucon would only grant the Commanvilles a delay on harsh terms, but Commanville claimed to have found a capitalist prepared to take over the debt and put money into a sawmill business if the guarantors would renew. Raoul Duval agreed, but Laporte refused because he would have to have backed his guarantee by raising a mortgage on his property.[84] No doubt under pressure from the Commanvilles, Flaubert twice begged Laporte to renew, but Laporte, who had nothing firmer than the Commanville assurances that they would repay, refused, explaining his reasons on 20 September. He told Flaubert that to avoid a break in their friendship, he must deal directly with Commanville, so that Flaubert would thus not have to take one side or other. 'Know well, my good Giant, that I will always love you with all my heart.'[85] Since Flaubert was so well aware of Laporte's difficulties and of having caused them, it appears that the Commanvilles must have succeeded in convincing him that Laporte, in refusing, was behaving as less than a friend, for on 8 October Flaubert mentioned to Mme des Genettes the egoism of a man he had believed to be his most intimate friend.[86] At the same time the letters reveal his panic at never knowing what was happening and the 'dementia' caused by his antipathy to business affairs.[87] In December he told Caroline that he was continuing to think of his ex-friend Laporte very often; this was something he had not swallowed easily,[88] and at the end of the month he sent her a copy of Laporte's New Year letter, saying he was not going to reply to it.[89] What we may not know are the pressures put on Laporte which caused him to send Flaubert (of all people) a writ, demanding repayment of 13,000 francs, which on 5 February 1880 Flaubert forwarded to the Commanvilles. It seems more likely that Laporte was himself under pressure from Faucon than that this represented a revolt against what Sartre maintains was Flaubert's treatment of Laporte as a vassal.[90] Flaubert was still in a state of incomprehension on the 6th.

This cruel break in relations has evoked partisan accounts by, on the one side, the supporters of Flaubert and Laporte (who included René Dumesnil, whose first wife was a Laporte) and on the other by Caroline's niece who, in attempting to put the record straight, was no less partisan. For the full story we must probably await the volume of Professor Bruneau's correspondence dealing with these years, but the fact that Caroline turned Laporte away when he came to Flaubert's funeral is surely indicative of her animus against him? It is difficult even to imagine the effect of this break on Flaubert, for whom friendship was all-important.

After the break with Laporte, at the end of September 1879, although Flaubert was signing his letters to Caroline as 'Le Vieillard de Cro-Magnon', he was reading proofs, commenting at length on a number of books sent to him by younger writers, and in November touring his property with his scientist friend Pouchet. A day before his 58th birthday he wrote one of many letters exhibiting the side of his nature that made George Sand christen him a 'troubadour'; letters in which all the warmth of his nature and his response to beauty in women led him to conduct flirtations on paper with them:

> I kiss your beautiful eyes, your beautiful eyebrows, your. . . . Ah! everything beautiful in your person. In twenty-four hours, tomorrow 12 December, your unworthy slave will be 58! I would rather offer you no more than 25! Never mind, the heart remains young.[91]

The truth of this last sentence is self-evident, though not everyone would agree that Mme Brainne was his last love.[92]

It was an exceptionally cold winter; his housekeeper made a coat for Julio out of an old pair of trousers. Flaubert's genius for description had not left him: 'Not a boat on the water, not a passer-by on the road. It is like a tomb of complete whiteness in which one lies, buried.'[93] On 14 December Turgenev spent twenty-four hours at Croisset before going to Russia, which 'vexes me extraordinarily.'[94]

On 24 January 1880 Flaubert confessed to Mme des Genettes that the insupportability of human stupidity had become '*an illness*, and the word is feeble',[95] but next day he told her that he had at least three or four letters to write every day, two or three volumes sent by young writers to read per week, not counting what he had to read for *Bouvard et Pécuchet*, for which he had had to absorb over 1,500 volumes.[96] He was overjoyed to read Maupassant's *Boule de Suif* ('C'est un chef d'œuvre'), he told Caroline on 1 February,[97] asking her on the 3rd when 'this *devastation*, pecuniary and moral', would end.[98] Also that month he was seriously worried by a threat to prosecute Maupassant and the editor and printer of a journal which published two pieces of verse by him. In the end, only the publication of Flaubert's open letter to *Le Gaulois*, recalling the *Bovary* trial, prevented this. Although on 15 February he told Caroline that he was still worried by 'this continual uncertainty',[99] as ever he was moved by the signs of spring, noting on the 29th, as he made 'a long tour' of the gardens, that the terrace would be green in a week and violets and primroses were showing.[100] In April he read with emotion Maupassant's dedication of his first published volume 'À l'illustre et paternel ami que j'aime de toute ma tendresse, à l'irréprochable maître que j'admire avant tous'. By then Flaubert believed that at least the Commanville affairs were going better; as he told Turgenev on 4 March, Ernest had got funds to restart a sawmill at Rouen and when the contract was signed, he would go to Odessa to procure timber.[101] On 28 March Flaubert gave an Easter dinner party (which he paid for out of some money kept hidden for that purpose) for Maupassant, Goncourt, Zola, Daudet, and Charpentier, who all spent the night at Croisset. The food was excellent, the wine flowed, and Flaubert was at the top of his form.[102]

Though earlier that month he had told Caroline that *Bouvard et Pécuchet* was giving him 'un mal de chien', on 22 April, when he was keenly looking forward to spending some time in Paris with her (at the apartment they now shared), he told her that he would have completed the first volume except for two final scenes.[103] He told the Princess on the same day that he would pack for Paris in a fortnight and would, of course, rush to the rue de Berry (her Paris home).[104] The Saint Polycarp dinner arranged on 27 April that year (which happened to be Juliet's birthday) was brilliantly stage-managed by Lapierre and Maupassant, who devised congratulatory telegrams including ones from the archbishop of Rouen and the Italian cardinals. On 2 May he asked Mme des Genettes if she would be in Paris at the end of that month or at the beginning of June: 'How I long to see you.'[105]

There was really only one serious blot on the horizon. On 17 September 1879 he had agreed to publish *Le Château des cœurs* in a periodical he detested – *La Vie moderne*, launched by Charpentier in April that year and edited by Gautier's son-in-law, Émile Bergerat. The first scene appeared in the number for 24 January 1880, and Flaubert became more and more disgusted with the way in which it was being published, complaining of the 'infantile illustrations'[106] ('Oh illustration! modern invention made to dishonour all literature').[107] This 'parody of the text' made him bitterly regret that he had, for once, failed to stick to his own principles of refusing to allow his work to be illustrated. In the meanwhile he had, on 23–24 January, asked Caroline to '*keep all the numbers*. . . . Because I will send all my copies to Juliet'.[108] This is the last mention of Juliet in the correspondence, but if Flaubert continued to send her his copies of *La Vie moderne*, she must have received all except the last, because that number appeared on 8 May, the day of his death. The January letter to Caroline is eloquent testimony of the fact that he was thinking of Juliet until the end; the fact that he was still sending her copies of his writings does not admit of any doubt that she had entered his life at many levels, if not such profound ones as had Élisa Schlésinger, and after over two decades, only death broke this tie.

On Saturday 8 May, the day before he was to leave for Paris, Flaubert died suddenly, after a very hot bath. The doctor who saw him (his own doctor was not available) diagnosed apoplexy – the then customary term for a stroke – exactly as would be expected from the deepening red of his complexion and from the strains put on him by worry and working under pressure. All who admire Flaubert must rejoice that he was spared 'the insulting paralysis',[109] but feel some sense of outrage at Ledoux's claim that he had attempted to strangle himself in his bath (how?) and that, with the complicity of the doctor, the family camouflaged this.[100] It is sufficient to say that Ledoux was never able to produce the evidence of a police report he claimed would substantiate this.

IX Caroline and Juliet

Ah mon pauvre Flaubert! Voilà autour de ton cadavre des machines et des documents humains, dont tu aurais pu faire un beau roman provincial!

JOURNAL DES GONCOURT, 14 May 1880

Caroline

One would think that Edmond de Goncourt had confused Flaubert with Balzac. What had provoked this comment was a report, via Maupassant, of what happened immediately after Flaubert's death. According to this, Ernest Commanville was talking all the time about the money to be made out of Flaubert's works and giving the impression that he would be capable of blackmailing the surviving recipients of the love letters.[1] If this report can be believed (for it is, of course, a partisan account), it would be of considerable interest to know who Ernest considered as candidates for blackmail. He certainly knew that Louise Colet was dead and if, as seems very probable, he knew of the nature of the relationship with Juliet, he must surely also have known that it would hardly be lucrative to blackmail a governess. If Flaubert had kept any notes from actresses, they would have been only too glad to proclaim their relations with him.

Maupassant told Goncourt that the evening before the funeral, soon after dinner (at which he and José-Maria de Heredia were present), Commanville took him into the summer house, detaining him an hour while making false protestations of affection, and he also passed on what he can only have learned from Heredia – that during that time Caroline took Heredia on a bench in the garden, telling him that she needed the devotion of a man of the world who would represent and defend her against her own family. She burst into tears and moved her head in such a way that Heredia believed she was going to throw herself into his arms; at one point she was alleged to be inviting him to kiss her. Ernest, it was said, had put Caroline up to this to get Heredia to take a hand in some sharp practice with the Achille Flauberts.[2] It is perhaps sufficient to say that this is a highly malicious account, and one retailed by a master of fiction. However, if Heredia really did describe Caroline's behaviour in anything like these terms, her own account of their subsequent relations, as narrated by her niece, seems the more extraordinary. According to this, during later meetings with him there developed on her side 'a kind of elegiac friendship, romantic and sentimental', but Heredia (himself a married man) gave her cause to consult her father-confessor, the Dominican Père Didon, whose help she had sought in 1879 and who now insisted that this relationship must not go beyond friendship. She submitted, but not so Heredia, who broke off relations with her.[3] Thus once more Caroline was obliged to deny the promptings of her heart.

There was at least some truth in the statement that Caroline needed someone to defend her from the members of her own family – the Commanvilles were right in believing that Julie Flaubert and her daughter Juliette Rocquigny would give her no quarter. When the family assembled to decide the succession, Achille was dying in the south of France; his wife and daughter had a long-standing grievance since, in their estimation, Mme Flaubert had unduly favoured Caroline in leaving Croisset to her. And they knew that Flaubert had been ruined and that the Commanvilles were heavily in debt. They therefore refused the succession, coldly intimating to Caroline, through a lawyer, that they had no intention of paying Ernest's debts.[4] However, the major debts appear to have been settled shortly before Gustave's death – in February 1880 he told Caroline that Faucon's *acte* (i.e. a settlement with the creditors) would probably be signed on 26 February,[5] and his letter of 14 March to her (and of the 4th to Turgenev) indicate that Ernest did raise the money and the sawmill would reopen.[6] The extent of the Commanvilles' remaining debts or new obligations is not clear.

Caroline has been severely criticized for selling Croisset immediately after her uncle's death – in point of fact, after his estate was wound up, for the sale took place in May 1881. But money was not her sole reason for selling; as she told a friend on 11 June that year, her husband had never been well there;[7] the indications were that he already had tuberculosis. And the house had become extremely dilapidated.[8] She was therefore telling the truth in saying, in the same letter, that it was a heavy charge on them. It was purchased ostensibly by a private person for 180,000 francs, but he seems to have been put up to buy it by the owner of a distillery, because a month later it changed hands for the same sum. Two months later demolition began, and by 1885 a large distillery was in operation, which was, in turn, followed by a paper factory. We know from her niece how much its demolition did hurt Caroline, for when she used to visit the house of Dr Parfait Grout, opposite Croisset, she always refused to go with her little nieces to a hillock which opened up the view of that distillery belching black smoke.[9]

Caroline has likewise been harshly criticized for not making provision for the preservation of all Flaubert's manuscripts, notebooks, dossiers, etc., and the collection of books in his library. Her niece states that Caroline's view was that 'it was absolutely necessary to preserve all of them',[10] and in order to do so, she took in paying guests recommended by Gertrude Tennant. However, as Professor Bruneau has noted, at some time or other she sold a large number of the books which had belonged to her uncle, including Creuzer's *Religions de l'Antiquité*, before she bequeathed the rest to Louis Bertrand; moreover a certain number of books not previously sold did not form part of the legacy to him but were sold at Antibes on 28, 29, and 30 April 1931.[11] Hence when Bertrand bequeathed what remained to the Canteleu-Croisset *mairie*, the library had already suffered amputations and some additions. As for the manuscripts, notebooks, dossiers, etc., although Caroline did leave the major manuscripts to public institutions (divided between Paris and Rouen), a very large number of manuscripts, some of the notebooks, the whole great collection of *ébauches* and *brouillons* for *L'Éducation sentimentale* as well as the item entitled in the sale catalogue 'Renseignements pour l'éducation sentimentale', and the collection of objects in Flaubert's study were sold. All too many valuable items disappeared altogether; some in private hands have been inaccessible to scholars. Mme Chevalley-Sabatier believed that it would not have displeased Caroline to know that they had come into the hands of collectors and turned up for sale from time to time, since this 'could only contribute to keeping Flaubert's memory alive'. But this reflects a total failure to appreciate the contribution to the greatness of Flaubert's achievements which emerges from the study of the youthful works and his notebooks, scenarios, and drafts of the major novels.

After the sale of Croisset Caroline, who had also her untouchable dowry settlement, was the richer by 180,000 francs minus whatever had to be paid to creditors, but that the Commanvilles were far from being reduced to the plight of the Herberts after Richard's bankruptcy we know from Edmond de Goncourt's record of a dinner with them in February 1884. They lived in a small, wealthy, bourgeois home in Paris. Its luxuriousness, the silky wall-coverings, and the calm, satisfied affluence of its owners made him rather sad and reminded him of poor Flaubert's last days, 'completely ruined by this well-to-do couple and reduced to smoking penny cigars'. Goncourt was not charmed by his fellow guests, whom he described as 'formerly pretty' wives of stockbrokers, baronesses married to painters, journalist blue-stockings, men of the world engaged in linguistic studies, and professors of cuneiform.[12]

Coming now to the publication of Flaubert's letters, it looks very much as if Caroline must have taken the decision to publish them very soon after his death – again his niece is misleading in saying that she did not decide to publish until the favourable reception of the letters to George Sand (she seems to have meant the volume published in 1884, although she actually mentioned the one published in 1904 containing the joint Flaubert–Sand correspondence). In fact Caroline first published her uncle's letters to George Sand in Juliette Adam's *Nouvelle revue* in December 1883–January 1884,[13] but since she also had to deal with the proofs of *Bouvard et Pécuchet* (which first appeared in the same periodical between December 1880 and March 1881) and was by no means content to let the letters be published verbatim, she must have been working on them well ahead of their publication, for it seems that she must herself have made the 'edited' copies which were published. In all her uncle's letters, in all the series published during Caroline's lifetime (when she held the copyright), not only had anything from phrases to entire paragraphs been deleted, but in some cases she 'improved' her uncle's phrasing or his punctuation, as in a letter to Turgenev in which Flaubert's 'tâchons . . . de nous tenir le bec hors de l'eau' became 'tâchons de nous tenir la tête levée hors de l'eau'.[14] But since she made no deletion or correction marks on the manuscripts,[15] she must have made the copies herself. (It is not surprising that she made an occasional mistake, as in writing 'Saint Antoine' for 'Saint Julien'.)[16] A very large number of the letters was omitted *in toto*.

It is essential to know how Caroline set about publishing the letters before considering why every reference to Juliet was suppressed when she came to publish her uncle's *Lettres à sa nièce Caroline* in

1906, for she reserved these letters from the first edition of the general correspondence published in 1887–93, and it is only in them that any references to Juliet occur. (The elimination of Juliet persisted in the 9-volume Conard edition as well, since it appeared before Caroline's death.) One cannot attempt to answer the question why these particular suppressions were made before at least sampling other ones made by Caroline, to guess at her principles in making them. Thanks to the fact that the suppressed passages are enclosed in parentheses in the CHH edition (unfortunately an opening or closing parenthesis is often omitted), it is not difficult to discover that Caroline suppressed all passages which she believed were too intimate (or indecent) or which might give offence to those still living. Uncomplimentary comments on the Achille Flauberts, on Alexandre Dumas *fils*, even on Turgenev's excessive 'enslavement' to the Viardot family,[16] occasional animadversions on the Princess were suppressed, as were most of the passages on the Commanvilles' financial ruin and Flaubert's often pathetic requests for money. What might be termed a second category of suppressions (but here Caroline was decidedly inconsistent) concerns phrases or sentences deemed unimportant, such as greetings or minor messages. There remain cases in which it ranges from being difficult to impossible to divine Caroline's reasoning – why, for instance, in a letter to Mme Roger des Genettes of March 1876 did she omit Flaubert's recommendation to her to read Zola's *Son Excellence Eugène Rougon*, which he described as powerful and of great breadth, and on which he was curious to know her opinion?[17]

In the light of these omissions, with one possible exception (the 1872 letter referring to his 'chère compagne', quoted on p. 117), the elimination of Juliet seems to have no special significance, for all the phrases in which her name occurs or in which 'the governess' is mentioned come in the 'unimportant' category. Even the 1872 phrase is innocent enough, although a number of people might willingly have read more into it. And another reason for these suppressions suggests itself – Caroline's well-attested snobbishness. There is ample evidence of it in her exaggeration of Mme Flaubert's more aristocratic forebears, in her slighting dismissal of the Milman's Row house as 'minuscule', and in her comments on Marianne's acquaintance with the aristocracy and on life at Lyndon Hall. Her nieces referred to her as 'la dame si bien'.[18] Hence Caroline may have wished to suppress all trace of a relationship between her uncle and a mere governess.

Neither the explanation suggested by Mme Chevalley-Sabatier nor that suggested by Professor Bart seems to be the right one. Mme Chevalley-Sabatier, in suggesting that when Caroline read the letters she felt resentment at discovering that the ties between her uncle and her governess were closer than she believed, seems to overlook the fact that, as is shown in Chapter VII, Caroline must have been aware of the nature of their relations from at least 1872. Even so, had she found a series of love letters written by Juliet, still more explicit of what had been going on, or had she read her uncle's letters to Laporte, she might have been shocked by them and experienced a revulsion from Juliet. As, however, will be seen, she did not find Juliet's letters, and Laporte kept his letters from Gustave during his lifetime. (He died in 1906.)[19] Professor Bart's suggestion that the references to Juliet were suppressed because the Herbert family was still alive could, surely, only be valid had there been anything scandalous in the letters Caroline saw; the very innocent mentions of her in the ones she did see could only have bestowed distinction on the obscure Herbert family, who would thus be known as the friends of so celebrated an author. The far from obscure Gertrude Tennant, when she was Stanley's mother-in-law, was described by Léon Daudet, on a visit to London, as a member of the élite because she 'appears in Flaubert's memoirs'.[20]

What of Juliet's letters to Gustave? It seems unquestionable that Caroline did not find them, for the year before his death, in May 1879, not long after the accident to his leg, Flaubert told Laporte: 'Yesterday I spent *eight hours* sorting and burning letters, a long delayed job, and my hands are shaking from tying up packets'.[21] This precisely corroborates Maupassant's account, which he published 'about 1891' on the occasion of the inauguration of Flaubert's memorial in Rouen and which was included in a little collection published by Georges-Émile Bertrand in 1947. Exactly a year before Flaubert's death, Maupassant wrote, Flaubert told him he wanted to burn all his old letters, setting some aside. 'I do not want anyone to read them after my death, but I do not want to do this all alone.' He had therefore arranged for Maupassant to spend the night at Croisset. After dinner they went into Flaubert's bedroom, adjoining his study, and there Maupassant saw, behind a curtain, a great trunk (no doubt the one Flaubert buried during the Franco-Prussian war) and they each took one end of it to carry it into the study. It was full of papers. Flaubert said: 'There is my life. . . . I want to keep part of it and burn the other part.' He told Maupassant to take up a book. The first letters were insignificant ones; then he took out the long ones by George Sand, and others. He set aside many to be kept, but one glance at the rest sufficed for him to fling them into the fire. Hours passed; from time to time Flaubert murmured a name, making a regretful gesture. He read few of these intimate papers, as if he wanted to be done with them, and then set to and burned piles of them. At 4 a.m. he suddenly found a little packet tied up with ribbon in the midst of the letters. In it was what Maupassant described as 'a little silk dancing shoe' with a faded rose in a lace-edged handkerchief inside it. Flaubert kissed these relics and then burned them, wiping his eyes. It was daylight before he finished.[22]

That slipper was not a dancing-shoe; it was Louise Colet's slipper, or pair of slippers (perhaps Maupassant overlooked one of them), which Flaubert had written about in August 1846, in one of the most superb of his love letters. He told Louise that when the evening had come and he was alone, quite certain of not being disturbed, when everyone else was asleep, he opened a drawer and took out 'my relics', which he spread out on his table, the little slippers first, the handkerchief, her hair, the sachet containing her letters.[23]

Eight hours is a very long time considering that Flaubert read few of these intimate letters he burned, so that, alas, at least many hundreds must have gone on to that pyre. It surely can hardly be doubted that among them were all Louise's and Juliet's letters; almost certainly also most of Laporte's. For there is a good deal of independent evidence to confirm Maupassant's account. It is, of course, well known that George Sand's letters survived; indeed, in February 1880 Flaubert told Mme Brainne that he had looked through all her 164 letters before sending them to Maurice Sand, who wanted to publish his mother's correspondence.[24] And it seems clear that when Caroline sorted the surviving letters, she did not find the enormous bundles of 'the Muse's' letters, for she tried to purchase her uncle's letters to 'the Muse' from Louise's daughter, Mme Bissieu, but – as she herself acknowledged – she was obliged to publish copies (not autographs) of only 138 of these letters,[25] and at that (as has been seen, p. 98), only on condition that *vous* was to replace *tu* throughout. Since no one, let alone an astute business woman like Caroline, would have traded many hundreds of autograph letters for these copies, it must surely be evident that Louise's original letters went up in flames?[26] As for Laporte's letters, the fact that the Lovenjoul library possesses only two letters and a note of his indicates that Flaubert burned the replies to almost all of the 180 letters and notes he wrote to Laporte between 1866 and 1879.[27] And this is, surely, also the explanation of the failure to date to find a single one of Juliet's letters written during a period of twenty years? Maupassant was right too about the unimportant letters; as Antoine Albalat reported when he saw some twenty enormous bundles of papers at Caroline's eventual home, the Villa Tanit at Antibes, some of the most insignificant notes had been piously kept.[28]

Maupassant's account of the reason why Flaubert conducted this holocaust is likewise completely convincing, and there is an interesting parallel with Robert Browning, who also burnt letters because of his 'lifelong hatred of gossip-mongers' and his belief that a poet had as much right to a private life as anyone else.[29] Flaubert too knew of, and noted in a *carnet*, the duc de Morny's instructions that his love letters were to be burned.[30] And as long ago as 1859, Flaubert (after the publication of Louise's *Histoire de soldat*) had written: 'The moment one is an artist, messieurs the grocers, registry clerks, customs clerks, boot-makers and others amuse themselves with your personal affairs. . . . I think, on the contrary, that the writer should leave nothing of himself except his works.'[31] Even earlier he had told 'the Muse' that he had burned many letters from Mesdames Didier[32] and Roger des Genettes which she had passed to him; her letters (Louise's) already filled a whole carton (and there were several years to run before the final break).[33] And then in 1874 the publication of Mérimée's *Lettres à une inconnue* had caused a sensation in Paris: 'even politics became a secondary consideration for the hour', according to the *Quarterly Review* for January 1874.[34] It was the publication of these letters that made Flaubert and Maxime Du Camp decide to destroy all their 'youthful letters', as Flaubert told Mme des Genettes on 2 March 1877, specifically telling Mme Brainne on the same day that 'the example of what has happened to Mérimée induced us to take this prudent measure'.[35] (Fortunately some escaped destruction.) But besides his wish to prevent posterity from knowing much about his private life, it seems unquestionable that Flaubert would also have thought of protecting someone so vulnerable as Juliet.

There remain two questions. First, what happened to any letters Juliet wrote after May 1879, for she must have written some, if only to acknowledge the copies of *La Vie moderne*? It seems highly probable that Flaubert would have destroyed these too, but one or two may have come too late. Presumably Caroline either returned these to her or destroyed them. And the second question is whether, when she was calling in her uncle's letters, Caroline may have asked Juliet to return hers. It is hard to believe that she would have thought of publishing these letters, since she must have known that they would have been extremely damaging to Juliet and her mother and sisters, who were, after all, friends of Caroline's. She may therefore not have asked for them; and if she did (in order to read them herself), their absence from the Fonds Franklin-Grout in the Lovenjoul library seems to indicate that she did not receive them (as will be further discussed) rather than that she destroyed them.

After the death in 1883 of 'Mamzelle Julie', the Flauberts' devoted servant, by which time Achille, his wife and daughter, and Caroline's paternal aunt were all dead, she felt that her last links with the past had dissolved. Since also Père Didon had advised her to move south because of Ernest's incurable disease, she bought a piece of land at Antibes and built the villa which she called Villa Tanit (the name of the Carthaginian goddess in *Salammbô*). She continued to make a stay in Paris each spring, where she regularly visited her old friend Frankline Grout, who had married Auguste Sabatier. Ten years after Ernest's death (he died in 1890), Caroline asked Frankline if her brother Franklin (chief alienist of a well-known hospital at Passy) was disposed to marry her – she knew he had loved her and believed that this was one of the reasons why he had never married. It evidently was so, and they married that autumn, so that Caroline belatedly had the happiness always hitherto denied to her. The Villa Tanit became a literary, artistic, and musical centre, Franklin at first continuing his practice but then spending more and more time at Antibes before he retired there. He died in 1921. Caroline at 84 remained alert, impressive, a little authoritarian, in full command of all her faculties, indeed continuing to paint and sketch, as Willa Cather recorded when she met her at Aix-les-Bains shortly before Caroline died in 1930.[36]

Juliet

We know all too little about Juliet's life after Flaubert's death; unfortunately no diarist recorded a visit to Milman's Row. Juliet, it seems, must have learned of his death from Caroline, and she probably saw an obituary which appeared in *The Times* on 10 May 1880, which at one point confused Gustave with Achille. Recording that Gustave had died of apoplexy in Rouen the previous day, at the age of 58, it continued:

> He intended starting that day for Paris as a rest from a work entitled 'Bouvard et Peluchet [*sic*]' on which he was engaged. He at first adopted his father's profession – that of surgeon – but soon deserted it for literature; and after several slight attempts he won notoriety in 1856 by a Government prosecution for immorality against his 'Madame Bovary'. He was acquitted, and the novel, the fruit of eight years' labour, had a great run. Six years later he published 'Salammbo', a picture of life in old Carthage; in 1869, 'Education Sentimentale'; and in 1875 the 'Tentation de St. Antoine'. The same year his 'Candidat' was brought out on the stage, and he has since written some minor works.

It is fitting to spare a thought for Juliet's unrecorded grief.

It will be recalled that Juliet's well-off uncle William Herbert had died in 1863 (p. 60); her cousin, his daughter Elizabeth, who with her husband James Hopgood were prominent in the well-to-do Clapham society of the day, was still alive, so that Juliet and her sisters had not yet benefited from the reversionary clauses in William's will (see p. 61). The first of Juliet's sisters to die was the youngest, Adelaide, in 1886; as we learn from the *Calendar of Grants of Probate* at Somerset House, it was Juliet, not her two elder sisters, who was the sole executrix, and since it was again she who was granted administration or probate after her mother's death in 1881 and after Augusta's death in 1894, she appears to have been the most responsible member of the family. Her mother's effects were first sworn at £551, but resworn as nil in 1896. It is unexpected to find that Adelaide did not die penniless but left a personal estate of £570. Elizabeth Hopgood died in 1892 and had drawn up her will shortly after Adelaide's death. In it, she instructed her trustees to set aside shares of her estate for her niece and cousins. Six thousand pounds went in equal shares to Marianne, Augusta, and Juliet Herbert – 'all of them children of my deceased uncle Richard Herbert a brother of my said father' – for their respective lives, with a reversion to the Reverend George William Herbert. She bequeathed her freely disposable estate to her husband. Thus all three surviving Herbert sisters benefited after her death, and it is gratifying to know that at long last they were comparatively well off. Augusta (aged 67) left £1,195; Marianne, who died in 1894 aged 74, left £5,079. Since the Reverend George William Herbert died in November of the same year,[37] Juliet was Marianne's sole beneficiary.

It must have been after Marianne's death, when Juliet was alone, that she decided to leave Milman's Row in order to be near her cousin Emma Harris Harris, wife of Henry Harris, who lived at Etheldon Road, Shepherd's Bush. Juliet's own will[38] shows that in 1900, when she drew it up, she was living at 27 Ingersoll Road, Shepherd's Bush, where she died in the presence of Emma Harris on 17 November 1909 of 'disease of Heart, duration unknown, syncope 10 days'.[39] Her effects amounted to £5,329. She left everything to her cousin Emma.

What of Flaubert's letters and the inscribed copies of his and Bouilhet's books she had been given? We think it almost certain that she must have destroyed both, probably before she moved from Milman's Row, if not sooner. It is at least possible that Gustave may have warned her to destroy the letters, but Juliet was clearly no fool and may not have needed any warning. Even if this supposition is wrong and Juliet, like Jenny Dacquin (Mérimée's 'inconnue'), could not bear to destroy Gustave's letters – very different ones, it must be emphasized, from Mérimée's, in which Jenny is always addressed as 'vous' – it is not readily credible that her cousin Emma could have made anything of them. The very characterless feminine handwriting exhibited in her signature on the will and the total improbability that she could read French argue strongly against the preservation of these letters.

Despite a search of the catalogues of the major London dealers for a decade after her death, we have not been able to trace any of the inscribed copies of the books (or of any autograph letters). Yet as it has not been unknown for items connected with Flaubert to disappear but then to reappear, the infinitely desirable possibility of the discovery of the trunk in an attic or a bank, already mentioned in the Introduction to this book, cannot be entirely ruled out. And if any of the letters do come to light, they must, we believe, be even more interesting now that Juliet herself is at least less shadowy than at the outset of our research.

Plate 1. Flaubert by Nadar

Plate 2. The Flauberts' house at Croisset, seen from the Seine. Painting by Thomsen. The house has now been demolished, but the pavilion on the left of the picture remains

Plate 3. The Thames end of Milman's Row, Chelsea. Drawing by Walter W. Burgess. The Herbert family lived in one of the eighteenth-century terraced houses nearer the King's Road

Plate 4. Cremorne Gardens, Chelsea, showing the dancing platform. Painting by P. Levin

Plate 5. The Bal Mabille, a celebrated Second Empire Paris pleasure garden. Nineteenth-century engraving by Provost

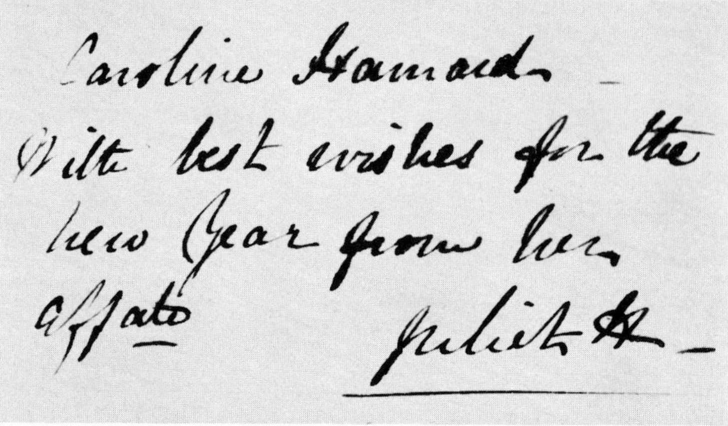

Caroline Hamard —
With best wishes for the
new Year from her
affate
Juliet H —

Plate 6a. Juliet's handwriting in a book she gave to Caroline Hamard

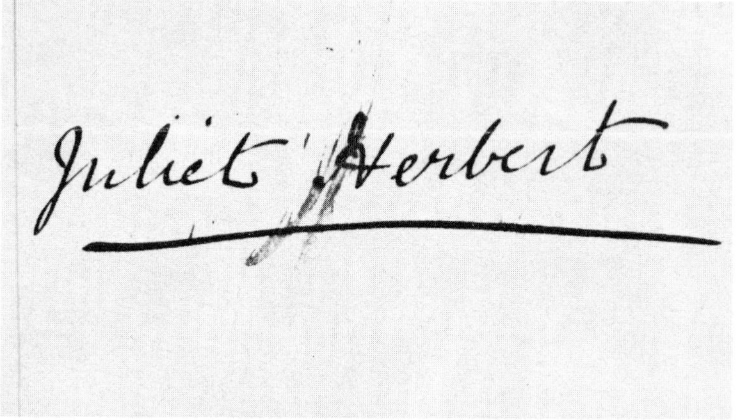

Juliet Herbert

Plate 6b. Juliet's signature on her will, drawn up in 1900

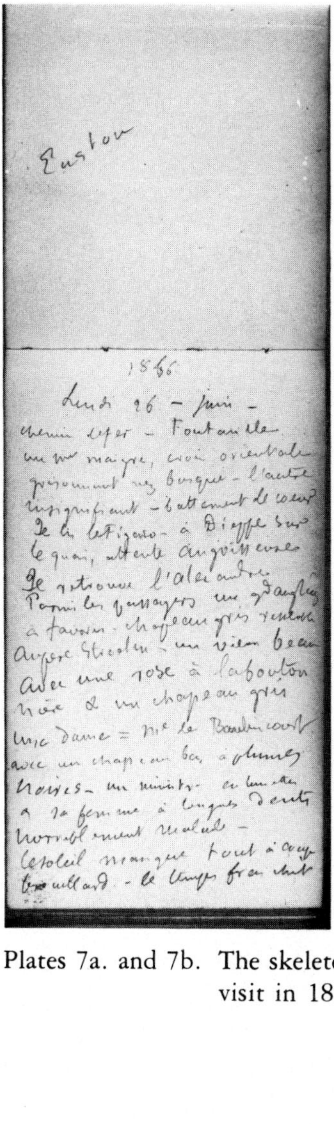

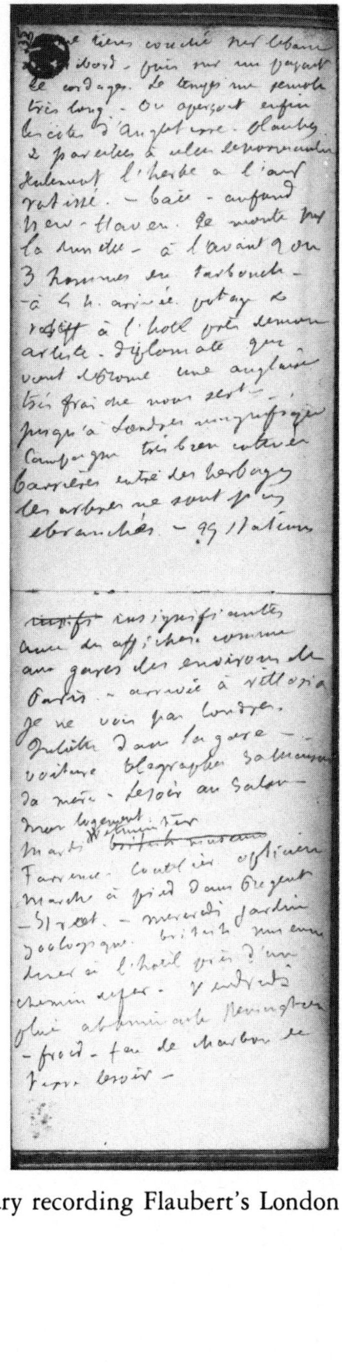

Plates 7a. and 7b. The skeleton diary recording Flaubert's London visit in 1865

bridge-water [illegible]
en [illegible] St James Park
[illegible] - ~~[illegible]~~
national galery
dîner à l'hôtel - [illegible]
tout. la journée dans les jardins
dîner à [illegible] heures en famille
champagne - [illegible] - [illegible]
à 8 h. promenade sur le bord
et sur le quai jusqu'à
Cremorne [illegible] - [illegible]
clair de lune -
lundi - galerie [illegible] de Westminster
à grosvenor house - promenade
dans hyde-Park - [illegible]
de l'arche - Wellington - [illegible]
[illegible] à l'entrée des champs
Elysées - une [illegible]
folle - acheté un guide des
chemins de fer - retourné à

Kensington - où je regarde
des tapisseries flamandes -
dîner chez [illegible] -
Mardi - temps magnifique
soleil brûlant - Hampton Court
mercredi Regent's park [illegible]
[illegible]
jeudi Sydenham - route
caillouteuse - [illegible]
Orage - chaleur - dîner dans
la grande salle près de la fenêtre
ouverte - [illegible]
chapeau -
vendredi - chemin de fer
souterrain [illegible]
Farmer jardin - où [illegible]
[illegible] - [illegible]
un mangeur dans [illegible]
au chemin de fer de
Charring - cross [illegible]

[illegible] renseignements -
dîner à [illegible]
samedi - bateau - palais de
Westminster - Pont -
national galery. [illegible]
Verrey - rentré à 8 h [illegible] -
[illegible] - longue conversation
le matin. pluie et soleil
[illegible] les [illegible]
[illegible] - dîner à [illegible] h
toute la journée à [illegible]
(chambre [illegible])
- [illegible]
lundi, matin, pluie vent
froid - chauffé à [illegible]
écrit des lettres, [illegible]
d'Orsay [illegible] pendant
[illegible] dormant

~~[illegible]~~ . horticultural
Garden - Kensington
Gardens
Mardi - London bridge
[illegible] garden - sur
la tamise joute de canotage
Soleil ardent -
mercredi promenade sur
le Pont - départ à 9 h
[illegible] -

Abbreviations used in the Appendices and Notes

BAF	*Bulletin des Amis de Flaubert.*
BHVP	Bibliothèque historique de la ville de Paris.
BL	British Library.
BN	Bibliothèque nationale.
Bruneau, *Corr.*, i	Flaubert, *Correspondance*, i (janvier 1830 à avril 1851), ed. Jean Bruneau.
CHH *OC*	Flaubert, *Œuvres complètes* (Paris, Club de l'Honnête Homme, 1971–5).
GLC	Greater London Council.
LOV	Bibliothèque Spoelberch de Lovenjoul, Chantilly.
PRO	Public Record Office.
RHLF	*Revue historique de littérature française.*
Seuil *OC*	Flaubert, *Œuvres complètes*. Paris: Éditions du Seuil, 1964.

Appendix I
Flaubert's Skeleton Diary in *Carnet de Voyage 13*

For the sake of clarity, each day recorded starts a new line, is italicized, and is given an initial capital letter. Parentheses enclose interpolations, including punctuation omitted by Flaubert (e.g. full points at the ends of lines). Words cancelled by Flaubert (all omitted in the CHH transcription) are scored through, as in the MS; additions or second thoughts are enclosed in angle brackets. Accents omitted have been restored and words joined together have been separated. For the CHH readings, see vol. 8, pp. 342–3 and for the fullest account of Flaubert's orthography, Naaman, *Lettres d'Égypte*.

1866[1]

Lundi 26 – juin –
Chemin de fer – Fontanelle[?][.][2] un mr maigre croix orientale[,] grisonnant[,] nez busqué – l'autre insignifiant – battement[3] de cœur[.] Je lis le Figaro[4] – à Dieppe sur le quai, attente angoisseuse[.] Je retrouve l'Alexandre[.][5] Parmi les passagers un gd anglais à favoris – chapeau gris ressemble au père Stroelin[6] – un vieux beau avec une rose à la boutonnière et un chapeau gris[.] Une dame = Mme de Baulincourt[7] avec un chapeau bas à plumes noires – un ministre – en lunettes et sa femme à longues dents[,] horriblement malade – le soleil manque tout à coup – brouillard – le temps fraîchit[.] Je me tiens couché sur le banc du[?] tribord – puis sur un paquet de cordages. Le temps me semble très long. – On aperçoit enfin les côtes d'Angleterre – blanches et pareilles à celles de Normandie, seulement l'herbe a l'air ratissé. – baie – au fond

[1] See above, p. 73.

[2] Fontenelle? – see above, p. 79. CHH omits.

[3] CHH: *battements*.

[4] Then an opposition paper.

[5] This was the new steam packet which made her maiden voyage in 1863, reducing the time taken by the crossing. Flaubert would certainly have seen her before 1865 when visiting Caroline in Dieppe, and Juliet would have sailed on her in 1863 and 1864.

[6] i.e. Stroehlin – see above, p. 80.

[7] i.e. de Beaulaincourt – see above, p. 80.

New-Haven. Je monte sur la dunette – à l'avant 2 ou 3 hommes en tarbouch – à 4 h. arrivée. potage et rosbiff[8] à l'hotel[,] près de moi un[?][9] artiste – diplomate[10] qui vient de Rome. Une anglaise très fraîche nous sert – jusqu'à Londres magnifique campagne très bien cultivé[,] barrières entre des herbages[.] les arbres ne sont pas ébranchés – qq[11] stations ~~insif~~ insignifiantes avec des affiches comme aux gares des environs de Paris – arrivée à Vittoria.[12] Je ne vois pas Londres. Juliette dans la gare – voiture[,] télégraphes[,][13] sa maison[,] sa mère – Le soir au salon – mon logement.
Mardi – ~~British museum~~ ⟨Westminster⟩ Farrence – coutelier opticien. Marche à pied dans Regent-Street.
Mercredi jardin zoologique, british museum. dîner à l'hôtel près d'un chemin de fer.
Vendredi pluie abominable Kensington – froid – feu de charbon de terre le soir –
Samedi – ~~Kensington~~[14] ⟨bridge-water colection[15] en vue de St James Park.⟩ National galery. dîner à l'hotel –
Dimanche toute la journée dans le jardin[.] dîner à 2 h. en famille[.] champagne – jardin – Salon[.] à 8 h. promenade sur le Pont et sur le quai jusqu'à Camorne =[16] bastringue – le soir[.] clair de lune –
Lundi – galerie du duc de Westminster à grosvenor-house – promenade dans hyde-Park – assis près de l'Achille-Wellington – ça rassemble à l'entrée des champs Élysées – une vieille femme folle – acheté un guide des chemins de fer – retourné à Kensington – où je regarde des tapisseries flamandes – dîner chez Juliet –
Mardi – temps magnifique, le soleil brille – Hampton Court[.]
Mercredi Kiew[17] ⟨le tavernier[?] [illegible word] et sa femme⟩
Jeudi Sydenham – route caillouteuse – le Palais. Orage – chaleur – dîner dans l'angle salle près de la fenêtre ouverte – retour délicieux – chapeau –

[8] CHH: *rosbeef.*
[9] CHH: *mon.*
[10] CHH: *artiste diplomate*; the omission of the dash transforms the meaning.
[11] Abbreviation of *quelque.*
[12] CHH: Victoria.
[13] CHH: *télégraphe.*
[14] The CHH omission of the erasure is responsible for the failure to see that the 'bridge-water colection' entry is an addition to Saturday and not to Friday.
[16] CHH prints a full point instead of the equals sign.
[17] CHH: *rien*; the entire addition is omitted.

Vendredi – chemin de fer souterrain – hornesey[18] Mrs[19] Farmer. Jardin – on coupe et roule le gazon – Farrens[.] Un changeur dans haymarket – au chemin de fer de Charring-cross pr[20] des renseignements – dîner à la maison[.]
Samedi – bateau. palais de Westminster – Pont – National gallery – dîner chez Verrey – rentré à 8 hr/d[21] –
Dimanche – longue conversation[,] le matin pluie et soleil. Mlle Adelaide coupe des concombres – dîner à 2 h – toute la journée à la maison. ⟨ illegible words ⟩.[22]
Lundi, matin pluie[,] vent[,] froid – chauffé à la maison[.][23] écrit des lettres, lu Rédemption d'Octave Feuillet pendant que J. dormait.[24] ~~Mardi~~ horticultural Garden – Kensington Gardens[.]
Mardi – Longdon[*sic*] bridge. temple's garden – sur la tamise joûte[25] de Canotiers[.] Soleil et vent –
Mercredi. promenade sur le Pont – départ à 7 h. de la maison –

[18] CHH: [*un mot illisible*].
[19] CHH: M.
[20] Abbreviation of '*pour*'.
[21] Abbreviation of '*heure et demi*'.
[22] CHH: (*c̈hancelière*, *crinoline*), omitting the equals sign.
[23] CHH: *cuisine*.
[24] CHH: . . . d'Octave Feuillet. *Foutu embêtement pendant que* Juliette *dormait*.
[25] The u appears to have a circumflex.

Appendix II
Gérard-Gailly's Note on Bergerat's *Le Chèque*

In 1971 the late M. Émile Gérard-Gailly, the eminent authority on Flaubert, published an article in the *Bulletin des Amis de Flaubert* stating that a novel by Émile Bergerat, *Les Drames de l'honneur: Le Chèque* (published in 1893) was inspired by an actual cheque drawn in favour of Flaubert by 'a young English governess, apparently the one who looked after the little niece Caroline at Croisset'. By this 'cheque', she undertook to pay 'her own person' to Flaubert when he wished. Gérard-Gailly maintained that this 'cheque' was not 'honoured' then and there because it would have been dangerous and indelicate for the engagement to be fulfilled at Croisset, 'between the mother and the little niece', or even on an escapade to Rouen. 'It was necessary to wait for the return of the young governess to her home in England. Then, on some pretext, Flaubert paid a visit to London' where, Gérard-Gailly says he was assured by M. Francis Ambrière, it was 'honoured'. It was M. Ambrière, he states, who showed him this 'cheque' in the office of the *Mercure de France*; it was 'exactly like that of Bergerat's novel' except that it was a real cheque. No precise date is given.

In the novel by Bergerat the heroine writes twenty-five blank cheques in favour of a young man whose family was ruined by her father; he then filled in each cheque with some part of her anatomy. (Bergerat gives as examples her hands, arms, hair, and lips, but discreetly draws a veil over the rest.) Gérard-Gailly introduces his article by describing a visit to Bergerat's son Théo and his wife when they were staying at a villa belonging to the Bergerats between Dinard and Saint-Lunaire, when Gérard-Gailly had recently read *Le Chèque*. It was twenty-five years after this visit, when Bergerat was dead, that he was discussing Flaubert with M. Ambrière who, according to Gérard-Gailly, produced the actual 'cheque' drawn in Flaubert's favour in the office of the *Mercure*. 'I cited Bergerat's novel, which he did not know, to my colleague, and he did not doubt that Bergerat based his novel on it.' Gérard-Gailly went on to state that Bergerat (who was Gautier's son-in-law) was a great friend of Flaubert in his last years and 'despite his old motto 'Conceal your life', Flaubert liked talking about his with some of his close friends, and he must have told Bergerat the story of the English governess which resulted in the novel *Le Chèque.*[1]

Since this English governess can only have been Juliet, and the existence of such a 'cheque', if genuine, must radically affect any portrayal of her character (even if could be believed that it was a private joke between Gustave and Juliet), I wrote to M. Francis Ambrière to ask if he could throw any more light on it. I was able to tell him how much out of character it appeared to be with a Victorian English governess and with Juliet's home background, and to say that if he still had this document and could send me a photograph of it, it would be possible to ascertain its genuineness by comparing the signature with Juliet's signature on her will. At the same time I mentioned several unanswered questions which it raised – for example, had the 'cheque' been 'honoured' in England, as stated, it must have returned into Juliet's possession, and she would hardly have been likely to have kept such an extremely compromising document.

M. Ambrière most kindly replied on 18 November 1978, informing me that until he received my letter, he was unaware of the existence of Gérard-Gailly's article, since for the past thirty years he has ceased to be 'an *active* flaubertist' and does not read the *BAF*; he therefore did not know that Gérard-Gailly had invoked his testimony, and at first was astonished: 'I have *never* heard any mention of a cheque concerning the relations between Juliet Herbert and Flaubert, and in consequence I have *never* told anyone the story Gérard-Gailly attributes to me. I was even momentarily indignant.' M. Ambrière then gave me this explanation. In 1938 he found, at a dealer in autographs, a document which did constitute an engagement 'to pay Flaubert her own person'. He published this, he believed, in a weekly, but was able to quote the text by heart forty years later. (This item in his collection of autographs appears to have vanished, no doubt during World War II.) It read: 'I engage, when the bathroom of the town house I am having built in the rue Chateaubriand is finished, to yield my person to sieur Gustave Flaubert, who may use or abuse it as he wishes.' Only the signature of this 'cheque' was not Juliet Herbert's but that of the so well-known courtesan Esther Guimont, mistress of Émile de Girar-

[1] *BAF*. no. 37, Jan. 1971, pp. 37–8.

din (who was paying the bills for the house in question). M. Ambrière adds that this little tale amused all flaubertists and it could well be that at the time he told it to Gérard-Gailly, but he in 1971 was a very old man and his faculties were beginning to betray him, which is how he came to transfer to Juliet Herbert what M. Ambrière had told him of Esther Guimont.[2]

M. Ambrière kindly offered to try to find the article he published at the time, but was unable to do so, since the Germans, who occupied his apartment during World War II, used many of his papers as fire-lighters. I therefore consulted the *Mercure de France* (but found no article by him) and various bibliographies and indexes to periodicals with negative results until, at the suggestion of Dr A. W. Raitt, my collaborator and I went through the unindexed notes which appear at the end of each number of the *Mercure*. There we eventually found, under the heading 'Les Journaux' in volume 291 for 1 April 1938 – 1 May 1939 (pp. 193–5), a note stating that M. Ambrière had published an article, 'Quand Flaubert prenait livraison de la Guimont', in *L'Intransigeant* of 2 March 1939, which was summarized, and the note included the text of the 'cheque'. M. Ambrière, writing forty years later, had indeed remembered its wording with total accuracy, except for the substitution of 'town house (hôtel)' for 'house (*maison*)' and of 'as he wishes (*selon sa volonté*)' for 'as he pleases (*selon son plaisir*)', and except for the omission of 'I have sworn this (*Je l'ai juré*)'. The date of this actual 'cheque' is given only in the note in the *Mercure*: 23 March 1859.

[2] 'Je n'ai *jamais* entendu parler de chèque en ce qui concerne les rapports de Juliet Herbert et de Flaubert, et par conséquent, je n'ai *jamais* tenu à quiconque les propos que Gérard-Gailly me prête. J'en étais même indigné sur le moment. . . . Il est exact qu'en 1938 j'ai trouvé chez un marchand d'autographes un document qui constitue, comme vous dites, un engagement 'à payer à Flaubert sa propre personne'. Je l'ai publié quelque part, dans un hebdomadaire je crois (je retrouverai l'article si cela vous fait plaisir), mais sans le moindre recherche je puis vous en citer le texte à quarante ans d'intervalle, étant doué de quelque mémoire: 'Je m'engage, quand la salle de bains de l'hôtel que je fais construire rue de Chateaubriand sera prête, à livrer ma personne au sieur Gustave Flaubert qui en usera et en abusera selon sa volonté.' Seulement, la signature de ce chèque n'est pas Juliet Herbert, c'est la courtisane bien connue Esther Guimont, maîtresse d'Émile de Girardin (qui faisait les frais de l'hôtel en question).

'Cette petite histoire amusa tous les flaubertistes, et il se peut bien que je l'aie racontée à l'écpoque à Gérard-Gailly. En 1971 il était fort vieux, ses facultés commençaient à le trahir, et voilà comment il aura transféré sur Juliet Herbert ce que je lui avait conté d'Esther Guimont.'

This date is important for, as has been seen (p. 63), Juliet was no longer permanently at Croisset – she had left by 8 September 1857 and was not to return except during the summers of 1859–61 (and possibly 1858). She was in England in March 1859, a year when Flaubert was in Paris from mid-February until May. M. Ambrière's interpretation of this 'cheque' is that Esther Guimont wrote it to disembarrass herself of Flaubert, at least for the moment and perhaps for good. But it looks very much as if at some time or other Flaubert discovered that the workmen had left the rue Chateaubriand, for it seems inconceivable that, if the 'cheque' was still among his papers, he would not have consigned it to the flames that evening Maupassant described (p. 141) when Flaubert was sorting the sheep from the goats. If the 'cheque' was 'honoured', it must, of course, have returned to Esther and, as will be seen, this seems to be the explanation why it came into the hands of a dealer in autographs.

Esther Guimont (or Guimond, as the name is sometimes written) was a well-known, if not notorious woman of obscure origins who 'probably started as a *grisette*'.[3] The *Mercure* note summarizing Ambrière's article states that she was born no one knows where, in a more than modest social sphere; she could scarcely write and her language, when excited, was that of a fishwife. It was François Guizot who plucked her from a seamstress's workshop and paid for her first apartment and its furniture. (Guizot, as French ambassador in London in 1832–40, was of all French statesmen the one most esteemed in Victorian England; as recently as 1947 he was described as 'incorruptible, commanding, high-minded, severe'.[4]) The 'honourable M. Guizot' was succeeded as her lover by, among others, Hugo, Sainte-Beuve, Musset, Émile de Girardin, and Nestor Roqueplan. She plumed herself on having contributed at least to the *dénouement* of *La Dame aux camélias*. She used to visit Alexandre Dumas *fils* when he was at a pensionnat, and once when he visited her she was semi-delirious with typhoid fever, during which she poured out her more intimate life history and he immediately began writing the famous scene of the agony of Marguérite Gauthier.

Arsène Houssaye recounts an incident at the ultra-exclusive Jockey Club (told him by Prince Radziwill) when the society women were overcome at the entrance of Esther and other women of the *demi-monde*. They sent the master of ceremonies to tell them that

[3] Houssaye, *Man About Paris*, p. 329.

[4] Pope-Hennessy, *Monckton Milnes*, p. 123.

they had no right to be there. Esther replied that she was there at the pleasure of 'ces messieurs' and if she did not belong to the world of these ladies, she did to that of these gentlemen. On leaving, she got her coachman to drive beside the coach of a countess and improvised a song which 'all Paris' was singing next day. According to Houssaye, she was the darling of the gilded youth because of her gaiety; one met her even at diplomatic suppers and she knew all the statesmen. He adds a valuable explanation of why the 'cheque' written in Flaubert's favour was preserved after it must have come back into her hands: she made a habit of selling autographs – she told Roqueplan and Houssaye that she had 800 letters from Girardin, who refused to buy them.[5] No doubt Flaubert did likewise and she disposed of this one to a dealer. Esther died in 1879.

Did she add one or more ingredients to Rosanette in *L'Éducation*?

Whether or not Bergerat based his novel on this document is not really relevant to a study of Flaubert's relations with Juliet, but Gérard-Gailly's statement that Bergerat was an intimate friend of Flaubert's does not seem to be supported by the evidence of the correspondence.

[5] Arsène Houssaye, *Les Confessions: Souvenirs d'un demi-siècle 1830–80* (Paris: Dentu, 1885), ii. 329.

Appendix III
The *Choses Vues* and Flaubert's Writings

Did Flaubert see several 'curious things' in London which were 'very useful' for *L'Éducation sentimentale*, as he told Caroline when he wrote to her from London in 1865 (p. 73), and did he see anything useful for any other work?

L'Éducation sentimentale

It is very doubtful if the first question can be fully answered until it has been possible to study Flaubert's notes, scenarios, sketches, the entire dossier for *L'Éducation* which remained inaccessible while it was in the possession of Sacha Guitry, and also the item entitled 'Renseignements pour l'éducation sentimentale' which was sold at Antibes (p. 101). The dossier is now in the Bibliothèque nationale but will not be available for study until 1980, and then the work of decipherment and collation will necessarily take considerable time. It is possible, for example, that in a sketch later discarded Flaubert may have used an English background for the early history of one of the characters, or that he originally intended to use one of the paintings or pieces of pottery described in *Carnet 13*, but later changed his mind. (In the published novel the pieces of pottery at Arnoux's factory at Creil are described only in generic terms as majolica, faïence, Etruscan and Oriental china.) There is, however, one scene which may – it is necessary to be tentative – owe something to one place Flaubert visited in London in 1865: Cremorne Gardens. This is the 'Alhambra' pleasure garden (incorrectly termed a 'dance-hall' in the Penguin translation by Robert Baldick) at the top of the Champs-Élysées where his friend Deslauriers took Frédéric Moreau to try to distract him from the anguish of his hopeless love of Mme Arnoux.

Flaubert's Alhambra had recently opened, and it went bankrupt in its second season 'on account of a luxury that was premature in this type of establishment'. Here is his description of it:

Two parallel arcades in the Moorish style extended right and left. The wall of a house took up the whole of the far end, opposite, and the fourth side, where the restaurant lay, was designed to look like a Gothic cloister with stained-glass windows.

A sort of Chinese roof sheltered the platform on which the musicians played; the ground all round it was covered with asphalt; and there were some Venetian lanterns hung on poles which, seen from a distance, formed a crown of multi-coloured lights above the dancers. Every few yards there stood a pedestal supporting a stone basin from which a slender jet of water rose into the air. In the shrubberies plaster statues could be seen, Hebes and Cupids, all sticky with oil paint, and the countless paths, spread with bright yellow sand, carefully raked, made the garden look much bigger than it was.

Students were strolling up and down with their mistresses; shop-assistants strutted about with walking-sticks between their fingers; school-boys puffed at cheroots; old bachelors stroked their dyed beards with combs; there were Englishmen, Russians, South Americans, and three Orientals in tarbooshes. Courtesans, working-girls, and prostitutes had come along in the hope of finding a protector, a lover, a piece of gold, or simply for the pleasure of the dance; and their tunic dresses in sea-green blue, cherry-red, and mauve, went swirling past among the laburnums and the lilacs. Nearly all the men had check suits; some were wearing white trousers, in spite of the coolness of the evening. The gas-lamps were lit. . . .

The orchestra, perched like monkeys on the platform, scraped and blew with a will, while the conductor, standing in front of them, beat time mechanically. The dancers were crowded together and in high spirits; hat ribbons, coming undone, brushed against cravats; boots disappeared under skirts; and all this jumped up and down in time with the music. . . .[1]

There was an actual, very well-known pleasure garden or *bal champêtre* in Paris at the time, situated between the avenue of the Champs-Élysées and the avenue Montaigne. The son of the proprietor of an originally small open-air dancing establishment in 1844 transformed it into a vast garden, illuminated by innumerable lights and globes and with a grotto, shrubberies, arbours, and a kiosk for the orchestra. Many of the lights were fixed on the leaves of metal palm-trees. This was the Bal Mabille, one of the most celebrated pleasure haunts in Paris under the Second Empire and already by 1847 the subject of a poem by Gustave Nadaud dedicated to the

[1] *L'Éducation sentimentale*, I.v (trans, by Robert Baldick for the Penguin *Sentimental Education*, 1964, pp. 80–1).

'Reines de Mabille'. It closed in 1880.[2] Many writers, including Baudelaire, Arsène Houssaye (then editor of *L'Artiste*), and Taine, described the Mabille and its frequenters and it was portrayed in engravings and in a drawing by Jules de Goncourt,[3] so that it is possible to note immediately that it lacked precisely the features which caused Flaubert to christen his pleasure-garden the Alhambra – the Moorish-style arcades.

Flaubert himself – in *Carnet 13* – provided the clue which enables us to see the genesis of his Alhambra, in an otherwise cryptic sentence: 'Les bains Deligny disposés en Allambra [*sic*]', an idea enthusiastically endorsed by Bouilhet who, in September 1865, wrote: 'I entirely agree to the name Alhambra – *it is very good*'.[4] As has been seen (p. 74), the 'bains Deligny' phrase occurs among notes written at the back of *Carnet 13* which belong to the late summer or autumn of 1865 and Flaubert is likely to have communicated this idea to Bouilhet as soon as it came into his head. It seems worth recalling that when he had visited the Crystal Palace on 6 July that year, he must have seen its Alhambra court, constructed from facsimiles, and this may have given him the initial idea for his Alhambra. If it did, when he had returned to Croisset he thought of another Alhambra model closer at hand and one he knew far better – the Deligny baths. These baths, where Flaubert used to swim when he was in Paris, are still in existence on the Quai d'Orsay, and are depicted in an engraving by Grandville and described in the first volume of *L'Illustration*. They were constructed within a Moorish-style courtyard and the bathers promenade in galleries with Moorish columns (Flaubert's 'arcades in the Moorish style'). Contrasting this style with the classical style of 'l'école-Petit', *L'Illustration* described the Deligny architecture as 'coquettish, sumptuous, elegant as a vast boudoir', and 'lacy, festooned, full of arches and ogives like a Moorish palace. It is a floating Alhambra, an Alcazar built on piles.'[5]

We therefore begin to see how Flaubert made a composite *bal champêtre* out of the Bal Mabille and the Bains Deligny, but some

[2] P. Larousse, *Dictionnaire universel du XIXe siècle*; *Bulletin du Musée Carnavalet*, June 1972.

[3] *Vie et opinions de . . . Graindorge*, pp. 37–42.

[4] 'J'adopte parfaitement le nom d'Alhambra – *c'est très bien*' (LOV C, XI 1865, f. 744).

[5] *L'Illustration*, vol. 1, Mar.–Aug. 1843.

elements in his Alhambra are not found in either. The 'Venetian lanterns hung on poles' forming 'a crown of multicoloured lights above the dancers' exactly coincide with those shown in the Mabille lithograph which is reproduced in the Carnavalet Museum's bulletin for June 1972, but what about the 'sort of Chinese roof' over the orchestra platform? It is, of course, not a very precise description, and the top of the kiosk depicted in the same lithograph could certainly fit it, but a far more definite Chinese roof in a pleasure garden Flaubert had seen was the Cremorne Gardens pagoda. Since some of the other Cremorne features appear in Flaubert's Alhambra, it seems at least probable that he recalled this pagoda, even if he also simultaneously recalled the Mabille orchestral platform. And Flaubert's basins with their slender jets seem also to derive from Mabille's 'élégantes vasques de marbre ornées de fleurs',[6] which Taine described as 'sham Corinthian vases',[7] but it does seem as if Cremorne inspired Flaubert's plaster statues, a feature absent from the Mabille descriptions and the engraving. Cremorne had plaster Cupids and Venuses;[8] for the frequenters of such places, Hebe was, of course, as appropriate as Venus. One conspicuous feature of Flaubert's Alhambra is absent from both Cremorne and Mabille – the highly picturesque restaurant designed to resemble a Gothic cloister. One's appreciation of this happy invention is heightened by the knowledge that it was not imported from either of the actual pleasure-gardens and even more so by the piquant irony of the introduction of a simulated cloister in which the Alhambra clientele partook of refreshments. The house taking up the whole of the far end seems to coincide with Taine's description of 'an enormous house' which overhung Mabille, but in contrast with Flaubert's sandy paths, Taine found the Mabille gravel hurt his feet. Lastly on the physical features, it is not unimportant to note Flaubert's omission of the Mabille metal palm trees, conspicuously shown in the lithograph reproduced by the Carnavalet Museum.

The frequenters of Flaubert's Alhambra coincide precisely with the Mabille habitués, although the translation inevitably loses the tone and subtle distinctions of the women of the *demi-monde*, termed by Flaubert 'lorettes', 'grisettes', and 'filles', but not 'courtisanes', for courtesans were distinguished by their elegance and worldly

[6] Larousse, op. cit.
[7] Taine, op. cit.
[8] See Holme.

manners,[9] as Flaubert's three categories of women were not. 'Lorettes', 'grisettes', and 'filles' are aptly defined in a note to the English translation of Arsène Houssaye's memoirs; the first, named after Notre-Dame-de-Lorette, were women who had risen to a middle-class position but were emphatically not courtesans. 'Grisettes' were working girls so poorly paid that they depended, during the week, on 'mature' lovers to pay the rent and for necessities but went out with a young lover on Sundays and had a young man of their own class in the wings to marry eventually. 'Filles' were prostitutes.[10] At Mabille, 'virtue did not flourish at all',[11] so that women of good social standing and even the petty bourgeoisie did not go, but many male writers, artists, 'lions' of the day, capitalists, pleasure-seeking youths, and blasé rich voluptuaries went regularly, as did the foreign visitors.[12] Taine noted many Germans, Italians, above all Englishmen,[13] who therefore correctly headed Flaubert's list of foreigners. Cremorne, on the other hand, may have had a more respectable clientêle in 1865 at least. It is stated that when Taine himself (visiting London in the 1860s) described it as 'a sort of bal Mabille' frequented by *lorettes*, he was misled by the appearance and behaviour of boisterous servant girls and shop girls out for an evening's pleasure,[14] but this this statement ignores – as Taine did not, for he studied *Statistical Abstracts* and did not rely on impressions – the abysmally low wages of the shop girls and servant girls of the period and the fact that many of them too were forced to supplement their wages in the same way as the *grisettes*.[15] It is also difficult to believe that no women of easy virtue frequented Cremorne, as they certainly frequented Vauxhall. The costumes described by Flaubert belong, of course, to the 1848–58 decade, and do not match those depicted in the much later Carnavalet print or the Goncourt drawing – or those he saw at Cremorne in 1865.

[9] See the definitions of *courtisane* in *Trésor de la langue française*.

[10] See the editor's note to 'In the *Demi-Monde*', in *Man About Paris: the confessions of Arsène Houssaye*, trans. and ed. by H. Knepler (London: Gollancz, 1972), pp. 73–4.

[11] *Bulletin du Musée Carnavalet*, June 1972.

[12] Ibid.

[13] *Vie et opinions de . . . Graindorge*, p. 42.

[14] Holme, p. 189. For Taine's description see his *Notes sur l'Angleterre*, pp. 46–8.

[15] See George Gissing. *The Odd Women* (London: Nelson, n.d.); Charles Booth, *Life and Labour of the People of London*, i (London: Williams & Norgate, 1889), ch. viii: Women's Work.

When we know its real-life components, we can see in Flaubert's Alhambra a minor but illustrative example of the distance between the model and the work of art, it may help us to appreciate the infinitely vaster work of transformation that has gone on in this great novel as a whole, as in all Flaubert's mature works of imagination.

Hérodias

Turning to the second question posed at the beginning of this chapter, there seems reason to believe that one thing Flaubert saw in London was useful for him, though not for *L'Éducation* but for *Hérodias*, one of his *Trois Contes*. This was one of the Assyrian bas-reliefs collected by Austen Henry Layard, which Flaubert saw in the Kouyunjik Gallery at the British Museum in 1865. (Kuyunjik, to use the modern spelling, was the citadel of Nineveh built by Sennacherib.)

Without studying Flaubert's manuscript plans, notes, and scenarios for *Hérodias*, or until they are the subject of the careful, scholarly publication devoted to *Un cœur simple*,[16] any answer to this question must likewise be tentative, but there seems at least a strong presumption that Flaubert recalled this particular bas-relief. He was writing *Hérodias* eleven years later, but he did not forget *choses vues* which impressed him at the time – it was the much earlier Eastern journey of 1849–50 which partly inspired *Salammbô*, and in writing *Hérodias* he evidently recalled his visit to Jordan and the Dead Sea, and probably the Turkish fortress high up on a terrace where he and Maxime spent a night in 1850.[17]

Hérodias opens with a description of the citadel Machærus on its high rocky hill, on which, as Josephus relates, Herod had built a fortified stronghold and a magnificent palace.[18] In Flaubert's tale, when the Proconsul Vitellius visits Machærus, he demands to know what lies behind the door of a rock chamber, of which only 'the Babylonian', who was then summoned, had the key. The Babylo-

[16] See *Plans, notes et scénarios de 'Un Cœur simple'*, 1er ed. intégal, introd. F. Fleury (Rouen, 1977) and G. A. Willenbrink, *The Dossier of Flaubert's 'Un Cœur simple'* (Amsterdam: Rodopi, 1976).

[17] Bruneau, *Corr.*, i. 673.

[18] Flavius Josephus, *The Works*, Whiston's trans., rev. by the Revd. A. R. Shilleto (London: Bell, 1903), v. 142.

nian had a bow on his shoulder and a whip in his hand; his bandy legs [the legs of a rider] were tightly laced up with multicoloured cord, while his great arms emerged from a sleeveless tunic and a fur cap shaded his face. His beard was curled in ringlets. In the rock chamber 'perhaps a hundred' white horses were kept in case of siege. Their hair was 'bouffant' on their foreheads and they had very long tails, but above all they were 'marvellous beasts, supple as serpents, light as birds'.[19] In this the horses of Machærus recall the celebrated Chinese flying horse, unknown to Flaubert, but also, strikingly, the description in *Carnet 13* of the Assyrian bas-reliefs at the British Museum depicting 'three grooms leading three horses by the bridle attached to the mouth, marvellous in movement and design, above all the first horse, which is slightly bending its left leg' (see p. 81).[20] As anyone visiting the Assyrian galleries in the British Museum today can see, this is an extraordinarily accurate description of the bas-reliefs numbered 124795–7, one of which (the one in which the horse most corresponds with Flaubert's description) is reproduced in the handbook, *Assyrian Palace Reliefs in the British Museum* (1970). But it is necessary to ask if Flaubert's horses derived instead from his very extensive reading for *Hérodias*.

Flaubert's documentation for this tale, including the 'Fiches de lecture', has been reproduced in part (with that for the other *contes*) in volume 4 of the CHH *Œuvres complètes*, but by some extraordinary oversight, folio 666 is omitted (while folios 665 and 667 are reproduced).[21] Folio 666 is, however, crucial since, as C. A. Burns's article, 'The Manuscripts of Flaubert's *Trois Contes*', published in 1954, reveals, the notes on this folio were headed '*Layard*', and a footnote suggested that this indicated a reference to 'some work by Sir Austen Layard, perhaps his *Monuments of Nineveh*'.[22] Flaubert no doubt consulted not only this work but also Layard's *Nineveh and Its Remains* (1847); in fact 'Layard: Ormuz' appears as an entry in the *Carnets de lecture* published in the CHH volume 8, although it is clear that this note was one made for the *Tentation*.[23] Neither of

[19] *Hérodias*, II (Seuil *OC*, ii. 192).

[20] 'Trois palefreniers conduisant trois cheveux par la bride attachée au barbillon, merveilleux de mouvement et de dessin – surtout le premier cheval qui plie un peu la jambe gauche' (f. 62).

[21] CHH *OC*, iv. 611–12.

[22] *French Studies*, Oct. 1954, p. 320.

[23] CHH *OC*, viii. 389.

these works by Layard reproduces or describes the British Museum bas-reliefs in detail, and none of the illustrations depicting horses recalls Flaubert's description of the horses of Machærus, for the horses in Layard's plates are either very static or are depicted as galloping in a stylized manner. In *Nineveh and Its Remains* Layard did, however, specifically say that the horses represented in the sculptures appeared to be of 'noble breed' and 'evidently drawn from the finest models', and he quoted Habakkuk on the horses of the Chaldeans: 'They are swifter than Leopards and more fierce than the evening wolves'.[24] Yet this stirring description – certainly already known to so ardent a reader of the Bible as Flaubert – does not fit 'marvellous beasts, supple as serpents, light as birds' so well as the particular bas-relief which he described as 'marvellous in movement and design', which happens to be the very one (no. 124795) reproduced in the British Museum's handbook, in which the suppleness and movement of the horse are so very striking. In all the bas-reliefs the horses have their hair bouffant on their foreheads and tails so long that they reach their hooves. And it scarcely needs saying that Flaubert's reading of Layard must have recalled the bas-reliefs, if it was not the visit to the Kouyunjik Gallery that set him reading Layard's books.

Flaubert's Babylonian is clearly a composite figure, for neither in the museum's bas-reliefs nor in Layard's illustrations do grooms carry bows, but only warriors shooting from horseback or the soldiers in the plate entitled 'Female captives brought to the conquerors' in *Monuments of Nineveh* (plate 8). Again, all Layard's grooms like those in the bas-reliefs, are bare-legged and barefoot; it is the warriors who have laced leggings. All, of course, have beards curled in ringlets. There seems no archaeological warrant for Flaubert's fur cap – the grooms in the bas-reliefs have their hair secured by fillets. Layard describes 'conical caps, apparently formed by bands or folds of felt or linen', but these were worn not by Assyrians but by people of another race; the Assyrian warriors wore skullcaps, probably of iron.[25]

Juliet herself was seemingly not the prototype of any of Flaubert's characters. There was no role for her in the conception of the women characters in the novels and tales he wrote after she went to Croisset

[24] *Nineveh and Its Remains* (London: Murray, 1867), p. 235, quoting Hab. i. 8.
[25] Ibid., pp. 88 and 234.

(*L'Éducation, Salammbô*, the *Trois Contes*). But the absence of any mention of her, or of any character sketches which could conceivably be held to resemble her, in the notebooks containing his scenarios for the unwritten novels may in fact reflect Flaubert's high opinion of her rather than the converse for, as is well known, there are few truly sympathetic characters in his novels, and in the unwritten *Sous Napoléon III* in particular the names of actual friends or acquaintances in the noteboooks do not appear in a flattering light. It is notable that Gertrude and Harriet Collier appear to their disadvantage, Harriet as one of three sisters who all demoralize men, one because she is bourgeoise and limited.[26] It thus seems that if it can be demonstrated that it was Juliet who sent the Calves' Head Club dossier to Gustave, if or when the 'Renseignements pour l'éducation sentimentale' can be recovered and studied, this was the only positive contribution she made to his writings, other (it is reasonable to suppose) than being an intelligent listener and correspondent to whom he is surely bound to have described the stages of the work in progress?

[26] See Durry, pp. 258–9 and 339.

Notes

(For abbreviations, see p. 147)

INTRODUCTION
THE QUEST FOR JULIET HERBERT

1 *Flaubert et sa nièce Caroline* (Paris: La Pensée universelle, 1971), p. 213 n. 90.
2 *Flaubert* (New York: Syracuse University Press, 1967), p. 391.
3 Ibid., p. 362.
4 CHH *OC*, xv. 131, no. 2218.
5 *Mémoires d'un fou*, xv and *Novembre* (Seuil *OC*, i. 240 and 270).
6 Bruneau, *Corr.*, i. ix.
7 *Flaubert the Master* (London: Weidenfeld, 1971), p. 52.
8 CHH *OC*, viii. 342 n.1 and see index entry.
9 Ibid., xiii. 266, no. 462 ('vérifié sur la copie de René Descharmes', BN MS 23831).
10 Ibid., xiv. 282–3, no. 1337, n.l.
11 LOV VI 1860, f. 288.
12 PRO HO107/1472.
13 PRO RG9/30.
14 PRO RG10/73.
15 Chevalley-Sabatier, p. 90.
16 GLC P89/18 X16/83.
17 GLC P89/MRY1/194.
18 GLC DL/T/56 6.
19 Denoting a semi-detached house, sometimes written as 17A.
20 GLC DL/T/56 7.
21 *Thomas Cubitt, Master Builder* (London: Macmillan, 1971), p. 262.
22 Spencer in *French Studies*, 8, Apr. 1954 (drawing also on the findings of Miss C. B. West); Bruneau, 'Madame Bovary jugée par un 'Fantôme de Trouville', *Revue de litt. comparée*, avr.-juin 1957, pp. 277–9. The often repeated statement that Flaubert stayed with Gertrude and Harriet Collier in London in 1866 arose because of the suppression of all mention of Juliet in the correspondence. It recurred as late as 1972 in *L'Album Flaubert*; iconographie réunie et commentée par Jean Bruneau et Jean A. Ducourneau (Paris: Gallimard, 1972).
23 CHH *OC*, xii. 321.
24 Bruneau, *Corr.*, i. xvii-xviii.

I CROISSET AT MID-CENTURY

1 Bart, p. 9.
2 Her husband Hippolyte died on 21 April 1851 (J. F. Jackson, *Louise Colet et ses amis littéraires*, New Haven: Yale University Press, 1937, p. 161).
2 See Bruneau, *Corr.*, i. 811–15, and for the discovery of this document see his preface, pp. xvii-xix.
3 Ibid., p. 162 n.3, at p. 927 and p. 208 n.1, at p. 946.
4 Caroline Commanville, *Souvenirs sur Gustave Flaubert* (Paris: Ferraud, 1895), p. 42. These souvenirs, entitled *Souvenirs intimes*, are included in vol. 1 of the Conard edition of the *Correspondance* but without the delightful illustrations of the volume cited here.
5 *Lettres de Gustave Flaubert à George Sand*, précédées d'une étude par Guy de Maupassant (Paris: Charpentier, 1884), p.lxx (hereafter referred to as Maupassant).
6 *Correspondance entre George Sand et Gustave Flaubert* (Paris: Calmann-Lévy [1904]), p. 60.
7 Commanville, *Souvenirs*, pp. 48–9.
8 *Souvenirs littéraires*, i.299 (cited in Bruneau, *Corr.*, i.309 n.1 at p. 1010).
9 Commanville, *Souvenirs*, pp. 43–4.
10 Maupassant, p.lxx.
11 Ibid., p. lxxi.
12 Bruneau, *Corr.*, i.280.
13 *Madame Bovary*, III. v.
14 *Voyage en Orient: Égypte* (Seuil *OC*, ii. 553).
15 *Corr. entre Sand et Flaubert*, p. 11.
16 Émile Zola, *Les Romanciers naturalistes* (Paris: Charpentier, 1910), pp. 176–7; Maupassant, pp. lxiii-iv; *Journal des Goncourt*, ed. Ricatte (Monaco: Société d'Imprimerie, 1956–8), 29 Oct. 1863; *Catalogue de la succession Franklin-Grout—Flaubert*, Paris, 18–19 novembre 1931.
17 *Journal des Goncourt*, 1863.
18 Zola, p. 177.
19 Bruneau, *Corr.*, i. 720.
20 Ibid., pp. 253 n.2, 294 n. 6, 427 n.3, 494 n.1.
21 Zola, p. 176. The two Japanese chimeras in the vestibule described by Zola were the much later gifts of Flaubert's friend Edmond Laporte.
22 See Spencer, *French Studies* 8 (1954), p. 103.
23 Bruneau, *Corr.*, i. 66.
24 See ibid., p. 15 n. 2, at p. 844.
25 Commanville, *Souvenirs*, p. 23.
26 *Journal des Goncourt*, 29 Oct. 1863 (trans. by Robert Baldick, *Pages from the Goncourt Journal*, London: OUP, 1962, p. 91).
27 André Maurois, *Lélia, ou la vie de George Sand* (Paris: Hachette, 1952), p. 481.

George Sand said 'La mère de Flaubert est une vieille charmante'.

28 Bruneau, *Corr.*, i. 369.
29 *Journal des Goncourt*, Jan. 1872.
30 Bruneau, *Corr.*, i. 459.
31 *Voyage en Orient: Égypte* (Seuil *OC*, ii. 551).
32 Bruneau, *Corr.*, i. 623.
33 CHH *OC*, xiii. 274, no. 467.
34 Bruneau, *Corr.*, i. 761 (Flaubert's italics).
35 ibid., p. 720.
36 CHH *OC*, xiii. 255–6, no. 462.
37 Bruneau, *Corr.*, i. 270 and 281.
38 Ibid., p. 468.
39 See letter to Caroline, Feb. 1867 (CHH *OC*, xiv. 331, no. 1419).
40 Ibid., p. 245, no. 1265.
41 *Flaubert*, p. 8.
42 Bruneau, *Corr.*, i. 646 n.5, at 1100–1.
43 Ibid., p. 333.
44 Ibid., pp. 369–70.
45 Commanville, *Souvenirs*, p. 44.
46 CHH *OC*, xv. 32–3, no. 2009.
47 See her crisp memento of the sums 'I have given you', in Bruneau, *Corr.*, i. 766.
48 Ibid., p. 725.
49 Ibid., p. 646.
50 Ibid., p. 725, at p. 1125.
51 CHH *OC*, xiii. 231, no. 444.
52 *Lettres inédites de Gustave Flaubert à son éditeur Michel Lévy*; corr. présentée par Jacques Suffel (Paris: Calmann-Lévy, 1965), pp. 26 and 61–2.
53 *Lettres inédites à . . . Du Camp, F. Fovard, Mme Adèle Husson . . .*, publiées par Auriant (Sceaux: Palimugre, 1948), pp. 74–6.
54 CHH *OC*, xiv. 228–9, no. 1226.
55 Ibid., p. 296, no. 1362.
56 Bruneau, *Corr.*, i. 477.
57 In her unpublished *Heures d'autrefois*, cited Chevalley-Sabatier, p. 29.
58 Bruneau, *Corr.*, i. 688.
59 Ibid., p. 469.
60 Chevalley-Sabatier, p. 53.
61 Commanville, *Souvenirs*, pp. 51–6.
62 Ibid., p. 86.
63 CHH *OC*, xvi. 308–10, no. 3575.

II GUSTAVE FLAUBERT 'NEL MEZZO DEL CAMMIN'

1 *Pensées intimes* (CHH *OC*, xi. 595). This work, which dates from 1840, was published under the title *Souvenirs, notes et pensées intimes*, with a foreword by Lucie Chevalley–Sabatier (Paris: Buchet et Chastel) in 1965, but with many errors in decipherment. The MS was recently acquired by the Bibliothèque nationale (Fr. N. A. 15809).
2 Maupassant, p. lxxxv.

3 CHH *OC*, xiii. 590, no. 722.
4 Zola, p. 181.
5 Maupassant, pp. lxxiii-iv.
6 *Voyage en Orient: Égypte* (Seuil *OC*, ii. 554).
7 Ibid., p. 697. One sentence in the text reproduced here from the Conard edition was suppressed. Messrs Sotheby sold an autograph MS text including this sentence on 16 May 1978, which they kindly permitted us to examine before the sale.
8 CHH *OC*, xiii. 530, no. 633.
9 Commanville, *Souvenirs*, p. 18.
10 CHH *OC*, xiii. 463, no. 571.
11 Maupassant, p. lxxvi.
12 Suffel, *Gustave Flaubert* (Paris: Éditions Universitaires, 1958), p. 20.
13 M.–J. Durry, *Flaubert et ses projets inédits* (Paris: Nizet, 1950), pp. 345 f.
14 CHH *OC*, xiv. 310, no. 1389.
15 *Journal des Goncourt*, 28 Jan. 1863.
16 CHH *OC*, xiv. 404, no. 1540.
17 Zola, p. 187.
18 *L'Éducation sentimentale*, II. ix.
19 Bruneau, *Corr.*, i. 314.
20 This caricature by Lemot, which was published in *Parodie* in September 1869, is reproduced in many biographies and in the Classiques Garnier edition of *Madame Bovary*.
21 *Mémoires d'un fou* (Seuil *OC*, i. 234).
22 Ibid.
23 Seuil *OC*, i. 197.
24 *Mémoires d'un fou* (ibid., p. 234).
25 Zola, p. 203.
26 Commanville, *Souvenirs*, p. 76.
27 Bruneau, *Corr.*, i. 394.
28 Maupassant, p. lxxv.
29 *Journal des Goncourt*, 29 Mar. 1862; *E. and J. de Goncourt, with letters and leaves from their journals*, compiled and trans. by M. A. Belloc and M. Shedlock (London: Heinemann, 1895), p. 181.
30 Bruneau, *Corr.*, i. 43.
31 Zola, p. 186.
32 Juliette Adam, *Mes sentiments et nos idées avant 1870* (Paris: Lemerre, 1905), p. 162.
33 *Journal des Goncourt*, 21 Feb. 1861.
34 *Souvenirs littéraires*, i. 225.
35 *Flaubert the Master*, p. 4 n. 5.
36 *Flaubert*, p. 20.
37 Avrahm Yarmolinsky, *Turgenev: the Man, His Art, and His Age* (New York: Orion Press, 1959), p. 44.
38 R. Dumesnil, *Gustave Flaubert* (Paris: Desclée, 1932), p. 441.
39 *Journal des Goncourt*, Nov. 1858. As early as 1843 Sainte-Beuve had noted that Byron and Sade had 'perhaps been the greatest inspirers of our moderns' (*Portraits contemporains*, Paris: Lévy, 1870, iii. 430).

40 G. D. Painter, *Marcel Proust* (London: Chatto, 1965), ii. 268–9.
41 Zola, p. 187.
42 CHH *OC*, xiii. 614, no. 747.
43 *Mémoires d'un fou* (Seuil OC, i. 232).
44 Bruneau, *Corr.*, i. 99.
45 Professor Bruneau lends the weight of his great authority to the findings of the Syracuse University Faculty of Medicine that this illness was epilepsy (ibid., p. 202 n. 2 at p. 943). The illness has been a gift to critics belonging to the Freudian psychoanalytical school (see J.-P. Sartre, *L'Idiot de la famille*, Paris: Gallimard, 1971, ii. 1786 ff).
46 Bruneau, *Corr.*, i. 38.
47 CHH *OC*, xiv. 15, no. 832.
48 Bruneau, *Corr.*, i. 647.
49 National Gallery, *Masterpieces of European Painting in the National Gallery, London* (1965), p. 46.
50 Zola, p. 186.
51 Maupassant, p. lxxiii.
52 Bruneau, *Corr.*, i. 588.
53 *Journal des Goncourt*, 11 May 1859; Adam, *Mes sentiments*, p. 162.
54 Maupassant, pp. lxxxiii-iv.
55 Reproduced in numerous biographies, this portrait appears also on the dust-jacket of Bruneau, *Corr.*, i.
56 *Souvenirs littéraires*, i. 254.
57 Philip Spencer's article in *French Studies*, 1954, is the most important source for the Collier family; later scholarship showed that the Trouville meeting occurred in 1842 (see Bruneau's *Les Débuts littéraires de Gustave Flaubert 1831—45*, Paris: A. Colin, 1962, pp. 533–4). It is now possible to add that the Collier family descended from Henry Collier of Whitechapel (will dated 1701) and produced many admirals and colonels; for their family tree see *Miscellanea Genealogica et Heraldica*, ed. J. J. Howard (London: Hamilton, 1880), new ser., iii. Captain Collier's children were George Baring Browne, Clarence Augustus, Herbert Cromwell, Gertrude Barbara Rich, Adeline, Harriet (sometimes called Henrietta), and Clementina Frances.
58 George Aïdá (the name was later changed to Aïdé) was the son of an Armenian merchant in Constantinople. He lived in Vienna, spoke a number of European languages, and visited Regency London. He was killed in a duel in Paris when Hamilton was aged four. His eldest son Frederick (b. 1823) died in an accident at Boulogne in 1831. Charles Hamilton was born in Paris in November 1826 and was taken back to England by his mother in 1831. When he was with the Colliers at Trouville he was 15, and next year he went to Bonn University and later into the Army, from which he retired as captain in 1853 (*Dictionary of National Biography*, Suppl. 1906, vol. i). Much later, he was a friend of Henry James, who described him as 'the Diane de Poitiers of our time' (see Leon Edel, *Henry James: The Master*, London: Hart-Davis, 1972, v. 97).
59 Bruneau, *Corr.*, i. 359.
60 Ibid., p. 177 and n. 7.
61 Spencer, *French Studies*, 8, 1954.

62 Bruneau, *Corr.*, i. 402–3.

63 Burke's *Landed Gentry*, 1898; family tree in Howard; and Register of Marriages, St Catherine's House, July, Aug., and Sept. 1847. Charles Tennant's age (then 54) appears in the 1851 census return for Russell Square (PRO HO107/1507).

64 See *Gentleman's Magazine*, Sept. 1830 and *Annual Register*, 1832; Spencer states that he was M.P. for many years (no doubt this was family tradition). Among petitions he presented was one to protect landowners etc. from 'the evils arising from pauperism and a redundant population' with a view to systematic colonization (see Barrow's *Mirror of Parliament*, 23 Dec. 1830). It is hardly surprising that he was not elected to the Reform Parliament.

65 See Howard.

66 PRO HO107/1507. Adeline had married Colonel Gordon.

67 30 Aug. 1855, to Bouilhet (CHH *OC*, xiii. 510, no. 607).

68 PRO HO107/1475.

69 PRO RG9/166.

70 CHH *OC*, xiii. 586, no. 717.

71 Bruneau, *Revue de litt. comparée*, avr.-juin 1957, pp. 277–9.

72 Mrs Belloc Lowndes, *The Merry Wives of Westminster* (London: Macmillan, 1946), p. 125.

73 That this was the general opinion, even in enlightened circles in England at the time, is shown by the notice in the *Saturday Review* of 6 June 1857 by Fitzjames Stephen (later the eminent judge and member of the India Council) who wrote in almost identical terms of the 'coarseness' of Flaubert's 'so-called *realism*', which was, 'if possible, exaggerated by the most flagrant breaches of taste in point of style', and Thackeray branded it as a 'heartless, cold-blooded story of the downfall and degradation of a woman' (Mary Neale, *Flaubert en Angleterre; étude sur les lecteurs anglais de Flaubert*, Bordeaux, 1966, pp. 10–11 and 12n.). Theodore Zeldin has recently stated that the public prosecutor was right in accusing Flaubert of writing an immoral book, 'a dangerous work' (*France 1848–1945*, ii, Oxford: Clarendon Press, 1977, p. 817). It is of some interest that Gertrude Tennant's future son-in-law, H. M. Stanley, thought *Salammbô* was such a masterpiece that it was the last work before Shakespeare and the Bible he discarded to lighten his luggage (Neale, p. 40 n.).

74 *The Times*, 14 July 1890; Belloc Lowndes, p. 122.

75 1871 census return, PRO RG10/135. He died there in September 1872 (*Miscellanea Genealogica*).

76 *Les Débuts littéraires*, p. 523; *Corr.*, i. 101 n. 3, at p. 894.

77 *Les Débuts littéraires*, pp. 370–1.

78 *Flaubert*, p. 20.

79 C. Bauchard, 'En marge de 'L'Éducation sentimentale': Le premier mari de Mme Arnoux', *RHLF*, avr.-juin 1954; Starkie, *Flaubert the Master*, p. 119.

80 Bruneau, *Corr.*, i. 480.

81 *Souvenirs littéraires*, i. 481; see also Bruneau, *Corr.*, i. 1071–2.

82 Bruneau, *Corr.*, i. 601.

83 Ibid., pp. 637–8.

84 Ibid., p. 704.

85 Ibid., p. 1072.
86 CHH *OC*, xiii. 330, no. 494.
87 C. Gothot-Mersch, *La Genèse de Madame Bovary* (Paris: José Corti, 1966), p. 291.
88 Baudelaire, *OC*, texte établi . . . Claude Pichois (Paris: Gallimard, 1976), ii. 80.
89 Dumesnil, p. 486.
90 CHH *OC*, xiii. 316, no. 489.
91 Bart, p. 347.
92 CHH *OC*, xiv. 317, no. 1395.
93 Gothot-Mersch, p. 202.
94 Bruneau, *Corr.*, i. 397.
95 CHH *OC*, xiii. 584, no. 714.
96 Maupassant, p. 274.
97 CHH *OC*, xiii. 396, no. 530.
98 See A. Y. Naaman, *Les Lettres d'Égypte de Gustave Flaubert* (Paris: Nizet, 1965), p. 86 n. i; for Du Camp's allegation, see *Souvenirs littéraires*, i. 251.
99 Seuil *OC*, p. 732.
100 Bruneau, *Corr.*, i. 418 and 429.
101 Ibid., p. 397.
102 CHH *OC*, xiii. 203, no. 425.
103 *Journal des Goncourt*, 21 Nov. 1862.
104 Ibid., 20 Oct. 1862.
105 Bruneau, *Corr.*, i. 101 n. 6, at p. 895.
106 Douglas Siler, *Flaubert et Louise Pradier:* le texte intégral des 'Mémoires de Madame Ludovica' (Archives des Lettres Modernes, vi, 1973 (3), no. 145). I am grateful to Professor Bruneau and Dr A. W. Raitt for drawing my attention to this important source.
107 Bruneau, *Corr.*, i. 221.
108 Ibid., p. 799 n. 2, at p. 1145.
109 Siler, p. 5.
110 *L'Album Flaubert*, p. 98.
111 *Catalogue de la succession Franklin-Grout*, Paris, 18–19 novembre 1931.
112 *Essais de Montaigne*, liv. 1, ch. xxv.
113 Bruneau, *Corr.*, i. 980; see also Jackson.
114 Bruneau, *Corr.*, i. 350.
115 Ibid., p. 241.
116 *L'Album Flaubert*, p. 68.
117 Quoted by Rose Macaulay in *Crewe Train* (London: Collins, 1926), p. 213.
118 Bruneau, *Corr.*, i. 481.
119 'Des maîtres les plus grands les œuvres les plus belles,/Auprès du beau vivant, compare, que sont-elles?/Corrège et le Poussin, Titien et Raphael' (*L'Art et l'amour*, cited by Jackson, pp. 180–1).
120 *L'Album Flaubert*, p. 68.
121 Du Camp, *Souvenirs littéraires*, ii. 566; J. F. Jackson, *Louise Colet et ses amis littéraires*, pp. 147–60.
122 'Memento du 27 juin 1851' (Bruneau, *Corr.*, i. 812–13).
123 In the preface to *Corr.*, i. xvii-xix.

124 Ibid., p. 815.
125 Ibid., p. xxix.
126 Ibid., pp. ix-x.
127 Ibid., pp. 817, 819, and 821.
128 Ibid., p. 823.
129 Ibid., p. 418, and CHH *OC*, xiii. 390, no. 528.
130 Ibid., p. 443.
131 Ibid., p. 452.

III ENGLISH GOVERNESSES AT CROISSET

1 Gervas Huxley, *Lady Elizabeth and the Grosvenors* (London: Oxford University Press, 1965), p. 147.
2 Ibid., p. 56.
3 Cited in W. F. Neff, *Victorian Working Women* . . . 1832–50 (London: Allen & Unwin, 1929), pp. 157–8.
4 Ibid., p. 155.
5 Cited ibid., pp. 154–5.
6 W. H. C. Armytage, *Four Hundred Years of English Education* (Cambridge University Press, 1970), p. 130.
7 Mrs Gaskell, *Life of Charlotte Brontë* (London: Smith, Elder, 1871), p. 227.
8 Vol. 84, Dec. 1848–Mar. 1849, review of *Vanity Fair* and *Jane Eyre*.
9 Gaskell, p. 128.
10 *Speak Memory* (London: Weidenfeld, 1967). Cf. Lady Elizabeth Belgrave's statement on the quantities of 'Scotch' governesses in Moscow in 1827, who were 'much prized' as being able to teach the children English, though in fact they spoke broad Edinburgh and Aberdonian (Huxley, p. 143).
11 *Quarterly Review*, vol. 84, Dec. 1848–Mar. 1849, p. 178.
12 See D. Beale, *Reports Issued by the Schools' Inquiry Commission on the Education of Girls* (London: David Nutt, [1870]).
13 Mackenzie Bell, *Christina Rossetti*, 2nd ed. (London: Hurst & Blackett, 1898), p. 24.
14 *Quarterly Review*, vol. 119, Jan.–Apr. 1866, p. 510.
15 James Bryce's evidence to Schools' Inquiry Commission (Beale, pp. 74–5).
16 *Madame Bovary*, II. xii.
17 Beale, pp. 74–5.
18 Bruneau, *Corr.*, i. 246.
19 On Caroline Anne Heuland see *BAF*, no. 23, Dec. 1963 and Bruneau, *Les Débuts littéraires*.
20 Seuil *OC*, i. 240.
21 Spencer, *French Studies*, 8 (1954), p. 100.
22 Bruneau, *Corr.*, i. 852.
23 Ibid., p. 137.
24 For example, F. & J. Fargues, French and silk dyers, Spitalfields, and F. P. Fargues, copperplate printer, 47 Berwick Street are listed in Robens London Directory for 1833.
25 Bruneau, *Corr.*, i. 198 and 199–200.
26 Ibid., p. 202.

27 Ibid., p. 219.
28 Ibid., p. 546.
29 *Notes de Voyage: Égypte* (Seuil *OC*, i. 614).
30 G. Simon, 'Victor Hugo et Louise Colet', *Revue de France*, 15 mai 1926.
31 A note by Hugo records the enclosure of an important letter to Jules Janin and a letter to Louise in a third letter to M. Savoye (then in Milton Street, Dorset Square), who was asked to put these in the post addressed to Flaubert at Croisset (Hugo, *Œuvres poétiques*, Pléiade ed., Paris, 1967, ii. 423–4).
32 CHH *OC*, xiii. 352, no. 506.
33 Ibid., p. 360, no. 511. The Conard and CHH notes to Flaubert's letter to Louise of 27 March 1853 (CHH no. 489) stating that the governess addressed the letters and packets are therefore not quite correct.
34 See Starkie, *Flaubert: The Making of the Master* (London: Weidenfeld, 1967), p. 216. On Hugo's losing the address, see his letter of 12 Oct. 1853 (CHH *OC*, xiii. 419, no. 543).
35 PRO RG9/791.
36 p. 7: 'Nous descendîmes chez l'ancienne institutrice de ma mère, Mrs Farmer, dans un quartier un peu en dehors de la ville.' Professor Bruneau, who has a typewritten copy of *Heures d'autrefois*, kindly contributed verbatim extracts from it. Mme Chevalley-Sabatier described Mrs Farmer as 'l'ancienne institutrice de Gustave et de sa sœur' in *Gustave Flaubert et sa nièce Caroline*, which drew on *Heures d'autrefois*.
37 It was published as 'calendrier d'un séjour chez Juliet Herbert' in vol. 8 of the CHH *OC*, which erroneously includes *Carnet de voyage 13* (the MS in the BHVP) among the *Carnets de lecture*.
38 CHH *OC*, xiv. 68, no. 914.
39 Ibid., xv., no. 3688, misdated September 1869 on the basis of the Conard date.
40 Bruneau, *Corr.*, i. 589.
41 Ibid., p. 589 n. 2, at p. 1081.
42 CHH *OC*, xiii. 157, no. 397.
43 Chevalley-Sabatier, p. 36.
44 Bruneau, *Corr.*, i. 711.
45 'Je ne m'amusais guère dans le home anglais de Mme Farmer, confinée dans la nursery avec de tout petits babies, n'ayant pas le droit de cueillir une fleur au jardin, moi qui étais maîtresse entière de celles de Croisset.'
46 CHH *OC*, xiii. 144, no. 381.
47 Bruneau, *Corr.*, i. 314.
48 CHH *OC*, xiii. 151–2, no. 388. The sentence in this letter cursing the presence on this walk of 'your jolly old oaf of a cousin' (*Votre gros bon garçon de cousin*) cannot have referred to Hamilton Aïdé, then aged 25 and in the army, as the editors of the *Supplément* (i. 143 n.) believed might have been the case. There can have been no shortage of cousins in the numerous Collier family.
49 *Flaubert à l'Exposition de 1851* (Oxford: Clarendon Press, 1951).
50 *Heures d'autrefois*, pp. 7–8. 'Un après-midi on m'emmena dans un pensionnat où des demoiselles défilèrent devant ma grand-mère. C'étaient des institutrices. Le choix tomba sur Miss Isabelle Hetton [*sic*], une brune assez jolie, quoique gravée de petite vérole. Il fut convenu qu'elle nous rejoindrait en France.' Mme Chevalley-Sabatier called the governess 'Miss Isabelle Helton'.

51 *L'Éducation sentimentale*, II. iii. (Seuil *OC*, ii. 76).
52 Chevalley-Sabatier, p. 37.
53 Ibid., p. 36.
54 CHH *OC*, xiii. 183, no. 416.
55 Ibid., p. 372, no. 516. The index omits a reference to this letter, which demonstrates that Isabel Hutton was still at the Flauberts' in July 1853.
56 By the editors of the CHH *OC* in the note to the letter cited in n. 55 above.
57 Ibid., xiii. 312, no. 489.

IV JULIET HERBERT AT CROISSET

1 John Summerson, *Georgian London* (Harmondsworth: Penguin, 1962), p. 223.
2 Thomas Smith, *A Topographical and Historical Account of the Parish of St Mary-le-Bone* (London: J. Smith, 1853).
3 Baptisms All Souls Church, Langham Place, 1829 (GLC DL/T/56 6).
4 Marylebone Church Baptisms (GLC P89/18 X16/83).
5 GLC P89/MRY 1/194.
6 1871 census return for Milman's Row, Chelsea (PRO RG 10/73).
7 Will of William Herbert, dated 19 Aug. 1858, proved 5 Oct. 1863 (Somerset House).
8 He is listed at that address in the London directories from 1823–4.
9 1851 census return for Farm Street, PRO HO107/1576.
10 William Herbert's will.
11 Hobhouse, p. 184.
12 Ibid., pp. 90–1.
13 GLC MDR10/301.
14 Obituary of William Herbert in the *Builder*, 26 Sept. 1863.
15 Sometimes numbered 16½.
16 GLC MDR10/374.
17 1832 London directories.
18 GLC *Survey of London*, vol. 39: *The Grosvenor Estate and Mayfair*, pt. 1, *General History* (London: Athlone Press, 1977).
19 GLC MDR1/383, 1832.
20 P. W. Kingsford, *Builders and Building Workers* (London: Arnold, 1973).
21 Richard was still listed at that address in the 1833 directory.
22 GLC DL/T/56 7.
23 PRO B3. 2562.
24 Thomas Cubitt was originally backed by two members of the Carpenters' Company (Hobhouse, p. 7).
25 PRO HO107/680.
26 Hobhouse, p. 253.
27 PRO HO107/1576.
28 He took his B.A. in 1852 (*Oxford University Calendar*).
29 Art-Union of London, *Annual Reports*, 1844–62.
30 William Herbert's will.
31 Ibid., and P.O. Directory 1856, vol. 1.
32 William Herbert's will.
33 She visited Juliet in 1870 when she came over during the Franco-Prussian war

and described the house and her visit in *Heures d'autrefois*, p. 25 bis.

34 LCC *Survey of London*, vol. 4: *The Parish of Chelsea*, pt. 2 (1913).

35 Thea Holme, *Chelsea* (London: Hamilton, 1972); David Piper, *The Companion Guide to London*, 2nd ed. (London: Collins, 1968), p. 199.

36 PRO RG10/73.

37 William Herbert's will.

38 'faible et bossue', *Heures d'autrefois*, p. 26 bis.

39 Will of Elizabeth Mary Hopgood, dated 4 Nov. 1886, proved 26 Mar. 1890 (Somerset House).

40 *Heures d'autrefois*, p. 25 bis.

41 Table of 'The Second Marquess of Westminster's Children', in Huxley.

42 Ibid., p. 160.

43 Beale.

44 CHH *OC*, xiii. 497, no. 597.

45 Ibid., pp. 517–18, no. 613.

46 Ibid., p. 529, no. 632.

47 Ibid., p. 530, no. 633.

48 Ibid., p. 531, no. 634.

49 'When I read Shakespeare, I become bigger, more intelligent, and purer', he had written in 1846, and again in the same year: 'The three most beautiful things created by God are the sea, *Hamlet*, and Mozart's *Don Juan*' (Bruneau, *Corr.*, i. 364 and 373).

50 CHH *OC*, xiii. 535, no. 638.

51 Ibid., p. 574, no. 700. At this date Flaubert always called her Juliette, so that this appears to be one of the CHH's 'normalization' of spellings.

52 Information kindly communicated by Professor Bruneau, who commented 'This volume has, of course, disappeared.' We were unable to see this catalogue.

53 Bruneau, *Corr.*, i. 437.

54 Bruneau, *Les Débuts littéraires*, pp. 203–5.

55 'Pouvez-vous l'aboucher (expression indécente) avec un de vos confrères d'outre-Manche?' (*Lettres inédites . . . à Michel Lévy*, p. 37).

56 Ibid., pp. 36–8 and 41.

57 BL add. MSS 46560–682.

58 CHH *OC*, xiv. 111, no. 986.

59 Edmund Gosse's *Swinburne* (London: Macmillan, 1917), cited by James Pope-Hennessy, *Monckton Milnes: The Flight of Youth* (London: Constable, 1951), p. 15.

60 'Si tu écris à Mme Flaubert, dis lui qu'elle recevra à la fin de la semaine les pantoufles de Mlle Juliette' (LOV C, III 1857, f. 41).

61 'Une autre chose de neuf, ici – le départ de l'institutrice me chiffonne aussi un peu – c'était une charmante fille, et j'ai peur qu'elle ne laisse un grand vide à ta mère – elles paraissaient s'arranger très bien ensemble' (ibid., f. 52).

62 Information kindly communicated by Professor Bruneau.

63 The sole genuine reference for it appears to be the second one given by Professor Bart (p. 392 n.3) to the catalogue of the Franklin-Grout sale at Antibes in 1931, which we unfortunately failed to see. However, like so many other Flaubert letters, this one may have been wrongly dated.

64 'Mme Flaubert a dû savoir ma courte apparition à Paris, par Mulot, que j'avais

chargé de lui remettre les pantoufles de Mlle Juliette' (LOV C, V 1859 f. 168).

65 Ibid., f. 202.

66 The only volume published that year (in August) was Bouilhet's *Poésies, festons et astragales*, yet Bouilhet wrote of the emotion Flaubert felt for the volume – the emotion produced by the feeling of abandoning its youth and nakedness to the public, as if Flaubert were the author. (He may have had a proprietary feeling for Bouilhet's book.) Bouilhet said: 'tu as bien fait d'offrir un volume à Mademoiselle Juliette. Ce que tu me dis de l'émotion produite sur toi par le dit volume ne me surprend pas du tout – j'ai éprouvé la même chose à *Melænis* et à ce dernier recueil. . . . c'est sa jeunesse et toute sa nudité qu'on abandonne au public' (ibid., f. 207). No poem in Bouilhet's later volumes, published posthumously, was dedicated to Caroline.

67 LOV C, V 1859, f. 210.

68 *Flaubert*, p. 392.

69 LOV C, VI 1860, f. 283.

70 'j'ai fait venir une *Melænis*, je l'expédie aujourd'hui – par la poste ou par le chemin de fer – je vais voir. J'y ai mis une dédicace à Miss Juliette' (LOV C, VI 1860, f. 286).

71 Ibid., f. 287^{v}.

72 'Mes bons souvenirs à Mlle Juliette' (LOV C, VII 1861, f. 380).

73 CHH *OC*, xiv. 91–2, no. 946.

74 *Nouvelle biographie universelle.*

75 CHH *OC*, xiv. 128, no. 1016.

76 Ibid., pp. 208–9, nos 1190–1.

V GUSTAVE'S FIRST VISIT TO JULIET

1 *E. and J. de Goncourt*, p. 198.

2 Du Camp related that when he and Flaubert were invited to dine with General Aupick (then ambassador) in Constantinople in November 1850, when Du Camp did not know that he was Baudelaire's stepfather, he told the general that he had just had a letter from Louis de Cormenin saying that he had met 'a Baudelaire' at Gautier's and thought well of him as a poet (*Souvenirs littéraires*, ii. 77–8). From this it does not seem as if either he or Flaubert knew or even knew of Baudelaire at that date. Du Camp added that from the general's expression, he knew he had committed a gaffe, though not why; he later stated that he got to know Baudelaire in the summer of 1852 (ibid., p. 84). Baudelaire's first letter to him is dated May 1852 (*Œuvres complètes, Correspondance générale*, Paris, Conard, 1953, pp. 7–8).

3 Information kindly communicated by Professor Jean Bruneau.

4 CHH *OC*, xiv. 193, no. 1161.

5 Ibid., p. 217, no. 1202.

6 Ibid.

7 Ibid., xiii. 398, no. 532.

8 Ibid., xiv. 197, no. 1169.

9 Ibid., p. 210, no. 1193.

10 Ibid., p. 217, no. 1203.

11 Ibid., p. 239, no. 1252.

12 'tu es bien heureux de vouloir [?] aller prendre l'air dans un beau pays . . . et je t'embrasse en te souhaitant un bon voyage (LOV C, XI 1865, f. 705v.)

13 'Je suis très surpris de ton voyage en Angleterre, vu qu'il n'était pas dans ton programme, et je me creuse la tête pour en deviner le motif. . . . Adieu, cher vieux, bien du plaisir dans tes diverses pérégrinations' (ibid., f. 707).

14 I am indebted to Dr A. W. Raitt for this suggestion.

15 *Nouvelle biographie universelle.*

16 I am indebted to Professor Jean Bruneau for this explanation.

17 CHH *OC*, xiv. 29, no. 851. Juliette Adam described the performance (*Mes premiers armes*, Paris: Lemerre, 1904, p. 212).

18 All information on Baden derives from C. Bauchard, 'Sur les traces de Gustave Flaubert et Madame Schlésinger', *RHLF*, jan.-mar.' 1953. (Professor Bruneau kindly drew my attention to this article.) Turgenev returned to Baden, after a visit to Russia, on 18 July (Henri Granjard, *Quelques lettres d'Ivan Tourguénev à Pauline Viardot*, Paris: Mouton, 1974, p. 135).

19 LOV XI 1865, f. 744.

20 'j'envie . . . la mirifique bière que tu bois en pays hérétique – car, ici, elle est détestable. . . . Fais une langue pour moi à John Bull – et tâche de ne pas gâter ton catholicisme au contact de la hideuse Réformation – c'est le dernier vœu de ton archevêque, Monseigneur' (ibid., f. 709).

21 CHH *OC*, xiv. 242, no. 1258.

22 Information kindly communicated by Dr A. W. Raitt.

23 *Nouvelle biographie universelle.*

24 I am indebted to Dr A. W. Raitt for this information.

25 CHH *OC*, xiv. 266, no. 1304.

26 Ibid., p. 283, no. 1338.

27 LOV C, XI 1865, f. 712.

28 CHH *OC*, xiv. 242–3, no. 1259.

29 Ibid., p. 243, no. 1260.

30 Meteorological data kindly supplied by the London Weather Centre; see also relevant issues of the *Illustrated London News*.

31 M. André Dubuc noted this label (though Strand appeared as Stand) in '*L'Éducation sentimentale* dans les carnets et notes de Flaubert', *BAF*, Dec. 1969, where he described the notebook as 'Carnet acheté à Londres en juin 1866'. The firm of Limbird appears in the 1865 and 1866 London directories.

32 Bryan's *Dictionary of Painters and Engravers*.

33 Milman's Row 1861 census (PRO RG9/30).

34 Born in Rouen in 1637, where he is commemorated by a plaque, he was educated by his uncle, Thomas Corneille.

35 Simona Pakenham, *Sixty Miles from England: the English at Dieppe from 1814–1914* (London: Macmillan, 1907).

36 Bruneau, *Corr.*, i. 151 n. 6, at p. 922.

37 Durry, pp. 331–2; Painter, i. 156–7.

38 Bruneau, *Corr.*, i. xxiv.

39 see e.g. *Illustrated Hand-book to London and Its Environs* (London: Ingram, Cooke, 1853).

40 Baedeker, *London and Its Environs*, 1879.

41 The CHH version has 'Lord Sigonier'.

42 The CHH reading 'Bridgewater, côte brune' caused some mystification.
43 *Dictionary of National Biography.*
44 Huxley, p. 60.
45 Cunningham's *Handbook for London*, 1849.
46 Holme, p. 196.
47 Warwick Wroth, *Cremorne and the Later London Gardens* (London: Stock, 1907).
48 *Illustrated Hand-book to London and Its Environs.*
49 *Guide-Chaix, Nouveau Guide à Londres pour l'Exposition de 1851* (Paris, 1851).
50 *Flaubert à l'Exposition de 1851.*
51 The dukedom was not created until 1874, when Hugh Lupus, the third Marquess, became the first Duke of Westminster (Huxley, p. 168).
52 Ibid., p. 59.
53 Nikolaus Pevsner, *The Buildings of England: Middlesex* (Harmondsworth: Penguin Books, 1951), p. 81.
54 *L'Éducation sentimentale*, III. 1.
55 There are several misreadings in the CHH version.
56 Professor Bart states that Flaubert and Juliet 'together . . . went down to Hampton Court and spent the night in a hotel. . . . Their lodging was near the bridge; they were on the third floor' (p. 463). There is no evidence that Juliet spent the night with Flaubert or even that she was with him at Hampton Court. If she was, he could have seen her off at the station or she could have gone home by steamer. The records of the Mitre were destroyed when it was taken over by Schooner Inns, but it does not seem credible that Juliet would have behaved in a way that was bound to shock or embarrass her mother and sisters. Professor Bart's 'third floor' for 'au 2d' reflects the American practice of calling the ground floor the first floor.
57 Bart, who reproduces this passage on p. 363 n., has misread 'voitures de maître dételées' as 'voitures du maître du télégraphe', which he translated in the text as 'carriages of the telegraph bureau'. There never was a post or telegraph office at this entrance to Hampton Court or in sight of the Mitre.
58 'Hotel de la mitre, près du pont, au 2d – je vois une prairie coupée par des lignes fréquentes d'arbustes, elles sont plus nombreuses à l'horizon et font bois – au premier plan une meule de foin – à droite la gare du chemin de fer – à la rive les canots – à la porte en face des voitures de maître dételées – la rivière vue en raccourci couleur d'acier pale – des barques dessus comme des mouches – petits nuages blancs[,] le ciel est satin bleu pale[,] la lune se lève' (ff. 52–51v.).
59 Flaubert's capital K resembles an R – hence the misreading 'Ruchiouk-Hânem' in the Conard *Notes de voyage*, which persists in the Seuil *OC* (ii. 574) and was retained in the CHH edition because this was the previous reading. The CHH editors misread 'Kiew' as 'Rien', but the w has a pronounced terminal upstroke.
60 Baedeker, *London and Its Environs*, 1879; see also H. Taine, *Notes sur l'Angleterre* (Paris: Hachette, 1872).
61 CHH *OC*, viii. 343.
62 *Flaubert, a Biography* (London: Faber, 1952), p. 156 n. 4.
63 CHH *OC*, xiv. 243–4, no. 1261. This letter was erroneously placed in August 1866 in the Conard edition but was redated by Gérard-Gailly.
64 CHH *OC*, xiv. 247, no. 1269, 14 Aug. 1865, redated by Gérard-Gailly.

VI THE SECOND VISIT TO JULIET

1 'J'ai fait une pièce de vers *pro Amoribus*, ou mieux *de Amoribus – vel Elegantius*: *ob amores* – à moins que je ne dise – *amorum causa* ce qui m'est parfaitement égal' (LOV B, XII 1866, f. 797. No precise date has been assigned to this letter but it is placed first in the sequence.)

2 Paris: Charpentier, 1874. The lyric poem 'Amour double' ('Il ne se peut pas qu'on aime/Deux maîtresses à la fois') is much too personal to fit this description.

3 L. Letellier, *Louis Bouilhet, 1821–69; sa vie et ses œuvres* (Paris: Hachette, 1919).

4 *Souvenirs littéraires*, i. 52.

5 'je ne t'envoie point *de Amoribus*, je veux y retoucher quelque peu' (LOV B, XII 1866, f. 799, assigned to 16 June).

6 CHH *OC*, xiv. 271, no. 1313.

7 *Journal des Goncourt*, 21 Feb. 1862.

8 Ibid., 18 Jan. 1864.

9 See letter of 7 July 1866 (CHH *OC*, xiv. 281–2, no. 1335).

10 Ibid., no. 1336.

11 'Je te conseille d'arrêter fortement ton plan – avant de te mettre en route – tu n'en voyageras qu'avec plus de joie. Je te prie de me rappeler, à Londres, au gracieux souvenir de qui de droit' (LOV B, XII 1866, f. 805, assigned to July 1866).

12 CHH *OC*, xiv. 264, no. 1300.

13 Ibid., p. 266, no. 1304.

14 'Tu as bien raison de ne pas te mettre en route avant de préparer fortement ton Chapître III – tu n'en voyageras qu'avec plus de plaisir' (LOV B, VI 1866, f. 805 bis, assigned to July).

15 F. Quintavalle, *Storia dell'unità italiana, 1814–1924* (Milan: Hoepli, 1926).

16 'c'est par la plus sage économie que je me prive de ce bon voyage comme de toute autre distraction . . .' (LOV B, XII 1866, ff. 801–2. This letter was assigned to June 1866 and is placed in the sequence ahead of those cited here in notes 11 and 14).

17 See Pakenham, and letter to Caroline 23 Mar. 1871 (above, p. 113).

18 CHH *OC*, xiv. 282–3, no. 1337.

19 Ibid., p. 283, no. 1338.

20 Thomas Stothard, 1755–1834, was a painter and book illustrator who was librarian of the Royal Academy in 1812. He painted the staircase of Burleigh House at Stamford and the ceiling of the Advocates' Library in Edinburgh and was an intimate friend of Flaxman, William Beckford, and Samuel Rogers. His pictures included 'Characters from Shakepeare' at South Kensington, and he illustrated Fielding, Richardson, Sterne, *Robinson Crusoe*, etc.

21 CHH *OC*, xiv. 592, no. 1892.

22 Ibid. p. 284, no. 1341 (dated 4 August in *Supplément*).

23 Ibid., p. 286, no. 1346.

24 Ibid., p. 287, no. 1347.

25 To G. Sand, 13 Apr. 1867 (ibid., p. 344, no. 1433).

26 Ibid., p. 341, no. 1428.

27 Ibid., p. 350, no. 1445 (precisely dated by Gérard-Gailly). No. 1437 makes it

clear that she had a slight stroke.
28 Ibid., p. 355, no. 1456.
29 Adam, *Mes sentiments*, p. 137.
30 CHH *OC*, xiv. 364, no. 1471.
31 Ibid., p. 365, no. 1473.
32 Ibid., p. 513, no. 1732, which perpetuates the wrong year (1869) given in the Conard edition (one of the errors noted by Gérard-Gailly).
33 Ibid., p. 370, no. 1482.
34 Ibid., p. 372, no. 1485.
35 Ibid., xvi. 3688, where the date appears as September 1869? – see Gérard-Gailly on Conard no. 1072.
36 CHH *OC*, xiv. 382, no. 1505.
37 Ibid., p. 350, no. 1446.
38 Ibid., p. 406, no. 1542.
39 Ibid., p. 455, no. 1623.
40 Ibid., p. 450, no. 1615.
41 *Supplément*, ii. 158 n.
42 CHH *OC*, xiii. 669, no. 818.
43 See article in *The Times*, 5 Feb. 1915.
44 H. Taine, *Notes sur Paris: Vie et opinions de M. Frédéric-Thomas Graindorge* (Paris: Hachette, 1905), pp. 184–5.
45 *Army Lists* till 1863; his transfer to the Indian Army (the Bengal Staff Corps) is only discoverable in the unindexed 'Promotions, Appointments, etc.' In 1870 he was gazetted captain in the 21st Lancers (the regiment was then in India).
46 Bruneau, *Corr.*, i. 114, n. 3, at pp. 901–2.
47 CHH *OC*, xiii. 586, no. 717.
48 *Dictionary of National Biography*.
49 Spencer, *Flaubert*, p. 179.
50 An antiquarian miscellany, published in 2 volumes in 1863–4; see i. 192–4.
51 Flaubert, *L'Éducation sentimentale*, texte établi et présenté par R. Dumesnil (Paris: Société les Belles Lettres, 1942), pp. 364–5.
52 *Journal des Goncourt*, 10 Dec. 1886. Professor Bruneau states that Caroline tried in vain to buy her uncle's letters to Louise Colet but succeeded only in acquiring copies (Bruneau, *Corr.*, i. xv).
53 BL Add. MSS 46642 (vol. lxxxiii, 1854–64).
54 I am greatly indebted to Dr A. W. Raitt for asking the interesting question whether it was Juliet who sent the dossier and for drawing my attention to Dumesnil's pictorial anthology.
55 Durry, p. 200 n.
56 CHH *OC*, xiv. 406–7, no. 1542.
57 Ibid., p. 481, no. 1677.
58 Ibid., p. 482, no. 1678.
59 Ibid., p. 485, no. 1685.
60 Ibid., p. 489, no. 1689 (dated between 22 and 25 June, this must have been written before the 24th, since on the 24th Flaubert told George Sand that Bouilhet had been advised to go south).
61 Ibid., p. 495, no. 1697.
62 Ibid., p. 496, no. 1698.

63 Ibid., p. 497, no. 1701.
64 Ibid., p. 512, no. 1731.
65 Classiques Garnier ed. of *L'Éducation sentimentale* (Paris, 1961), pp. 429–30.
66 CHH *OC*, xiv. 514, no. 1736.
67 Ibid., p. 520, no. 1756.
68 Ibid., p. 531, no. 1779.
69 *Lettres inédites de Gustave Flaubert à . . . Michel Lévy*, p. 148–9.

VII *1870–1872*

1 CHH *OC*, xiv. 575, no. 1866.
2 See Pakenham.
3 Alfred Cobban, *A History of Modern France* (London: Cape, 1962–3), ii. 200.
4 Zola, p. 183, but Zola's further statement that Flaubert was dazzled by the pomp of the Second Empire shows a misunderstanding of Flaubert's character.
5 CHH *OC*, xiv. 589–90, no. 1890.
6 Ibid., pp. 610–11, no. 1912.
7 As is stated ibid., p. 208 n.
8 To Caroline, 23 Dec. 1863 (ibid., pp. 186–7, no. 1146).
9 É. Gérard-Gailly, *Le Grand Amour de Flaubert* (Paris: Aubier, 1944, pp. 294–7); Chevalley-Sabatier, pp. 57–8.
10 Chevalley-Sabatier, pp. 58–9.
11 To Caroline, 5 Feb. 1865 (CHH *OC*, xiv. 225, no. 1222).
12 Ibid., p. 276, no. 1223.
13 Chevalley-Sabatier, p. 64.
14 See Jean Bruneau's preface to Chevalley-Sabatier, p. 8.
15 Ibid.
16 CHH *OC*, xiv. 266, no. 1304 and xvi. no. 3688 (wrongly dated 1869).
17 Chevalley-Sabatier, p. 85.
18 CHH *OC*, xiv. 590, no. 1890.
19 Starkie, *Flaubert the Master*, p. 184.
20 Chevalley-Sabatier, p. 86.
21 Not 'livres de piété' (ibid.).
22 Omitted by Mme Chevalley-Sabatier.
23 Not 'une petite école' (Chevalley-Sabatier, p. 86).
24 Mme Chevalley-Sabatier did not quote this paragraph and stated only that Juliet was governess of a wealthy family.
25 'J'étais descendu chez la mère de mon ancienne institutrice Juliet Herbert. Elle habitait une minuscule maison à Chelsea dont elle ne sortait jamais. Assise dans l'angle de la fenêtre du 'parlour', elle travaillait à l'aiguille ou lisait des livres édifiants. Très sourde, elle mettair à son oreille une sorte de casserole d'étain, quand elle faisait une question dont elle voulait entendre la réponse. Deux de ses filles vivaient avec elle. L'aînée, Marianne, était revenue au foyer après avoir été vingt ans chez le marquis de Westminster, dont elle avait élevé les enfants. Devenue sourde, elle aussi, elle portait enroulé autour de la taille plusieurs mètres de caoutchouc et quand elle voulait causer avec quelqu'un elle développait sa ceinture et vous présentait l'extrémité terminée par un cornet acoustique. C'était une personne fort instruite et qui, ayant fréquenté l'aristoc-

ratie anglaise, m'intéréssait par tout ce qu'elle m'en racontait.

L'autre fille, faible et bossue, mais au regard charmant, tenait une petite classe dans un quartier éloigné; elle rentrait tard le soir, exténuée et montait souvent se coucher sans 'supper'.

Mrs Herbert avait encore deux autres filles, toutes deux également institutrices. L'une d'elles était Juliet – à ce moment-là elle faisait l'éducation des Miss Conant. Je fus invitée à aller 'en visite' à Lyndon Hall, résidence des Conant. C'est ainsi que je fis connaissance avec l'existence anglaise à la campagne et elle me plut extrêmement' (*Heures d'autrefois*, pp. 265–6).

26 CHH *OC*, xiv. 590n6. The Conard edition has 'Lynton'.

27 Huxley, p. 172.

28 The Tennants are listed in the directories at 2 Richmond Terrace from 1869.

29 CHH *OC*, xiv. 593, no. 1892.

30 Ibid., p. 596, no. 1895.

31 Bruneau, *Corr.*, i. 70 n.5, at p. 882.

32 CHH *OC*, xiv. 602, no. 1901 and p. 598, no. 1897.

33 Ibid., no. 1902.

34 *Victoria History of the Counties of England: Rutland*, vol. 2 (London: St Catherine Press, 1935), where there is an illustration of the house.

35 Burke's *Peerage, Baronetage and Knightage* . . ., 105th ed., 1970. Their names and ages appear on a tablet in Lyndon church put up by Edward Conant's grandchildren.

36 Chevalley-Sabatier, p. 86.

37 *BAF*, Dec. 1974, p. 41.

38 CHH *OC*, xiv. 601, no. 1901.

39 On 30 April 1871 (ibid.)

40 *Souvenirs littéraires*, ii. 511.

41 CHH *OC*, xiv. 628, no. 1940.

42 Ibid., p. 630, no. 1943.

43 Ibid., no. 1944.

44 Ibid., p. 631, no. 1945.

45 Ibid., p. 630, no. 1945.

46 The Leicestershire Museums, Art Galleries and Records Service, to whom Sir John Conant kindly referred my enquiry, verified their absence from the 1871 census return for Lyndon Hall.

47 PRO RG10/104. The Conants are not listed in the P.O. London Directory.

48 Chevalley-Sabatier, p. 91.

49 Monsieur C. Simonet, Conservateur of the Rouen municipal library, kindly gave me particulars of the death of Baron Leroy.

50 Pakenham, p. 96.

51 CHH *OC*, xv. 32–3, no. 2009. For Turgenev's London address see LOV B, VI, f. 109; also Ivan Tourguénev, *Nouvelle Correspondance inédite* (Paris: Libraire des Cinq Continents, 1971), p. 193.

52 LOV B, VI, f. 113.

53 Dated by Gérard-Gailly.

54 CHH *OC*, xv. 120, no. 2193.

55 Ibid., p. 126, no. 2206.

56 Ibid., pp. 124–5, no. 2204.

57 Ibid., p. 123, no. 2202.
58 Ibid., p. 131, no. 2217.
59 Ibid., pp. 133–4, no. 2221.
60 Ibid., p. 133, no. 2220.
61 Ibid., pp. 135–6, no. 2225.
62 Ibid., p. 138, no. 2231.
63 Chevalley-Sabatier, p. 152.
64 CHH *OC*, xv. 148, no. 2246.
65 Chevalley-Sabatier, p. 103.
66 CHH *OC*, xv. 154, no. 2254.
67 Ibid. p. 154, no. 2255.
68 Ibid., p. 156, no. 2256.
69 Ibid., p. 154, no. 2255.
70 Ibid., p. 157, no. 2258.
71 Ibid., p. 159, no. 2261.
72 Lucien Andrieu stated that the sole reason was 'le souvenir de Juliet Herbert' (*BAF*, Dec. 1976), but Professor Bart (p. 633) suggested several additional reasons.
73 CHH *OC*, xv. 158, no. 2259.
74 Ibid., p. 159, no. 2261.
75 Ibid., p. 161, no. 2264.
76 Ibid., p. 164, no. 2269.
77 Ibid., p. 166, no. 2271.
78 Ibid., pp. 167 and 169, nos. 2273 and 2275.
79 *Correspondance entre Sand et Flaubert*, p. 336.
80 CHH *OC*, xv. 177, no. 2289.
81 Ibid., pp. 184–5, no. 2301.

VIII THE LAST YEARS, 1873–80

1 CHH *OC*, xv. 149, no. 2248.
2 To Mme Brainne, 9 July 1878, ibid., xvi. 62, no. 3137.
3 Ibid., xv. 197, no.2320.
4 Ibid., p. 287, no. 2471.
5 *Journal des Goncourt*, 17 Dec. 1873.
6 *Correspondance entre George Sand et Gustave Flaubert*, p. 394.
7 Letters to Mme Roger des Genettes, 1 May 1874, and G. Sand, 26 May 1874 (CHH *OC*, xv. 299 and 301, nos. 2496 and 2500).
8 Ibid., p. 322, no. 2527.
9 Ibid., p. 315, no. 2518.
10 Ibid., p. 334, no. 2545.
11 Ibid., p. 335, no. 2547.
12 Ibid. p. 342, no. 2558.
13 Professor Bart states that in 1874 Flaubert told the Princess that he had only been in Paris 48 hours when he had been there for some days, but according to no. 2553, he told her he had been in Paris for several days.
14 *Journal des Goncourt*, 4 May 1862.
15 *La Tentation de saint Antoine*, pt. iii (Seuil *OC*, i. 507).

16 Jean Seznec, *Nouvelles études sur la Tentation de saint Antoine* (London: Warburg Inst., 1949), pp. 111–12.
17 *Flaubert*, pp. 156–7.
18 CHH *OC*, xv. 512, no. 2859.
19 Jotting in notebook (Spencer, *Flaubert*, p. 157, citing Louis Bertrand).
20 30 Aug. 1846 (Bruneau, *Corr.*, i. 320).
21 See ibid., p. 605 n. 1.
22 CHH *OC*, xiii. 631, no. 770.
23 Ibid., xv. 376, no. 2634.
24 Ibid., p. 379, no. 2642.
25 Ibid., p. 382, no. 2650.
26 Francis Ambrière, 'Les Ennuis d'argent de Gustave Flaubert', *Mercure de France*, cclv (1934), pp. 519–34.
27 See Starkie, *Flaubert the Master*, pp. 231–2.
28 CHH *OC*, xv. 386, no. 2656.
29 15 Aug. 1875 (*Corr. entre Sand et Flaubert*, p. 424).
30 Ambrière, loc. cit., p. 521.
31 CHH *OC*, xv. 415, no. 2701.
32 8 Oct. 1875 (*Corr. entre Sand et Flaubert*, p. 424).
33 Ibid.
34 See e.g. letter to Mme Flaubert, 15 Dec. 1850 (Bruneau, *Corr.*, i. 719–20).
35 A. W. Raitt, 'Flaubert: Extract from *Un Coeur simple*', in Peter H. Nurse, ed., *The Art of Criticism; Essays in French Literary Analysis* (Edinburgh University Press, 1969), p. 214; see also his 'Flaubert and the Art of the Short Story', in Royal Soc. of Literature, *Essays by Divers Hands*, n.s., xxxviii (1975).
36 Maupassant, p. xix.
37 Yarmolinsky, *Turgenev*, pp. 202–5.
38 Letter to Benjamin Bailey, 22 Nov. 1817.
39 See above, p. 39.
40 CHH *OC*, xv. 464, no. 2779.
41 Ibid., p. 444, no. 2745.
42 Ibid., p. 459, no. 2773.
43 Ibid., p. 457, no. 2771.
44 Ibid., p. 460, no. 2774.
45 Ibid., p. 462, no. 2778.
46 Ibid., p. 487, no. 2813.
47 Bruneau, *Corr.*, i. 29 n. 2, at p. 856.
48 CHH *OC*, xv. 490, no. 2822.
49 Ibid., p. 494, no. 2829.
50 Ibid., p. 482, no. 2807.
51 Ibid., p. 483, no. 2809.
52 Ibid., p. 596, no. 3010.
53 Ibid., p. 597, no. 3011.
54 Ibid., p. 599, no. 3014.
55 Ibid., p. 600, no. 3015.
56 Ibid., p. 601, no. 3018.
57 Ibid., xvi. 71, no. 3153.
58 Ibid., pp. 82–3, no. 3170.

59 Ibid., p. 249, no. 3475.
60 Ibid., xv. 501, no. 2844.
61 Ibid., p. 552, no. 2921.
62 Ibid., p. 566, no. 2958.
63 Ibid., p. 541, no. 2904.
64 Ibid., p. 578, no. 2981.
65 Ibid., xvi. 46, no. 3106.
66 Ibid., p. 77, no. 3161.
67 Ibid., p. 92, no. 3189. This explanation seems to rebut Professor Bart's statement that a reason why Flaubert could not see Gertrude Tennant was almost certainly because he was with Juliet in Paris (Bart, p. 716). He situated this in 1879, but this was perhaps a typographical error.
68 CHH *OC*, xvi. 86, no. 3177.
69 Ibid., p. 97, no. 3199.
70 Ibid., p. 107, no. 3220.
71 Ibid., p. 110, no. 3224.
72 Ibid., p. 138, no. 3275 and p. 139, no. 3279.
73 Ibid., p. 165, no. 3317.
74 Ibid., p. 187, no. 3355.
75 Ibid., p. 201, no. 3380.
76 Ibid., p. 213, no. 3398.
77 Ibid., p. 202, no. 3380.
78 Ibid., pp. 209–10, no. 3393.
79 Ibid., p. 155, no. 3305.
80 Gustave Flaubert, *Lettres inédites à Raoul Duval*, commentées par Georges Normandy (Paris: Albin Michel, 1950), p. 23.
81 *Journal des Goncourt*, 15 Sept. 1879; see also M.-J. Durry.
82 CHH *OC*, xvi. 238, no. 3450 and p. 239, no. 3451.
83 See L. Andrieu, 'Un Ami de Flaubert: Edmond Laporte (1832–1906)'. *BAF*, Dec. 1976.
84 Ibid., pp. 228–9, no. 3430 and p. 254, no. 3483.
85 Ibid., note to no. 3483.
86 Ibid., p. 258, no. 3489.
87 Ibid., p. 273, no. 3513.
88 Ibid., p. 279, no. 3527.
89 Ibid., p. 289, no. 3546.
90 Sartre, i. 738–61.
91 CHH *OC*, xvi. 278, no. 3524.
92 See *L'Album Flaubert*, p. 193.
93 CHH *OC*, xvi. 281, no. 3529.
94 Ibid., p. 287, no. 3541.
95 Ibid., p. 300, no. 3565.
96 Ibid.
97 Ibid., p. 304, no. 3571.
98 Ibid., p. 311, no. 3576.
99 Ibid., p. 323, no. 3594.
100 Ibid., p. 335, no. 3611.
101 Ibid., p. 337, no. 3615.

102 *Journal des Goncourt*, 28 Mar. 1880.
103 CHH *OC*, xvi. 355, no. 3645 and p. 358, no. 3650.
104 Ibid., p. 356, no. 3646.
105 Ibid., p. 360, no. 3654.
106 Ibid., p. 319, no. 3589.
107 Ibid., p. 322, no. 3593.
108 Ibid., p. 298, no. 3561.
109 W. H. Auden, *The Ascent of F6*, II. ii.
110 See Dumesnil, *Flaubert*, app. A; *Lettres inédites à Tourguéneff*, ed. Gérard-Gailly (Monaco: Éditions du Rocher, 1946), pp. 224–7; Starkie, *Flaubert the Master*, pp. 301–3.

IX CAROLINE AND JULIET

1 *Journal des Goncourt*, 14 May 1880.
2 Ibid.
3 Chevalley-Sabatier, p. 182.
4 Ibid., p. 177.
5 CHH *OC*, xvi. 330, no. 3602.
6 Ibid., nos 3615 and 3618.
7 Starkie, *Flaubert the Master*, p. 305; Spencer, *Flaubert*, p. 244.
8 *Lettres inédites à Raoul Duval*, pp. 269–70.
9 Chevalley-Sabatier, p. 180.
10 Ibid., p. 181.
11 Bruneau, *Les Débuts littéraires*, pp. 22–3.
12 *Journal des Goncourt*, 7 Feb. 1884.
13 R. Descharmes and R. Dumesnil, *Autour de Flaubert*, ii (bibliographie et chronologie) (Paris, 1912).
14 *Lettres inédites à Tourguéneff*, p. 108.
15 I am indebted to M. Jacques Suffel and Dr Marcia Josephson who kindly checked one or two sample letters but they are not, of course, responsible for any error arising because it was impossible to check all the autograph letters.
16 *Lettres inédites à Tourguéneff*, p. 119n.
17 CHH *OC*, xv. 444, no. 2745.
18 Chevalley-Sabatier, p. 178.
19 Ambrière, *Mercure de France*, cclv. 519.
20 Léon Daudet, *L'Entre deux guerres*, iii (Paris: Nouvelle Lib. Nationaliste, 1915), p. 282.
21 CHH *OC*, xv. 203, no. 3383.
22 *Les Jours de Flaubert* (Paris: Éditions du Myrte, 1947).
23 Bruneau, *Corr.*, i. 308.
24 CHH *OC*, xv. 331, no. 3603.
25 Bruneau, *Corr.*, i. xv.
26 Professor Bruneau states that it is not known if Louise's letters were destroyed, and by whom, but he does not cite Gustave's letter to Laporte or Maupassant's article (Bruneau, *Corr.*, i. xviii n. 2).
27 *Catalogue de la Bibliothèque Lovenjoul à Chantilly* . . . par Georges Vicaire (Paris: BN, 1960).

28 *Gustave Flaubert et ses amis* (Paris: Plon, 1927), p. 2 (cited in Bruneau, *Corr.*, i. xix n. 1).

29 First reported by the notorious forger Thomas Wise, this destruction was treated with reserve until the publication of the Browning Institute's *The Brownings' Correspondence and Checklist* in 1978.

30 *Carnet 20*, f. 181 (see Durry, p. 313).

31 CHH *OC*, xiii. 667, no. 816.

32 Aglaé Didier, an intimate friend of Louise Colet, was the wife of Charles Didier (Bruneau, *Corr.*, i. 1020).

33 CHH *OC*, xiii. 446, no. 562.

34 Cited in the anonymous preface to *An Author's Love, being the unpublished letters of Prosper Mérimée's 'Inconnue'* (London: Macmillan, 1889), p. x. These are fictional letters; the genuine ones were burned during the Paris Commune.

35 CHH *OC*, xv., nos 2908 and 2910. For Du Camp's sense of outrage at the publication of these letters, see *Souvenirs littéraires*, i. 335.

36 'Une Rencontre', *BAF*, May 1974, pp. 19–30.

37 He died on 14 November 1894 and left £124,539 to his wife and children (will dated 29 Oct. 1886, proved 14 Dec. 1894).

38 Probate was granted on 15 Dec. 1909. For Juliet's signature, see plate 6b.

39 Registration District Fulham, 1909, no. 397.

Select Bibliography

Manuscripts

Bouilhet, Louis. Letters to Flaubert 1857–66, series C in the Fonds Franklin-Grout, Bibliothèque Spoelberch de Lovenjoul, Chantilly.

Flaubert, Gustave. *Carnet de voyage 13*, in the Bibliothèque historique de la ville de Paris.

Books and articles

Adam, Juliette. *Mes Premières Armes littéraires et politiques*. Paris: Lemerre, 1904.

— *Mes Sentiments et nos idées avant 1870*. Paris: Lemerre, 1905.

Albalat, Antoine. *Gustave Flaubert et ses amis*. Paris: Plon, 1927.

Ambrière, Francis. Les Ennuis d'argent de Gustave Flaubert. *Mercure de France*, cclx, 1934.

— Quand Flaubert prenait livraison de la Guimont. *L'Intransigeant*, 2 mar. 1934.

Andrieu, Lucien. Un Ami de Flaubert: Edmond Laporte (1832–1906). *Bulletin des Amis de Flaubert*, déc. 1976.

Armytage, W. H. C. *Four Hundred Years of English Education*. Cambridge University Press, 1970.

Baedeker. *London and Its Environs*. 1879.

Bart, B. J. *Flaubert*. New York: Syracuse University Press, 1967.

Bauchard, C. Sur les traces de Gustave Flaubert et Madame Schlésinger. *Revue historique de littérature française*, jan.-mar. 1953.

— En marge de *l'Education sentimentale*: le premier mari de Mme Arnoux. *Revue historique de littérature française*, avr.-juin 1954.

Beale, D. *Reports Issued by the Schools' Inquiry Commission on the Education of Girls*. London: Nutt, 1870.

Bertrand, Georges-Émile. *Les Jours de Flaubert*. Paris: Éditions du Myrte, 1947.

Bruneau, Jean. *Les Débuts littéraires de Gustave Flaubert, 1831–1845*. Paris: Colin, 1962.

— *Madame Bovary* jugée par un 'Fantôme de Trouville'. *Revue de littérature comparée*, avr.-juin 1957.

Chevalley-Sabatier, L. *Flaubert et sa nièce Caroline*. Paris: Pensée universelle, 1971.

Commanville, Caroline. *Souvenirs sur Gustave Flaubert*. Paris: Ferraud, 1895.

Cunningham's *Handbook for London*, 1849.

Du Camp, Maxime. *Souvenirs littéraires*. Paris: Hachette, 1882–3. 2 vols.

Dumesnil, René. *Gustave Flaubert*. Paris: Desclée, 1932.

— *Le Grand Amour de Flaubert*. Geneva, Éditions du Milieu du Monde, 1945.

Durry, M.-J. *Flaubert et ses projects inédits*. Paris: Nizet, 1950.

Flaubert, Gustave. *Lettres de Gustave Flaubert à George Sand*, précedées d'une étude par Guy de Maupassant. Paris: Charpentier, 1884.

— *Correspondance entre George Sand et Gustave Flaubert*, préface de Henri Amic. Paris: Calmann-Lévy, [1904].

— *Œuvres complètes de Gustave Flaubert. Correspondance*. Paris, Conard, 1926–33. 9 vols.

— *L'Éducation sentimentale;* texte établi et présenté par R. Dumesnil. Paris: Société les Belles Lettres, 1942.

— *Flaubert et L'Éducation sentimentale*. Paris: Société les Belles Lettres, 1943.

— *Lettres inédites à Tourguéneff,* présentation et notes par Gérard-Gailly. Monaco; Éditions du Rocher, 1946.

— *Lettres inédites à Maxime Du Camp, Me Frédéric Fovard, Mme Adèle Husson et 'l'excellent M. Baudry'*, publiées par Auriant. Sceaux: Palimugre, 1948.

— *Lettres inédites à Raoul Duval*, commentées par Georges Normandy. Paris: Albin Michel, 1950.

— *Œuvres complètes de Gustave Flaubert. Correspondance. Supplément*, recueillie, classée et annotée par René Dumesnil, Jean Pommier et Claude Digeon. Paris: Conard, 1954. 4 vols.

— *Sentimental Education*, trans. with an introduction by Robert Baldick. Harmondsworth: Penguin Books, 1964.

— *Œuvres complètes*, préface de Jean Bruneau, présentation et notes de Bernard Masson. Paris: Éditions du Seuil, 1964. 2 vols.

— *Lettres inédites de Gustave Flaubert à son éditeur Michel Lévy*, correspondance présentée par Jacques Suffel. Paris: Calmann-Lévy, 1965.

— *L'Album Flaubert*; iconographie réunie et commentée par Jean Bruneau et Jean A. Ducourneau. Paris: Gallimard, 1972.

— *Correspondance*, i (janvier 1830 à avril 1851), édition établie, présentée et annotée par Jean Bruneau. Paris: Gallimard, 1973. (Bibliothèque de la Pléiade.)

— *Œuvres complètes*; édition nouvelle établie, d'après les manuscrits inédits . . . par le Société des Études Littétaires Françaises contenant la collection complète des carnets. Paris: Club de l'Honnête Homme, 1971–5. 16 vols.

Franklin-Grout-Flaubert. Succession de Madame Franklin-Grout-Flaubert, *Catalogue des manuscripts, projets, notes et études, cahiers de Gustave Flaubert*. . . . Paris, Hôtel Drouot, 18 et 19 novembre 1931.

Gérard-Gailly, Émile. *Le Grand Amour de Flaubert*. Paris: Aubier, 1944.

— Datation de lettres de Flaubert. *Bulletin du bibliophile*, juillet, août-sept., and oct. 1947.

— Nouvelle datation de lettres de Flaubert. *Bulletin des Amis de Flaubert*, mai et déc. 1965, mai et déc. 1966, and mai et déc. 1967.

— Le Chèque. *Bulletin des Amis de Flaubert*, jan. 1971.

Goncourt, Edmond and Jules de. *Journal des Goncourt*, ed. R. Ricatte. Monaco: Société d'Imprimerie, 1956–8. 22 vols.

Gothot-Mersch, C. *La Genèse de Madame Bovary*. Paris: Corti, 1966.

Greater London Council. *Survey of London: The Grosvenor Estate and Mayfair*, pt. 1: General History. London: Athlone Press, 1977.

Guide-Chaix, Nouveau guide à Londres pour l'Exposition de 1851.

Hobhouse, Hermione. *Thomas Cubitt, Master Builder*. London: Macmillan, 1971.

Holme, Thea. *Chelsea*. London: Hamilton, 1972.

Houssaye, Arsène. *Les Confessions; souvenirs d'un demi-siècle, 1830–1880*. Paris: Dentu, 1885. 2 vols.

Huxley, Gervas. *Lady Elizabeth and the Grosvenors*. Oxford University Press, 1965.

Illustrated Hand-book to London and Its Environs. London: Ingram, Cooke, 1853.

Jackson, J. F. *Louise Colet et ses amis littéraires*. New Haven: Yale University Press, 1937.

Jacobs, A. F. Datation des lettres de Flaubert. *Bulletin des Amis de Flaubert*, no. 5, 1955.

— Datation des lettres de Flaubert (1879–1880). *Bulletin du bibliophile*, no. 6, 1955.

Naaman, Antoine Youssef. *Les Lettres d'Égypte de Gustave Flaubert, d'après les manuscrits autographes*. Paris: Nizet, 1965.

Neale, Mary. *Flaubert en Angleterre; étude sur les lecteurs anglais de Flaubert*. Bordeaux: Sobodi, 1966.

Neff, W. T. *Victorian Working Women*. London: Allen & Unwin, 1929.

Painter, G. D. *Marcel Proust*. London: Chatto & Windus, 1965. 2 vols.

Pakenham, Simona. *Sixty Miles from England; the English at Dieppe from 1814–1914*. London: Macmillan, 1907.

Sartre, J.-P. *L'Idiot de la famille*. Paris: Gallimard, 1971. 3 vols.

Seznec, Jean, *Nouvelles études sur la Tentation de Saint Antoine*. London: Warburg Inst., 1949.

— *Flaubert à l'Exposition de 1851*. Oxford: Clarendon Press, 1951.

Siler, D. *Flaubert et Louise Pradier*; le texte intégral des 'Mémoires de Madame Ludovica.' Archive des Lettres modernes, vi, 1973(3), no. 145.

Simon, G. Victor Hugo et Louise Colet. *Revue de France*, 15 mai 1926.
Spencer, Philip. *Flaubert, a Biography*. London: Faber, 1952.
— New Light on Flaubert's Youth. *French Studies*, 8, 1954.
Starkie, E. *Flaubert, the Making of the Master*. London: Weidenfeld, 1967.
— *Flaubert the Master*. London: Weidenfeld, 1971.
Suffel, Jacques. *Gustave Flaubert*. Paris: Éditions universitaires, 1958.
Taine, H. *Notes sur l'Angleterre*. Paris: Hachette, 1872.
— *Notes sur Paris: Vie et opinions de M. Frédéric-Thomas Graindorge*. Paris: Hachette, 1905.
Wroth, Warwick. *Cremorne and the Later London Gardens*. London: Stock, 1907.
Zola, Émile. *Les Romanciers naturalistes*. Paris: Charpentier, 1910.

Index